THE NEW POWER PROGRAM

NEW PROTOCOLS
FOR
MAXIMUM STRENGTH

. . . .

Dr. Michael
COLGAN

Apple Publishing Co. Ltd
VANCOUVER • CANADA

www.applepublishing.com

Printed in Canada

The Information contained in this book was prepared from medical and scientific sources which are referenced herein and are believed to be accurate and reliable. However, the opinions expressed herein by the author do not necessarily represent the opinions or the views of the publisher. Nor should the information herein be used to treat or to prevent any medical condition unless it is used with the full knowledge, compliance and agreement of your personal physician or other licensed health care professional. Readers are strongly advised to seek the advice of their personal health care professionals before proceeding with **any** *changes in* **any** *health care program.*

FIRST EDITION

Canadian Cataloguing in Publication Data
Colgan, Michael
The new power program : protocols for maximum strength

Includes Bibliographical references and index.
ISBN: 1-896817-00-9

1. Physical training and education   I. Title
GV546.C63 2001   613.7'1   C00-901540-X

Apple Publishing Company Ltd.
220 East 59th Avenue
Vancouver, British Columbia
Canada V5X 1X9

www.newpowerprogram.com
www.applepublishing.com

Tel (604) 214-6688 & Fax (604) 214-3566
Email books@applepublishing.com

10 9 8 7 6 5 4 3 2 1

To all the athletes
who have put their
faith in me to
help them build
their power

Also by Dr Michael Colgan:

- *Electrodermal Responses*
- *The Training Index*
- *Your Personal Vitamin Profile*
- *Prevent Cancer Now*
- *Optimum Sports Nutrition*
- *The New Nutrition: Medicine for the Millennium*
- *Hormonal Health*
- *Protect Your Prostate*
- *Beat Arthritis*
- *Progressive Health Series*
- *Colgan Chronicles Newsletter*
  (see www.colganchronicles.com)

Forewords

*"Michael Colgan has done it again. The **Power Program** will turn the world of weight training upside down. Always on the cutting edge. Keep up the great work."*
Larry Scott
Bodybuilding Champion and Top US Trainer

"Thanks to the Colgan Institute I'm running faster and feeling great."
Regina Jacobs
Multiple Olympian and 3000 meter record holder

"Dr. Colgan is a straight shooter. He presents the unbiased truth on heavy weight training as it pertains to sports conditioning. His factual research and analysis is easily applied by all."
Ted Arcidi
World's Greatest Bench Presser, Actor and CEO, Arcidi Strength Systems

*"I was pleasantly surprised to see that many of the concepts in the **Power Program** made up the foundation of the training strategy that helped build my successful bodybuilding career.*
*Today my goals are much different. I train to maintain lean functional muscle that does not compromise agility and endurance. The **Power Program,** again, has proven to be the perfect formula for this endeavour. I have never felt better. An incredible accomplishment that will likely become a household manual. Michael, all the power to you!"*
Franco Cavaleri, BSc.
Bodybuilding Champion, President, NuSport

"The Power Program is a dramatic advance in our knowledge of sports training."
Dr. Andrew Strigner
Harley Street Physician, London

"You have given me so much information to achieve the results I have. I thank you for your outstanding work."
Sonny Mollinelli
Author, Lecturer and Masters Fitness Champion

I have used the Power Program now for 15 months. Where conventional weight training failed, Dr. Colgan's expertise has packed on 26 lbs of muscle and strength. Not only will the program create power for you, but it will do wonders for your health."
Richard Hall
Touring Golf Professional

"Mike, God Bless, Thanks for everything. Your friend, Iron Bull."
Jimmy Pellachio
One of the World's Strongest Men

"You are my inspiration, Dr Colgan. Here's my latest body after using more of your advice." (See page 224)
Victoria Johnson
TV Host of Victoria's Body Shoppe, Prime Sports Network

"The best part, Michael, is that you walk your talk."
Arthur Lydiard
New Zealand Olympic Coach & World Renowned Trainer

"Mike, keep up your great work!"
Anthony Clark
World Champion Powerlifter

"Dr. Colgan, you are on top!"
Lee Lebrada
Bodybuilding Champion, President, Labrada Nutrition

"Michael, your knowledge has helped me immensely. Thanks for your devotion to science in sports. You are a mentor and a friend."
Cory Holly
Masters Bodybuilding Champion and Sports Supplement Designer

Dr. Colgan, thanks for your support and your many contributions to health."
Paul Chek
Acclaimed US Trainer and Rehabilitation Specialist

"Dr. Colgan, thanks to your program, my Olympic dream is becoming an Olympic reality."
Warrick Yeager
Top Athlete of the US Armed Forces

"Dr. Colgan, you are the best! Required reading for athletes."
Dr. Bill Misner
Masters Athlete, Author and Top Trainer

"Dr. Colgan, many thanks for your expert counsel."
Doug Benbow
Bodybuilding Champion, Trainer of Champions

"Thanks for a great program. I'm going for Gold."
Vern Moen
Swimming Champion and Olympic contender

"Colgan Institute programs: No hype, just 25 years of continuous improvement."
Irwin Sower
World Masters Traithlon Champion, World Masters Ultra-Distance Running Champion

"Thanks to your guidance, Dr. Colgan. I did it! I won my first big title, Mr. Quebec Natural 2000."
Steve Rockburn
Champion Bodybuilder

"Michael, thanks for helping me hit the bull's eye."
T'ai Erasmus
Shooting Champion and Olympic Contender

"Accolades to Dr. Colgan and the Colgan Institute. I am thrilled to have a set a five minute personal best and to have qualified for the 2000 Olympic Marathon Trials."
Laurie Corbin
Marathon runner and Olympic Contender

"Thanks for helping me reach my goals."
Karen Clark
Junior Iceskating Champion

"Your knowledge and programs are outstanding! Thanks for being there."
Dean Miller
Bodybuilding Champion and Natural Mr. America

*"The **Power Program** has made the difference!"*
Danny Smith
Motocross Champion

"Dr. Colgan is my hero, my lifesaver. I and my family are forever indebted to him."
Neville Yuen
Dropped from 390 lbs fat in 1997 to a muscular 185 lbs in January 2000

"I met Dr. Colgan in the late '70's. Ever since I have looked to him for cutting edge information. Thanks, Dr. Colgan, for the great impact you have made on mine and my family's lives."
Kevin Paluch
Champion Golfer

"The Power Program enabled me to have the strength and endurance to complete 7 Ironman Triathlons at age 55-65 in one year. This is a must for any athlete who want to achieve excellent results."
Michael J. Stevenson, Chairman
Healthy Lifestyle Corporation

Acknowledgments

Thanks to all the athletes who have used our programs over the last 25 years. You've taught me so much more about the miraculous apparatus of the human body than I ever learned at university. You started the gleam in my eye to produce a written and video weight training program that would offer all athletes the right stuff.

My colleagues and friends in sports medicine and training gave so unstintingly of their knowledge and became so enthusiastic about our power training that they finally triggered the conception of the Power Program. Too numerous to name here, many of the "fathers" of this book appear in the pages ahead.

From the mid-term of the pregnancy, thanks to those who so generously modelled the photos for me, great guys, Franco Cavaleri and Steven Macramalla, and lovely ladies, Melissa Canales, Leah Harvey, Lesley Simpson and Karen Reynolds.

In the third trimester, the unfailing help and humor of my secretary Marion Halliwell and the patience and support of my friends on Salt Spring Island, especially at the Roasting House, kept the discomfort and the final labor pains within bounds. I didn't scream and thrash about too much.

And, through the long drawn-out birthing, my publisher, Al Pazitch, provided the lifesaving computer expertise of Amy Pon to extract the final document.

Throughout the whole process, I give thanks for my wife and fellow scientist, Lesley, who forced reluctant me to take breaks and to go to the gym, fed me and cleaned me, and quietly took a mountain of other work off my shoulders, so that this book might come to birth.

Introduction

So many dumb exercises, so many daffy weight machines, so many useless gadgets litter gyms that I visit all over the world, it boils my blood. When I began working with athletes over a quarter century ago, men still swung Indian clubs and stretched steel springs in pretense at resistance training. And women stood in vibrating belts or pressed beefy booties on revolving wooden rollers, vainly believing they would shake or pummel off their fat.

Today it's isolation weight machines, with restrictive pads and straps and other gizmos that ensure only a particular muscle gets exercised. Exerting that muscle's new found strength in any free movement of sport virtually guarantees injury to untrained stabilizers and connective tissues. Then there's the stair steppers and suchlike, designed to soothe egos more than take off bodyfat, by moving the ankles about 3½ inches.

None of that nonsense insults you here. **The Power Program** is the latest update of the training system used by the Colgan Institute to increase the power of athletes at all levels, from weekend warriors to Olympic medallists, in the whole alphabet of sport. From archery, basketball and boxing, through skiing, track and field, and tennis, to America's Cup yachting, this program provides a system of weight training that fits with human physiology and the science of strength and speed development. It gives you all you need to re-build yourself as a body of power.

As we move into the new millennium, the value of the correct weight training is finally becoming apparent, not only to athletes but to everyone who wants a powerful, disease-resistant body. Dr Worthy of the American College of Sports Medicine puts it best:

> "Done correctly, weight training is the most efficient, effective, and safest form of exercise there is, and it won't be long before people realize it."[1]

In choosing this book you are already well on your way.

Michael Colgan
Salt Spring Island,
British Columbia,
July 2000

Contents

THE NEW POWER PROGRAM

Got Power

Athletes in a wide variety of sports continue to fall for weight training routines portrayed in muscle magazines, probably because the accompanying photos depict massive bodybuilders, who supposedly got that way (drug-free!) simply by following these routines themselves.

We all know it's a pile of pig pucky, but seeing still prompts believing. The net result is that most sports training with weights is confounded with useless and dangerous practices that do diddly to increase athletic power. Athletes are induced to train heavy all year, for hours at a time, doing endless sets of endless reps, gutting it out through injury and exhaustion, one more rep, go for the burn, get the pump, build the mass, gotta have pain to make the gain. I want to show you why every one of these strategies is counterproductive for building power.

Working with top bodybuilders for the past 25 years, I know they don't use them either. The only time you see the elite pictured in such flapdoodle is when they are paid to pose for magazine articles, the main purpose of which is to keep muscleheads drooling for the next new "killer" routine or "dynamite" supplement.

There are good training articles, particularly in Muscular Development magazine, but they are buried by the mass of thinly disguised magalogs, hellbent on acquiring the contents of your wallet. So my first task in The Power Program is to dump the garbage. I take no prisoners.

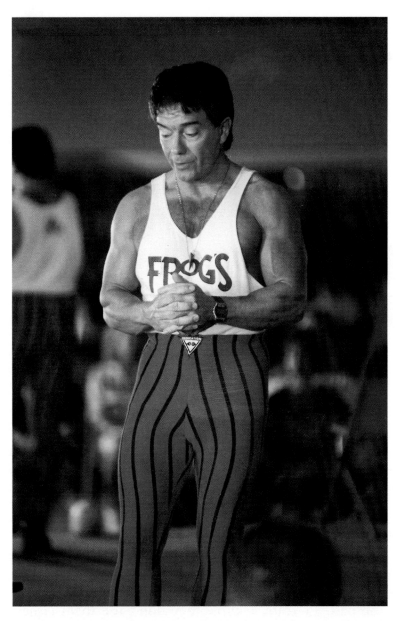

Until he developed his first periodization program in 1986, Michael Colgan had more than his share of injuries. Seen here, at age 60, he now trains injury-free.

Don't Train Heavy All Year Long

Unlike bodybuilders, who do not have to perform on the playing field, athletes should never train heavy all year long. A huge pile of scientific evidence shows that doing so inevitably produces overtraining, injury and long-term fatigue of the nervous system.[1,2,3] Any one or combination of the three can sideline you for months, and has sidelined many athletes for life.

Bill Kraemer of Penn State University and Steve Fleck, formerly of the US Olympic Committee, are prominent among sports training experts who have covered the evidence of overtraining and neural fatigue many times.[4] But I still get a ton of athletes, who are obviously not learning, referred to the Colgan Institute in desperation, after conventional weight training has done its damage.

Yet the solution is simple. The first step to athletic power is: **periodize your weight training**. That is, divide the year into cycles of different forms of weight work. But, before we get down to details, there's a lot more garbage to dump.

Don't Do Long Workouts

You see them every month in muscle mags, those long routines — apparently done all the time by the bozo in the photos — routines that would take hours to complete. Hokum for athletes for many reasons, a big one being your anabolic hormones. The most the human body can take of any heavy weight program is about 60 minutes. After that, hormone levels start to decline, neural fatigue sets in, and further weight work will not increase muscle power.[5]

Long workouts are not the best for muscle mass either. Mr Freaky himself, Dorian Yates, the top bodybuilder in the world during the '90s, whips in and out of the weight room in 45 minutes.

Athletes can't afford to spend hours in the weight room anyway. It takes too much of the time and energy they should be spending on skill training. Top levels of skill take 15 to 20 years to acquire. Once you get to the strength and power cycles of our power program, 60 minutes a day is all you need.

You Don't Need Many Sets Or Reps

For power training, if you can do six sets or more of any exercise, you are doing it dead wrong. Especially so if each set is typical bodybuilding training, and continues for 8 – 10 repetitions. As you will see

Hal Hessig is a fine example of training smart to build a great physique, rather than training long.

LARRY SCOTT first to h[...]
MR. UNIVERSE, & [...]

Master trainer Larry Scott knows all there is to know about overcoming injuries.

in chapters ahead, by the time you get to five reps, most of the fast-twitch power fibers of the muscles have fatigued and dropped out of the contraction.[6] If they're not working, they can't increase their power.

That's why the "one more rep" strategy doesn't work either. When you are fighting to squeeze out that last one or two reps in a typical bodybuilding set, almost all the power fibers have ceased firing.[6] All you are fighting is reduced muscle involvement. If muscle fibers are not firing, then they are completely unaffected by your efforts, even if you explode your eyeballs.

Don't Work Through Injury

You are just plain dumb if you work through injury. If I want to make sure one of my horses will be laid off for six months, all I have to do is make him jump a few gentle fences when he has a touch of tendonitis. Injured joints and connective tissues need rest in order to heal. Yet you see dopes in gyms all the time, wrapping sore knees and elbows, and grunting on through heavy weights.

It's no badge of courage to work out wrapped at every joint like an Egyptian mummy, more a badge of stupidity. My friend Mr Olympia, Larry Scott, is one of the best bodybuilding trainers in the world, with a wealth of experience in training champions for over 30 years. Heed his words of wisdom: "If you can't do an exercise without injury pain, don't do it at all."[7]

As Larry emphasizes, injuries to joints and connective tissue are usually localized. If you try different positions and planes of movement in various exercises, you can usually find one that allows you to exercise the bodypart without pain. Stick to that position and movement plane until the injury resolves. As a bonus, exercising in this way, rather than completely resting, will also speed healing.

Dump The Pump And Dodge The Burn

The celebrated "pump" is just a temporary increase in muscle size and hardness caused by an increase in blood and water flow to the muscles. Over a period, it increases muscle mass by growing more capillaries in the muscle and teaching it to hold more fluid. But it has nothing to do with athletic power.

The sought after "burn" is simply acid build-up. Whenever you exercise above tiddley-winks level, lactic and other acids accumulate in the muscles, lower the pH, and literally start to burn you. Increased acidity also interferes with neural transmission, stopping muscle contraction before the acid causes damage. Some of the lactic acid is

Dr Michael Colgan with Arnold Schwarzenegger at the Arnold Classic in 1993. Dr Colgan appeared at the Arnold Classic in Columbus, Ohio every year in the early 1990's. The greatest physique of all time, Arnold built a body that is both massive and functional.

then converted back to the primary energy molecule, adenosine triphosphate (ATP). Blood flow clears the rest, and the burn disappears. Over a period, the burn does increase muscle mass. But no part of it does anything much for power.

American fitness champion Nancy Popp shows that you don't need excess mass to have winning athletic power.

The Might Is Not In The Mass

The above bodybuilding gambits do work for building muscle mass. They increase muscle water content and muscle blood content. They increase the mass of the sarcoplasm, the soft tissue that surrounds muscle fibers. They thicken muscle fibers, especially slow-twitch endurance fibers, and cause some muscle fibers to split and form doubles.[6,8]

Anabolic steroids boost all these effects and can also cause muscles to grow fibers that are out of pennation. Out of pennation means they are out of alignment with the direction of muscle contraction. So they cannot function to increase the muscle contraction and make no contribution to its strength. Nevertheless, you do get much larger muscles. But they are soft and heavy with only a very moderate increase in power.

Elite athletes find that the bodybuilding methods slammed in this chapter often **reduce** their power. It's easy to understand once you realize that the human power equation is the same old equation that governs all force in the Universe: $E=MC^2$. The power a moving limb can produce is its mass multiplied by its velocity squared. You can see that velocity, not mass, is the biggie.

To move a limb at maximum velocity, the body uses the fast-twitch mass of its muscles. Any other mass is mostly along for the ride. And if you think excess mass doesn't slow you down, try running your best 400 meters wearing a 5 kg bodybelt.

Any introductory physics book will tell you that

the force required to move and accelerate an object from rest, increases as the mass of the object increases. So the larger the mass of a muscle for a given level of contractile force, the slower it can move, and the less power it can develop. Numerous conventional weight training strategies will make you bigger, slower and less powerful. No wonder some athletic coaches don't let their athletes anywhere near the weight room.

In sharp contrast, power training focuses on developing the maximum contractile force per pound of muscle mass. In the language of physics, the greater the force for a given mass, the more powerful the movement. You still grow an excellent physique, but a physique that gives you far greater power. As an athlete, you don't want excess mass. You want muscles that produce the greatest force in relation to their size.

Ultra-distance running champion James Bond (center) took the Colgan Institute Power Program to help him achieve his dream of winning the silver buckle in the Western States 100 mile race.

Periods And Peaks

Now we've thrown out the garbage, let's get back to the power. The first step is to divide your year in the weight room into periods. You have to time these periods so that you achieve a power peak just as the season for your sport opens. Never do the Power Program during the competitive season. Anyone who thinks they can train for power and compete at the same time is either Superman or an idiot. I've yet to meet Superman.

Colgan Institute training helped champion marathon runner, Laurie Corbin achieve her personal best time and qualify for the 2000 Olympic marathon trials.

Even for sports that go year round, you should plan your own competitive season and peak for it. Most of the elite know this well. In the sport of triathlon, for example, where we have worked with the best, top athletes often train to peak for only one or two races per year. Think about it. Mark Allen won the Nice triathlon in France seven years in a row, before changing his training to peak for the Hawaii Ironman, which he then won six times.

Some periodization programs get incredibly complex, with microcycles, mesocycles, recovery cycles, transitions, repeaters, etc.[2,3] We post the KISS principle — "Keep It Simple, Stupid!" — on the wall to remind us not to get too uppity. Athletes have enough to learn without imposing complicated schedules and a whole new language on them, just for the weight room component of their training.

Because many sports have a competitive season of about six months, in this book I divide power training on the same basis. That gives 25 weeks of every year to train for power, and one week of tapering before the season begins. The 25-week period you train for power is divided into an 8-week Extension-Connection Cycle, a 10-week Strength-Stabilization Cycle and a 7-week Power Cycle. During the competitive season we spend 10 weeks on a Link Cycle for speed and 15 weeks on a Maintenance Cycle. Then you get a week off!

For the personal programs we do at the Colgan Institute, the numbers of weeks in each cycle are adapted to the individual athlete's needs, dates of competitions and other factors. You can do the same adaptations to suit your sport. But every program we do contains at least a 6-week Extension-Connection Cycle, an 8-week Strength-Stabilization Cycle, a 5-week Power Cycle and an 8-week Link Cycle.

The full-year periodization table is laid out on the next page. Each cycle of the 25-Week Power Training is equally important for maximizing power, so I give each a chapter ahead. If you want power, this is **THE WAY.**

Power Principle 1: Periodize.

Accelerate
Add a celery garnish to your Bloody Mary as a reward for finishing your training.

52-Week Power Periodization

25-Week Power Training	Extension-Connection Cycle	8 weeks
	Strength-Stabilization Cycle	10 weeks
	Power Cycle	7 weeks
Taper		1 week
Link Cycle		10 weeks
Maintenance Cycle		15 weeks
Off		1 week

Power Parts

I have slammed conventional bodybuilding, because its focus on muscle mass is detrimental to athletes. Nevertheless, the techniques employed are superb for building mass. They make bodies **look** real good. Consequently bodybuilding has many thousands of adherents, and a thriving support industry of books, magazines, supplements and equipment. No wonder athletes fall for it. To help you avoid the hokum, here's a small peek at the history.

Competitive bodybuilding first developed out of old carnival strongman acts. It grew rapidly in the 1930's, after two Canadians, Joe and Ben Weider, adopted the activity as an advertising vehicle to build their vast nutrition supplement and weight equipment empire. They formed the International Federation of Bodybuilders to promote its growth. Born of the circus for the purpose of sideshow, competitive bodybuilding was never designed for athletes, and never incorporated the science that enables athletes to reach their power potential.

Science first impacted weight training over 60 years ago, when physicians such as Thomas De Lorme and Arthur Watkins, at Massachusetts General Hospital, began applying their revolutionary "Technics of Progressive Resistance Training" to rehabilitate patients who had suffered polio. By 1948, they had shown that three sets of an exercise, with progressive increases in weight each set to the maximum the patient could handle, causes rapid increases in muscle strength.[1]

Canadian Louis Cyr, the strongest man in history, still holds the record for the heaviest weight ever lifted — 1,968 kg (4,337 lbs) in a back lift. In 1896 he lifted a 250 kg (551 lbs) weight with one finger!

Back then, however, competitive bodybuilding was growing into a considerable cult, suffused with ritual exercises, mysterious routines, snake oil supplements, and all the glitter of the circus. The last thing its promoters wanted was their business exposed to the demanding standards of science. So they ignored it.

Instead they developed ever more cunning devices and routines, the more arduous and difficult the better. Not unlike dungeons and dragons computer games of today, they led the novice bodybuilder through progressive stages of ritual, each stage planned for quick obsolescence, until they snared both his mind and his wallet. In return, he got a nice physique and became somewhat stronger. But he developed little of the speed, agility, balance, coordination, power, or mental focus essential to athletic success.

Though their idols were the world's strongest men, such as the great Louis Cyr, bodybuilders of that time never approached real power. They gained the appearance but little of the substance.

No Performance Required

Recognizing their failure to produce athletic power, bodybuilding promoters quickly removed from their competitions all the old strength and agility tests that they had first adopted from circus strongman acts. Competitive bodybuilding became merely an exhibition of muscle size, shape and definition, with no tests at all to show that the muscles actually work.

From analyzing thousands of bodybuilders at the Colgan Institute over the last 25 years, we have found that many of the muscular systems built by bodybuilding do not work. The physiques **look** spectacular, but a lot of them are functionally so weak, slow and uncoordinated in the free movements that occur continuously in sport, they are a liability for anything more strenuous than miniature golf.

But the influence of clever advertising and promotion is so strong that, over the last 50 years, bodybuilding strategies have been blindly adopted worldwide as an effective way for athletes to train with weights. In consequence today, most gyms and athletes follow systems of weight training in which useless bodybuilding routines are intricately

A leader in applying science to weight training, powerlifting champion Ted Arcidi bears an uncanny resemblance in both looks and strength to the great Louis Cyr.

entangled with scientific weight training. In this book I undo those tangles, so that you can discard the ineffective, and focus your effort instead on the science that will build your power.

The legendary Jack Lalanne first alerted me to the difference between bodybuilding muscle and functional muscle when we were on a TV fitness show together in 1979. Still going strong at 85, Jack has proved his point. Since then, a lot of great trainers have helped me sort it all out. Canadian strength coach Charles Poliquin,[2] California super trainer Paul Chek, Professor Bill Kraemer of Penn State University, powerlifting champion Ted Arcidi, Olympic weightlifting coach Dragomir Cioroslan, Mr Olympia, Larry Scott,[3] bodybuilding champion Franco Cavaleri and a swag of others never adopted or long since tossed out the garbage. And my friend, Lee Labrada, with so many bodybuilding titles it would take a page just to list them, is also a fine athlete. So is the beautiful and elegant Lenda Murray, who reigned for six years as Ms Olympia, the ultimate bodybuilding accolade. But most gyms and athletes still follow practices primarily developed to grow muscle mass for the purpose of sideshow.

Lee Labrada, one of the smart bodybuilders, built both a world-class physique and a body that works.

If you are an athlete who has been using conventional bodybuilding as weight training carry out this test. Over the the next week, measure and record all your best strength, speed and power moves. Also record some measures of your agility, balance and coordination. Then follow the principles herein for the 25-week Power Training Cycles and measure again. The improvements should astound you.

Components of Power

Before you begin any weight training, you should know exactly which components of power that it benefits. A lot of weight training programs focus only on muscle mass and bodyfat. The Power Program, plus a good coach, trains you for them all.

Components of Power

1. *Anatomy. The length of the levers (bones), and the positions of attachment of tendons and ligaments.*

2. *Skill. The most important. The degree to which you have learned the correct movements for your sport, so they have become automatic neuromuscular sequences in the cerebellum of your brain.*

3. *Contractile mass. The number and size of the contractile fibers of your muscles.*

4. *Bodyfat. The amount of dead weight in fat your muscles have to carry.*

5. *Strength. The force at which your muscles can contract.*

6. *Balance. Your posture in standing and moving, and the balanced development of opposing muscle groups that yield it.*

7. *Flexibility. The elasticity of your muscles and connective tissues.*

8. *Coordination. The linking of muscle chains into smooth, complex movements.*

9. *Reaction speed. The efficiency of the neuromuscular connections between your muscles, nerves and brain.*

10. *Mental Focus.*

T'ai Erasmus, champion shooter, used a Colgan Institute program to help him gain his winning mental focus and coordination.

You can't change Factor 1, **Anatomy**, much. The length of your bones and the positions of tendon and ligament attachment are genetically determined, just like the color of your eyes. But a good coach can adapt your training to suit your particular structure.

I can't help you with Factor 2, **Skill** either. For skill you need the best coach you can get. Skill is learned and maintained only by constant practice. But practice makes permanent, not perfect. If you practice anything incorrectly, that's how your brain will learn it. Only a good coach can save you from learning your own mistakes.

But I can help you change the other power factors, dramatically — the **Contractile Mass** of your muscles, their **Strength of Contraction**, the **Bodyfat** you carry, your **Balance**, your **Flexibility**, your **Coordination**, your **Reaction Speed**, and your **Mental Focus**. We start the training for power where it all begins — with posture.

Power Principle 2: Train with weights for strength, balance, flexibility, coordination, reaction speed and mental focus.

Power Posture

The old Honda we keep at the beach house has wonky suspension, a downhill lean to starboard and judders noisily whenever you try a tight turn. It doesn't matter, because the car nevers run fast or far, and chugs the three miles to town and back just fine. So it is with the unbalanced bodies of most non-athletes. They chug along fairly reliably, but only at low levels of performance.

Contrast that image with a Ferrari 355. From its 380 horse-power, V8 engine to its 6-speed hydraulic transmission and computer-controlled suspension, everything is perfectly aligned and balanced so that the car can move and turn at top speed. If any component is even a hair out of true, performance bombs, because the tremendous power of the engine cannot be fully and smoothly applied.

When I first talk about balance in my training camps, uninformed athletes snicker and yawn, perhaps at the mental image of prissy girls parading with books on their heads. But once we demonstrate how correct posture dramatically improves performance, they sit up and learn.

As an athlete, you need the balance of a Ferrari. To apply the power you gain from the Power Program, you have to know how to balance your body and align it, so that it moves and turns at top speed with the least effort. It's not too difficult to learn.

From the ancient disciplines of Yoga and the martial arts, to the modern bodywork of Rolfing, and neuromuscular training of Feldenkrais and Alexander, the principles of body balance

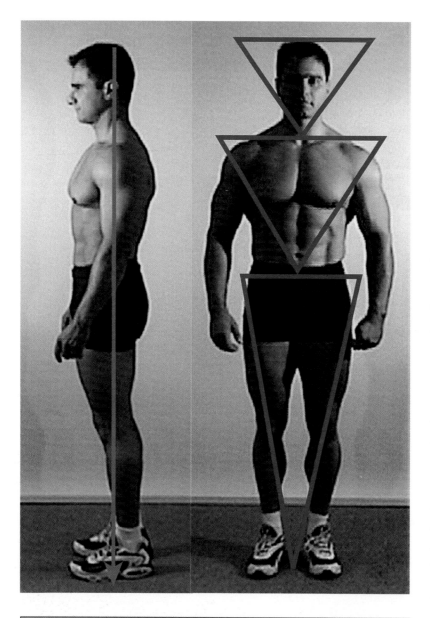

Bodybuilding champion Franco Cavaleri shows almost perfect standing posture. In the side view, the vertical line falls correctly just behind the meatus of the ear through the center of the shoulder, 2nd lumbar vertebra, hip and knee joints but just a little forward of the ankle. In the front view the tips of the three inverted pyramids are balanced at the centerline of the body.

have been known and taught for 5000 years. Taking advantage of such knowledge, I am writing this chapter with my friend and colleague Lee Parore of New Zealand, power trainer to the elite, including many of the All Blacks, the best rugby team on Earth. His forthcoming book, **Power Posture,** is a must for athletic coaches and trainers. With the help of Lee's expertise, I give you the basics here that will move you into the **posture of power**.

Body Balance

As the illustration shows, the human body is like three inverted pyramids balanced on top of each other. The pelvis and legs form the lower pyramid. At its center is the second lumbar vertebra, which forms the balance point of the middle pyramid, the flat top of which envelops the shoulders. The head forms the top pyramid, balanced on the cervical vertebrae of the neck, in the center of the shoulders. When the body is aligned in this way, it has the highest potential power.

In this power posture, seen most clearly in gymnasts, the head, trunk and pelvis are in balanced vertical alignment. The body requires the least muscular activity, and therefore the least energy expenditure, to hold itself upright against gravity. The body's center of gravity is also in a neutral position, from which movement can occur swiftly in any direction without the need for postural adjustment, and without losing the time that postural adjustment takes.

It's a bit like balancing a stack of dominoes. The more carefully you align each domino, the better balanced the stack. If you place even one domino out of line, then you have to place those above it out of line to compensate. Balance of the whole stack is compromised.

Take the common postural fault of running belly out with an exaggerated lordosis (inward curve) of the lower back. Your head and butt have to stick out to compensate. My friend and mentor, New Zealand Olympic coach Arthur Lydiard, calls it "running in a bucket." It slows you down because knee lift is compromised and your head and neck are fighting gravity every stride. It also leads to many back, hip and knee problems. Renowned Oregon runner, Steve Prefontaine, got a whole lot faster after coach Bill Bowerman, founder of Nike, corrected this fault in his posture.

Spinal Curves

Your spine has three natural curves: inward to the neck, outward at the upper back and invward again at the lower back. Feldenkrais showed us that optimal balance, and therefore optimal function, occurs when these three curves have the same angle, approximately 35°. Changing this angle by sticking your head out or your belly out, moves body mass outside the balanced vertical axis and dramatically reduces your power.

Running guru Arthur Lydiard, seen here with two of the great Olympians he trained: Peter Snell and Murray Halberg. Lydiard is a stickler for correct running posture.

Renowned Oregon runner, Steve Prefontaine, got a whole lot faster after coach Bill Bowerman (founder of Nike) corrected the common postural fault of running with an exaggerated lordosis (inward curve) of the lower back.

Try it yourself. Stand with your belly out and one hand up like a traffic cop stopping traffic. Get a friend to push your hand back, using just one or two fingers. See how weak you are. Now adopt the power posture. Suck your belly back into alignment and pull up on your anus. Hold your breath and push your head back into line by pressing your tongue hard against your palate just behind your front teeth. Let him try to push your arm again. Now we're getting powerful!

Balance Boosts Power

Whenever your body's center of gravity is outside your vertical center – located through the second lumbar vertebra – you are slower to move in any direction. In the language of physics, **whenever you stand with body mass outside the balanced vertical axis, the moment of inertia around the axis increases.** That simply means it takes more energy to move.

Your power is reduced in two ways. First, some of the energy that would otherwise be applied to movement is wasted just to maintain equilibrium in the unbalanced position. Second, your body has to return to equilibrium before initiating movement. You are slower off the mark and therefore less powerful, because, as we will see, speed is the biggie for power.

Standing and moving with correct posture takes a bit of hard work. But whenever you feel like saying "to hell with it" think of small, lightweight martial artist Bruce Lee. Standing erect in power posture, he could generate sufficient power from his 65 kg (143 lbs) body, to knock down a 100 kg (220 lbs) man with a one-inch punch.

Postural Pain

I hope you are convinced that if one part of your body is out of balance, other parts have to move out of balance to compensate. Otherwise you would fall over. So any postural imbalance induces other postural imbalances. If you stand belly out, for example, your whole structure has to change to compensate, putting stresses on your neck, shoulders, lower back, hips and knees. Remember it this way: poor posture is a pain in the neck.

And that's just standing still. Whenever you move rapidly, the stresses of poor posture are magnified manyfold. The common error of running with the head stuck too far forward, puts about 100 pounds of extra stress on the cervical vertebrae of the neck with every stride. The strongest neck will tweak after just a few miles.

I see heads stuck out all the time in marathon running, especially with novices. The common response to the aching neck is to hunch the shoulders, thereby transferring some of the stress to the upper back muscles. A few more miles and these tweak too, and the runners slow to a crawl. Even if they finish the race, at best the sore neck and upper back may persist for weeks, making training a misery. At worst, it will become a chronic injury, inhibiting training indefinitely, always ready to tweak whenever you make a big effort. All that pain and destruction of performance can be easily avoided simply by keeping your head erect, balanced on your neck, so that your eyes are level with the horizon.

Postural Stress

Poor posture does a lot more damage than merely slow you down. Your muscles have a minimum resting level of activity called **tone**, controlled by the central nervous system. When you are standing in balanced posture, the body is not still. It sways slightly in all directions, with the muscles continuously contracting and relaxing all over the structure to correct the sway. This slight movement, which you normally don't notice, is an automatic response that also relieves stresses on the joints and nerves and optimizes blood flow.

If your body is unbalanced it is under **postural stress**. Some muscles have to work too hard to correct swaying and become tight compromising their blood supply. Others hardly work at all and eventually become weak. Over a period, postural stress sensitizes the tight muscles. They then spend all day on red alert. Parts of the muscles and connective tissues become so sensitized, they create what are called **trigger points**, which increase muscle tension and pain, and dramatically reduce muscle strength. Trigger points are so named because they go off unpredictably whenever effort exceeds a certain threshold.

The pain is not only localized in the trigger point areas, but also radiates to other areas against which the muscle is pulling. Janet Travell, the world's leading expert on trigger points and their treatment,[1,2] explains them best. **A trigger point is a hyper-irritable point with reduced blood circulation, that occurs within a tight area of skeletal muscle or its associated fascia.** It causes stiffness, pain and weakness in the muscle and surrounding muscles and connective tissues. Muscle strength becomes unreliable, because neural inhibition may shut down the muscle at any time to prevent further injury.

For an athlete, trigger points are disastrous. Because of the pain and unpredictable loss of function, the athlete quickly learns to limit the contraction of those muscles to below the trigger point threshold. Once this occurs you can no longer apply full power.

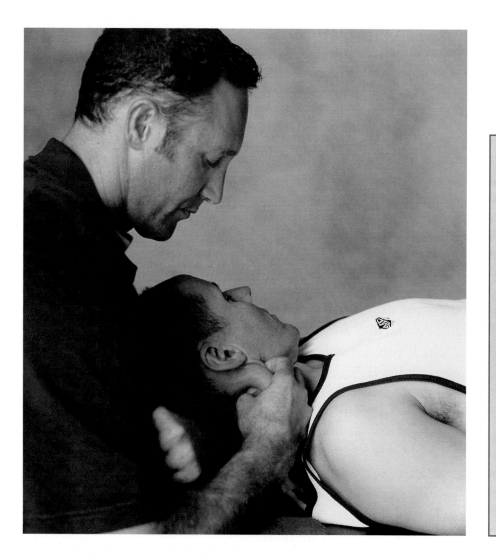

Lee Parore, trainer of some members of the New Zealand All Blacks rugby team, working on Brett Fairweather two-time aerobics champion, is an expert in trigger point treatment.

Trigger points develop not only from postural imbalances, but also from overuse, joint imbalance, imbalances in strength of agonist and antagonist muscles caused by faulty weight training, nutritional deficiencies, direct trauma and joint disease.[1,2] Whatever the source, whenever a trigger point is present, the athlete makes compensatory postural changes that lead to further problems.

Even if you have no injuries or tweaks, get assessed for postural imbalances and **latent trigger points** before you begin the Extension-Connection cycle of the Power Program. Unless you do, and take the steps to correct them, your increased power is sure to bring them out.

If you can find a bodyworker trained and certified in Rolfing or Feldenkrais **and** the Travell system, you are in luck. If you can't, then adopt at least the strategies covered in the rest of this chapter and in Chapter 4 on stretching.

Getting Power Posture

Where does your power come from? Sport (and life) occurs in an unstable, three-dimensional environment, so we better be sure of the source of our power. Oversimplified versions of martial arts – translated, I suspect, to suit Western brains – claim that all power comes from the ground. Some even wax lyrical about Mother Earth letting "Chi" flow into you by tapping into gravitational forces. More fanciful versions call on powers in the air or even "The Force" that binds all matter in the Universe. Shades of George Lucas!

Sounds pretty stupid when presented without the mystical trappings. And it is pretty stupid. There's no power in the ground, or in the air. The power is all inside you.

Martial artist and Colgan Institute trainer, Steven Macramalla, shows his explosive power in a flying kick.

The ground serves merely as a fixed point of leverage from which to apply your power. Even a gymnast up in the air on the high bar is using the ground as a lever. The bar is fixed to the frame, which is fixed to the ground. If it were not, then whenever the gymnast swung one way, the bar would go the other.

The better your body grips the ground or another fixed point of leverage, the more power you can release. That's why the horse stance of martial arts has feet fully planted and spread wide, pulling up and in with the inner thighs, to create tension so as to better hold onto the ground. And boxers know well that the real power punches come from a flat-footed, wide stance, with belly in and hard, to better transmit the energy. And without starting blocks, sprinters would start like cartoon characters, feet spinning uselessly as their enormous leg power breaks the grip between shoes and ground.

Hmm . . . has he been a good lad?

Guess so. Gently does it.

Shaun Adams, judo master on remote Salt Spring Island in British Columbia, Canada guides many young athletes on the right road to power.

Your Power Core

To best utilize the leverage of the ground, build your power posture from the ground up.[3] Leverage from the ground is trasmitted through the legs and through the hip joints to the pelvis. In combination with a strong transversus, obliques and back muscles to hold the organs, and hold up and stabilize the spine, the pelvic bone mass is the base of your **core** which transmits power up and down the body.[3] This bowl formed by the pelvis and its floor muscles and connective tissues coincides well with the power center or source of "Chi" (Chinese), "Ki" (Japanese) in many oriental disciplines. It is the center of your power.

Your core cannot do its job if your belly is out. Belly out distorts your spine and allows all your organs to flop around, in and out of the center of gravity. Belly up and in, by retracting the **transversus** muscle, is the only way to hold organs and spine firmly in your center.

Don't make the common mistake of training your **rectus abdominis** in an effort to flatten the stomach. The much admired eight-pack of muscle, running from ribs and sternum (breastbone) to pelvis, is not the structure for the job. Your eight-pack is designed and attached so as to pull the ribcage towards the pelvis. It has nothing, I repeat, nothing, to do with a flat belly.

Basic physiology shows that you cannot use your eight-pack to pull the belly up and in. The muscle fibers run top to bottom — the wrong way. So all those

Even exercising upside down doing hand-stand pushups, you need to keep a flat belly.

crunches and situps and belly-busting machines will *never* produce a powerful core. On the contrary, they will cause your belly to protrude!

Your belly and organs are held up and in by a thin corset of muscle called the **transversus,** which sits deep in the body on either side of the eight-pack, and attaches to the connective tissue behind it. Transversus fibers, as their name implies, run from the front of the body, straight across the sides to join into your back and to the sides of the pelvis. You will learn how to train the transversus for a guaranteed flat belly in Chapter 18.

Moshe Feldenkrais, originator of Feldenkrais training, showed us how body movements originate from the pelvis,[4] your power center. So the first step to power posture is feet firmly planted and pelvis balanced over them, with belly up and in. Seems obvious until you look around and see how many people stand belly out with legs shifting and unstable. They then have to stick their rear out to compensate. Like the unbalanced stack of dominoes, the neck then sticks forward, so the 10 - 20 pounds weight of their head is out of balance too. They run like Donald Duck and have more tweaks than you have hot dinners.

You can have a loose belly without sticking out your rear. Such people usually have too flat a curve in the lower back (less than 35º).[1] Top trainer Lee Parore calls these athletes "Pink Panthers." You should have your posture assessed to determine whether you are a Pink Panther or a Donald Duck. Both types need to pull the belly up and in. But only the ducks need pull in their rear. The panthers should do the opposite, that is, work to maintain a neutral spine by maintaining the curve.

Lift Your Anus

Folk tend to think of the pelvis (from the Latin word for "bowl") as a solid, bony bowl that holds the organs. Not so. The bones of the pelvis form only the sides of the bowl, leaving a big hole in the bottom.

The bottom of the bowl is made of muscle. If that muscle is not strong, then a strong transversus and obliques, which pull in the gut, try to push your organs out through the bottom of the bowl. Especially so during sports and weight training, where there are many instances of large, rapid increases in intra-abdominal pressure.

The clearest example of weakened pelvic floor muscles is after childbirth, during which the muscles become damaged by the action of the abdominals and uterine muscles in releasing the baby from the womb. Some birth training systems do a great job of teaching the mother-to-be to bear down on these muscles and damage them, but then fail to teach her how to repair them. That's one big reason behind the thriving US industry in diapers for older women.

Athletes with weak muscles of the pelvic floor can suffer similar incontinence problems. But the main reason for strengthening these muscles is to help you hold a firm gut for the transfer of power. The muscular floor of the pelvis is the base of your column of power. If it bulges, power dissipates. So, in addition to pulling the gut up and in for good posture, you should also pull up on your anus. I cover exercises for strengthening these muscles in Chapter 18.

Get Your Head Right

Body movements originate in the pelvis, but they are all directed by head movements.[4] If your head is out of place, usually by being stuck forward, nothing works properly. Your head makes up about one-tenth of your bodyweight. It sits naturally a tad forward of the center of gravity, a evolutionary design flaw inherited from our four-footed ancestors, which is why the strongest and largest neck muscles occur on the back of the neck. Otherwise we couldn't hold our heads up.[1]

Sticking your head further forward, however, dramatically increases compressive forces on the front of each vertebra by up to 100 pounds. You cannot operate at full power with your spine under such an unequal compressive load.

To help move the head back into alignment, press your tongue against your upper palate, just behind and above the teeth. This **tongue lock** is part of the power posture which links the head, neck and spine into the power center of the abdominals and pelvis.

Franco Cavaleri shows correct posture, including head position, for the deadlift.

Whenever you do a power move, use a firm tongue lock. It never fails to boost your power.

We have a rule in the weight gym which applies equally well to any tough move you have to make in life. Before moving any weight, center yourself — neutral spine, belly up and in, anus in, head in and balanced, tongue pressed on upper palate. Relax in this centered, balanced position and take in a full, slow breath. Then begin the a forceful move. Makes life a whole lot easier.

Power Principle 3: Learn Power Posture. Bum in, belly in, anus in, head in, and lock your tongue.

Fartlek
Runner who insists on
eating tofu.

Elastic Muscle

The length of your bones is set by your genetic heritage and childhood nutrition. It cannot be altered, except by arduous, long-term surgery and drugs. But the range of motion of your limbs and spine is determined more by the habitual movements you make. It can be improved dramatically by simply changing those movements.

Knowing how to improve your range of motion is crucial to athletic power. The length of your stride, the degree you can bend and twist without strain, the arc through which you can move your arms, even your speed of movement, all depend on the flexibility of your joints and the length and elasticity of your muscles. Muscles cannot apply their full power unless you can move limbs freely throughout their full range.

We all know well how a stiff neck or back or shoulder restricts our movements. Yet many athletes we ask, don't make the mental connection between the temporary limits imposed on movement by stiff muscles and joints, and the permanent limits imposed on performance by poor flexibility.

Most athletes do stretch, but often in a perfunctory or incorrect way, and with only a vague notion of the benefits. Many consider stretching an unimportant part of their training. I hope to convince you otherwise because, without good flexibility, you will ***never*** be able to apply your full power.

Stretching Prevents Injury, Boosts Speed

Some research shows little benefit from stretching. But when you examine the stretching programs used they are *pathetic!*.[1,2] And that's being kind. Controlled studies using decent stretching programs all show substantial reductions in muscle and connective tissue problems and more rapid healing of injuries.[3-6]

Numerous studies show that flexibility training also increases speed of movement. Why this is so was unclear until recent research by Terara et al at Kyoto University in Japan. They showed that flexibility training enables movements to be made with less energy.[7]

Important work by Wilson at the University of New England in Australia shows why flexibility reduces the energy required to move. Muscles that are more flexible show greater use of what is called **elastic strain energy**.[8] In practical words, you go off like a stretched rubber band.

You will learn more how stored elastic energy boosts speed of performance when you read The Vital Link in Chapter 25 and Plyometrics in Chapter 26. Anything that adds to your speed gives you a big edge on power.

Range Of Motion Boosts Power

The increased power of movement resulting from flexibility training is further enhanced by increased range of normal motion. In a representative study, Hortobagyi and colleagues at the University of Physical Education in Budapest, Hungary, trained healthy students in stretching, three times weekly for seven weeks. They used six exercises for stretching quadriceps, hips and hamstrings. Subjects were then tested for flexibility. The distance that subjects could stretch in front-to-back splits, for example, increased by an average of 9.5 inches for each leg, a total of 19 inches.[9]

At the Colgan Institute, we have improved the power of many runners by increasing the flexibility of their quadriceps, hips and hamstrings. Over our 8-week Extension-Connection Cycle, flexibility in the front-to-back splits improves by up to 12 inches for each leg, a total of 24 inches. This improvement translates into a passive increase in normal stride length of up to 4 inches.

Such an increase in stride length makes a big difference to performance. Here's a prime example from our files. The records show a runner who had a stride length of 53 inches before the stretching program, and a more powerful stride length of 56.8 inches after 8-weeks of

Michael Colgan demonstrating an abdominal stretch on the Swiss ball.

stretching. Before the program, we counted his strides in two 10Ks with a pedometer. He required an average of 7,417 strides to complete the race. After the stretching program, he completed a10K in 6948 strides, 469 fewer strides. Compared with the distance covered with his former stride length, that's an improvement of 633 meters.

Some coaches have criticized findings like these, saying that, though the stride is longer it is also slower, because the leg has to move a greater distance. Not so. As the studies above indicate, the lesser energy cost per stride enables the leg to move at a greater speed for a given level of energy. So the cadence or leg turnover speed of runners on stretching programs does not decline. And running times often improve dramatically.

For the runner noted above, his 10K time had been stuck between 40 and 41 minutes for a year, with a personal best of 40:02. Over the next six months he continued stretching and we used the pedometer to count his strides in several 10K races. He took 6923 – 7160 strides. Compared with his old stride, he gained between 400 and 700 meters in a 10K. His personal best time improved by a whopping 2:05 to 37:57.

Despite such findings, gym programs rarely work with range of motion as a component of athletic power. But that's going to change fast. Leading the charge is the Les Mills Bodybalance Program from New Zealand, which uses an integrated combination of yoga, balance and stretching exercises.

What Are You Stretching?

Stretching is not simple, despite the many books and charts on gym walls that make it seem so. Done wrongly, it is a source of many injuries on the playing field. Renowned marathon coach and former Olympian, Jeff Galloway, repeatedly warns runners against incorrect stretching, and some coaches reject it altogether. Here I tell you the right way, because the scientific evidence shows that the right stretching dramatically increases athletic power.[3-6]

First, you have to know what you are stretching. Numerous athletes we ask, believe they are trying to stretch not only muscles and their surrounding fascia, but also tendons and ligaments. No way José!

The tendons are thick, tough bands that connect your muscles to your bones. They are composed mostly of inelastic **collagen** fibers. That makes them about as stretchy as a heavy leather belt. You can tear tendons by extreme or ballistic stretching. **But tendons do not stretch**.

The ligaments are bands of fibers that connect bone to bone. They also contain collagen

Dr Jackie Mills and Don Christensen show the way in Les Mills' Bodybalance program, licensed to gyms in the US and New Zealand, which uses an integrated combination of yoga, balance and stretching exercises.

fibers but in a mix with a good proportion of stretchy **elastin** fibers. So ligaments do stretch. But should you stretch them? Generally, no. To do so renders the affected joint hypermobile and weak, because the over-length ligaments no longer hold the bones firmly together. The net result is multiple joint problems, including cartilage breakdown from uneven stresses and arthritis in later life. **Don't stretch ligaments**.

You do want to stretch muscles but their surrounding spiderweb of fascia makes it difficult. Fascia are the thin sheaths of connective tissue which surround and hold together muscles and individual bundles of muscle fibers. Although thin, fascia are composed mainly of collagen fibers, and are difficult to stretch.

Worse, fascia shorten with age, poor posture, and muscle imbalance. They also shorten during rest after exercise.[10] Shortened fascia are a big cause of the stiffness you feel the morning after a big workout. Shortened fascia shorten the muscles they hold and reduce their range of motion. So **you do want to stretch the fascia along with the muscles**.

How Muscles Stretch

I want to spell out how muscles stretch, because I have been guilty in the past of using lovely-looking stretches from books and videos, without thinking whether or not they work. Most of them don't.

As the drawing on the next page shows, each muscle is composed of bundles of muscle fibers called **fasciculi.** Each muscle fiber is made up

Lovely Karen Reynolds demonstrates a tensor fascia lata stretch with arms supporting the body to prevent reflex contraction of the hip muscles.

of 1000-2000 thread-like **myofibrils**. Each myofibril is a chain of short segments called **sarcomeres**. And each sarcomere is made up of pairs of short protein rods called **actin** and **myosin**. Muscles lengthen when these rods slide past each other. When the muscle is relaxed, the actin and myosin rods slide back to an habitual resting position. So each sarcomere has an habitual length. Correct stretching lengthens the muscle by causing the actin and myosin rods to adopt a new habitual resting position which lengthens the sarcomere.

Muscles also become longer by another adaptation to stretching only recently confirmed in studies on animals.[11] Regular stretching causes myofibrils to grow longer by growing new sarcomere segments. As yet there are no human studies, but I'll bet my back teeth they will hit the journals in the next five years. These are important findings for athletes, because the longer a muscle becomes, the greater its range of motion and the more power it can generate.

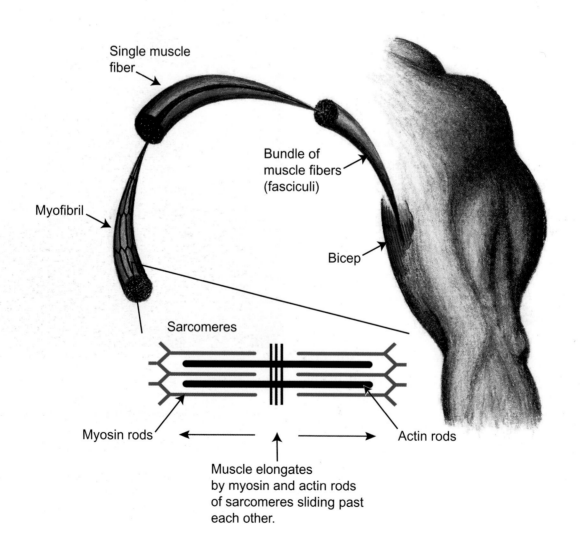

Single muscle fiber

Bundle of muscle fibers (fasciculi)

Myofibril

Bicep

Sarcomeres

Myosin rods

Actin rods

Muscle elongates by myosin and actin rods of sarcomeres sliding past each other.

Relaxation

I've sketched the basic physiology of flexibility because it shows why the grunt and groan stretching you commonly see in gyms is next to useless. If a muscle is contracted at the time of stretching, the actin and myosin rods cannot slide to a longer resting position. All you are doing is straining the tendons. Here's the key. **A stretch can change a muscle so that it is longer after being stretched, *only* if the muscle is relaxed while it is being stretched.**

Hamstrings provide a great example. Dozens of books show standing hamstring stretches, from simple toe touches to extreme one-leg ballet bar stretches. Unless the athlete has had extensive yoga or ballet training to relax the muscles, none of these stretches work. Whenever you bend from the waist in a standing position, the hamstrings contract automatically to stabilize the pelvis.[10] They cannot stretch because, unless you have had the right training, you cannot relax them. All you are doing is straining the muscle tendons and over-stretching the ligaments of the lower back. The first rule for successful stretching is: **relax the muscles being stretched**.

> *Maintaining flexibility is one of the keys to a long athletic career.*

Warmth

The second rule is warmth. Cold muscle means short, stiff muscle, and especially tight fascia, the hardest part to stretch. Studies show that a 10-minute warm-up greatly increases muscle elasticity.[10,12]

Though commonplace, jogging is *not* a good warm-up. Slow jogging delivers a vertical jarring force to the knees, hips, and back about four times that of fast walking. It causes muscles to tighten rather than relax. Use walking, cycling, rowing, stair-stepper or cross-country machines as your warm-up. Breaking a sweat is the criterion. **Always warm-up before stretching.**

Minimum Force

Excessive effort is a major reason folk fail to become flexible with regular stretching. Never force a muscle and never bounce. Pushing to pain, popular in some programs, brings only inflammation, injury, and shorter, tighter muscles. Comparison studies of low-force versus high-force stretching, show that the lower the force the greater the permanent lengthening of the muscle.[13]

Super flexible Melissa Canales demonstrates an extreme abdominal and back stretch.

Stretch only to the point of comfortable tension, then back off until the muscle relaxes. Then stretch again to a second comfortable point and back off again until the muscle relaxes. Repeat once more to reach the point of maximum comfortable stretch. **Always use minimum force.**

Breathing

Take slow even belly breaths throughout stretching. Belly breathing aids muscle relaxation. Exhale as you move into a new stretch position. Inhale as you back off. Exhale as you stretch again. **Belly breathe while you stretch.**

Long Duration

I've watched many athletes rushing through stretch routines, holding each stretch for 10 – 20 seconds, often forcing the stretch because they know it's too quick. Better not to stretch at all. The muscles never elongate, because they have insufficient time to relax. And the athletes complain they just can't get flexible.

Major muscles can stretch in a relaxed state to about 50% longer than their usual resting length. They will do it only if you wait. Especially, you have to allow time for the fascia, which are often reluctant to relax.

To move in and out of a stretch three times, while allowing the muscles and fascia to relax, takes a minimum of 60 seconds. It's a whole lot better to do 10 good stretches for two minutes each, than 30 in a rush. **Allow at least 60 seconds per stretch.**

Michael Colgan shows adductor flexibility in this extreme stretch.

Patience

You may be very tight when you begin a stretching program. Be patient. Every time you force a stretch you inhibit your progress. But if you persist for six months of correct daily stretching, results will amaze you. **Stretching is an exercise in patience.**

When To Stretch

Don't stretch after training. Your muscles are tight and full of the metabolites of fatigue. In that condition they are prone to stretch injury. After the muscles have relaxed from training, 30 minutes or so after, stretch in a hot tub or a hot shower with the water playing on the muscles being stretched. Stretching during your morning shower works well too. Most important is to stretch, after warm up, immediately before training. Think of it as essential preventive maintenance for your muscles.

After lying in the sun on the beach is a perfect time to stretch. Shown here is the correct form for the seated hamstring stretch, maintaining the normal inward curve of the lower back.

Advanced Stretching: PNF

The stretching method I've outlined is sufficient for the needs of most athletes. But some folk have tight problem areas, and some sports such as martial arts, gymnastics, and various events in track and field and winter sports demand extreme flexibility. For these we have developed a system called PNF-R, that is **proprioceptive neuromuscular facilitation plus rotation**.

The PNF part has been used by physiotherapists for more than 30 years. Studies with gymnasts show that PNF offers benefits additional to passive stretching, for both flexibility and performance.[14] The only problem is, you have to do most PNF stretches with a partner.

In the PNF version of the seated hamstring stretch, resistance is provided by a partner as the subject contracts the hamstrings, gluteals and lower back muscles to move out of the stretch. The final stretch often looks extreme, but is achieved without forcing.

Using the PNF technique to assist stretching the hamstrings.

CAUTION. You should find a certified bodyworker to teach you PNF. Learning the method on your own is hazardous. Most beginners tend to force the stretches and injure themselves. At our Sports Nutrition and Training Camps, we do a two-hour intensive training before allowing participants to use PNF on their own.

PNF Stretching

- Do an initial passive stretch to the point of mild tension. Inhale.

- Against partner resistance, contract the muscles that would move you out of the stretch for 5 - 10 seconds while exhaling. Start lightly and finish with a strong contraction. Inhale

- Exhale and move back into the stretch to a new point of tension for 30 seconds.

- Repeat this sequence twice more, each time moving a little further into the stretch, as the muscles which would move you out of the stretch lose tone and relax.

Maintaining a strong, flexible body is always an exercise in patience. Lesley Colgan with Michael Colgan at age 60, carrying a paragliding wing, heading up to the skyline before launching to fly over Queenstown in New Zealand.

Rotation Of The Joints

The new dimension we have added to our stretching program is **rotation (R)**. The technique itself is not new, however, and has been part of ballet training and some martial arts for hundreds of years. It is effective because of an important characteristic of human anatomy. We are designed so that all natural movements have a rotational component. To allow for that component, at the point of stretch, we get athletes to rotate the joint. With my friend, top trainer Steven Macramalla, we have used rotation to develop stretches that produce amazing gains in flexibility.

Whether you use PNF or not, employing rotation each time you stretch yields elongation of a much larger proportion of the muscle tissues and fascia involved. You also get the stretch while they are moving under torque at full extension, exactly the sort of stress your muscles and fascia undergo during the extreme movements of sport.

To summarize: each stretch starts with a passive stretch. If you have an experienced partner and have learned the technique, it continues with three sequences of PNF. (You can do almost as well without the PNF part.) Each stretch sequence ends with rotation of the joint at the point of greatest stretch. There is no better way to increase your range of motion and, along with it, your athletic power.

The Seven Keys To Stretching

1. Relaxation

2. Warmth

3. Minimum Force

4. Breathing

5. Long Duration

6. Rotation

7. Patience

Learn them by heart and repeat them to yourself every session.

Supposed Hamstring Stretch — Puts damaging stress on lower back ligaments. Hamstring cannot stretch because it is reflexively contracted to stabilize pelvis.

Supposed Hamstring Stretch — Puts damaging stress on lower back ligaments. Hamstring cannot stretch because it is reflexively contracted to stabilize pelvis.

Supposed Adductor Stretch — The Adductors cannot stretch because they are contracted to stabilize the pelvis.

Supposed Gluteus, Tensor and IT Band Stretch — The gluteus and tensor fascia lata cannot stretch because they are contracted reflexively to stabilize the pelvis. The IT band does not stretch because it is a tendon.

Avoid These Stretches

Hundreds of stretches litter athletic books and magazines. Some are excellent, others are OK but many are as useless as tits on a chicken. A few general principles will help you avoid them. First, as we've seen already, stretches should load muscles and fascia, not tendons, ligaments or joints. Second, the muscle must be able to relax in order to be stretched.

In general, any standing stretch in which you have to bend the torso towards the knees, such as toe touching, or ballet bar stretches, require a lot of training to do correctly. Unless you are expertly trained, the hamstrings contract reflexively to stabilize the pelvis, thereby transferring the stress to the lumbar ligaments. In addition, in most athletes, ballet bar stretches cause reflex contraction of the piriformis to stabilize the thigh, and also stress the sciatic nerve.

Some athletes at my lectures object that ballet dancers and gymnasts do these stretches all the time and can tie themselves into pretzels. Having worked with elite dancers and gymnasts, I agree that they do use extreme stretching exercises. But their sports demand extreme flexibility movements, and the ability to do them with relative safety is a result of years of stretching training. Even so, these athletes suffer more joint problems than athletes in other sports, and often require a whole chorus of bodyworkers to keep them viable.

Standing lateral stretches for the adductors and abductors don't work well either. In a standing position both these sets of muscles usually contract reflexively to stabilize the leg. They cannot stretch because they cannot relax.

A third rule in choosing stretches is: never put your knee in a weight-bearing position on the ground for any stretch. It's an invitation to ligament or cartilage damage. The common hurdler stretch and the kneeling quadriceps and hamstring stretches are the worst offenders.

Another bad effect of standing and seated stretches in which you bend the torso forward, is pressure on the sciatic nerve. Done repeatedly this pressure damages the nerve.

Initially, sciatic nerve damage is symptomless. It progresses insidiously over years, until it shows as a strong pain from the buttock down the back of the leg to the heel often radiating to the shin. It is the root cause of many chronic back and leg problems in athletes, especially as they age. You should do everything to prevent it. Use a thick foam pad whenever you stretch on the floor, and avoid stretches that put the sciatic nerve under stress.

Extreme Reverse Hurdler — Puts damaging stress on ligaments of lower back and knee.

Extreme Hamstring Stretch — Stretches hamstring but puts damaging stress on lower back ligaments..

Supposed Groin Stretch— Puts severe damaging stress on lower back ligaments.

Reverse Tailor — Puts damaging pressure on knee tendons and ligaments.

Quadricep Stretch — Puts damaging pressure on knee.

Hurdler Stretch — Puts damaging pressure on ligaments of knee.

The Right Stretches

For athletes, the weightbearing structures of the lower back, hips and legs need far more stretching than the non-weightbearing structures of the arms, shoulders and upper back. Impact stresses of running, jumping and side-to-side motion shorten the muscles and tighten the fascia. As a direct result, most athletes we test have sub-optimal ranges of motion in the lower half of their bodies.

We analyzed the research literature and the records of more than 9000 athletes in our computer database to find out which muscle groups cause the worst problems. Below are the muscles that athletes need to stretch most. And following are the best 15 stretches to do the job.

1. *Gluteus maximus, and associated lower back muscles for hip extension and lower back flexibility.*

2. *Piriformis and five other associated muscles at the side and back of the pelvis, for lateral hip rotation.*

3. *Iliopsoas, rectus femoris and tensor fascia lata, for hip flexion.*

4. *Adductors of the inner thigh for hip adduction.*

5. *Gluteus medius, gluteus minimus and tensor fascia lata for hip abduction.*

6. *Hamstrings for hip extension and knee flexion.*

7. *Quadriceps for knee extension. Rectus femoris of quadriceps for hip flexion.*

8. *Gastrocnemius and soleus for range of motion of foot, ankle and knee.*

9. *Lower back and lower abdominals for spinal rotation, flexion and extension.*

Power Principle 4: Stretch every day.

The Vital 15 Stretches

1. Gluteus Stretch

Lie on back. Bend one knee with foot flat on wall. Cross other leg over bent knee. As you become more flexible, you can use hands as shown or push with foot against wall to apply minimum force to increase the stretch. Rotate hip joint by drawing small circles with knee of stretched leg.

2. Piriformis Stretch

Stand at a bench a bit less than waist high. Lay one leg on bench as shown. Lean against bench and support torso with arms to allow piriformis and other hip lateral rotators to relax. Maintain normal spinal curve. Rotate joint by circling torso sideways, from over knee to over foot.

3. Iliopsoas Stretch

Lie on bench as shown. Hug knee to chest with hands to keep lower back close to bench. Allow other leg to hang freely over end of bench. After muscle has relaxed, use hands to increase stretch by applying minimum force to hanging thigh. Rotate thigh of hanging leg in hip socket by drawing small circles with knee.

4. Adductor Stretch

Lie on back with buttocks touching wall. Allow legs to slide sideways. After muscles have relaxed, use minimum force with hands on thighs to increase stretch. You should not feel tension at inner sides of knee or in groin. Rotate thighs in hip sockets by circling feet in both directions.

5. Abductor Stretch

Lie on bench as shown with upper leg crossed over lower leg. Allow upper leg to relax over end of bench. Rotate stretched thigh in hip socket by drawing small circles with foot.

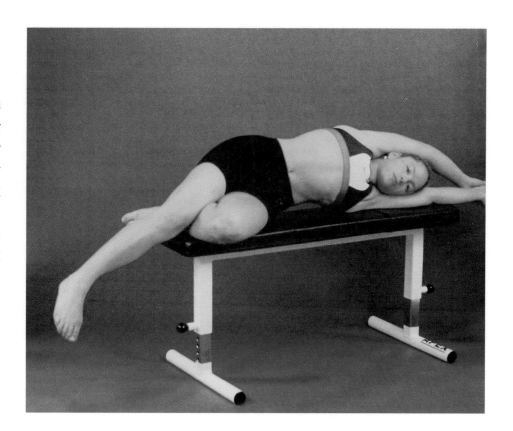

6. Hamstring Stretch

Lie as shown. To increase stretch, use minimum force to pull foot towards head. Rotate hip joint by circling raised leg out to side and back to center.

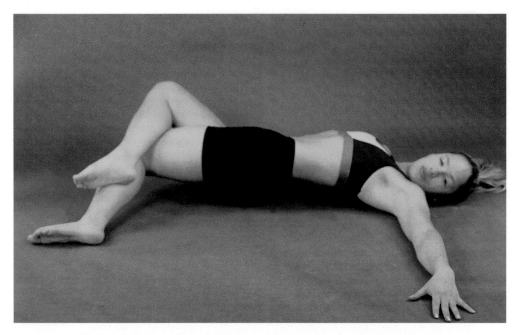

7. Hip Rotation

Lie as shown. After lower back and external oblique muscles have relaxed, use upper leg to press lower leg while twisting torso in o p p o s i t e direction. Rotate hip joint by drawing small circles with knee of stretched leg.

8. Quadriceps Stretch

Lie as shown. Hold ankle and pull upper heel into buttocks. Maintain normal lumbar curve. Rotate joints by drawing small circles with knee of stretched leg.

9. Gastrocnemius Stretch

Stand as shown. Keep rear heel firmly on floor. Maintain normal lumbar curve. Stretch by moving body towards wall. Rotate joints by drawing small circles with knee of unstretched leg

10. Soleus Stretch

Stand as shown in gastrocnemius stretch, but bend rear leg about 15°. Keep heel flat on floor. Don't lean further forward. Keep buttock above bent knee. Rotate joints by drawing small circles with bent knee.

11. Back Curl Up

Lie as shown. Hug knees to chest. Curl up more to increase stretch but keep head on pad and neck relaxed. Rotate spine by moving knees to one side then to the other.

12. Abdominal and Back Stretch

Lie on Swiss ball as shown. Extend arms to increase stretch. Rotate spine by tilting torso to one side then to the other.

13. Seated Spinal Twist

Sit as shown. Use elbow against knee to increase stretch. Rotate spine by gently rocking in and out of stretch.

14. Side Stretch

Sit as shown. Reach overhead towards foot to increase stretch. Rotate spine by gently twisting torso one way then the other.

15. McKenzie Stretch

Lie face down. Keeping hips on floor, push torso up with arms. Rotate by drawing circles with torso.

Upper Body Stretches

The Vital 15 Stretches cover the lower body which becomes most stiff in athletes. Shoulders, arms, chest and upper back also benefit from regular stretching, especially regarding their range of motion and ability to stand rotational stress.[3-6] To take advantage of these benefits without devoting even more the athlete's precious gym time to stretching, we incorporate upper body stretches into weight workouts by doing two opposing stretches in the rest period between each superset.

12 Top Upper Body Stretches

1. Arm Rotations

Swing one arm in 10 giant circles allowing it to fall like a lead weight in rhythm with exhaling. First swing anticlockwise with palm up as arm travels upward, rotating to palm down as arm travels downward.

Oppose this motion by swinging arm in 10 clockwise circles in rhythm with exhaling, with palm up as arm travels downward, rotating to palm down as arm travels upward.

2. Spinal Rotation

Hold post as shown with arms straight and palms facing each other. Rotate whole body away from post, exhaling at maximum point of stretch. Rotate in and out of the stretch in rhythm with breathing. Oppose this motion by spinal rotation on the opposite side.

3. Back Shoulder Stretch

Stand at bar with arms straight and palms up. Let head fall between shoulders, swinging first towards one shoulder, then towards the other, exhaling at the maximum point of stretch.

4. Back Shoulder Stretch

Do Stretch 3 with palms down.

5. Front Shoulder Stretch

Stand at bar with arms straight and palms down. Allow body to sink by bending knees. Stretch one shoulder, then the other, exhaling at maximum point of stretch.

6. Front Shoulder Stretch

Do Stretch 5 with palms up.

Do Stretches 5 and 6 in opposition to Stretches 3 and 4.

7. Arm Stretch Back

Stand at post as shown, with arm straight and palm facing forward. Rotate body away fron stretched arm, exhaling at maximum point of stretch.

Rotate in and out of stretch in rhythm with breathing.

8. Arm Stretch Back

Do Stretch 7 with palm facing backward.

9. Arm Stretch Forward

Stand at bar with arm straight across body and palm facing forward. Use other forearm to push away from post, exhaling at maximum point of stretch.

Rotate in and out of stretch in rhythm with breathing.

10. Arm Stretch Forward

Do Stretch 9 with palm facing backward.

Do Stretches 7 and 8 in opposition to Stretches 9 and 10.

11. Forward Hang

Hold bar as shown with arms straight and palms forward. Allow body to hang forward in a relaxed curve, exhaling at maximum point of stretch.

Rotate body side to side in circles in rhythm with breathing

12. Backward Hang

Hold bar as shown with arms straight and palms facing each other. Allow body to hang backward in a relaxed curve, exhaling at maximum point of stretch.

Rotate body side to side in circles in rhythm with breathing.

Do Stretch 12 in opposition to Stretch 11.

Extend And Connect

Your power in any movement is always limited to the strength of the weakest link in the movement chain. From the photo you can see that this chain is formed by four basic structures:

- The joints between bones.
- The ligaments joining bone to bone.
- The tendons joining muscles to bone.
- The muscles.

Most sports injuries do not occur to bones or muscles, but to joints, ligaments and tendons.[1] These injuries occur especially when the joints are in extension and rotation under load, just the sort of situation that occurs with athletic

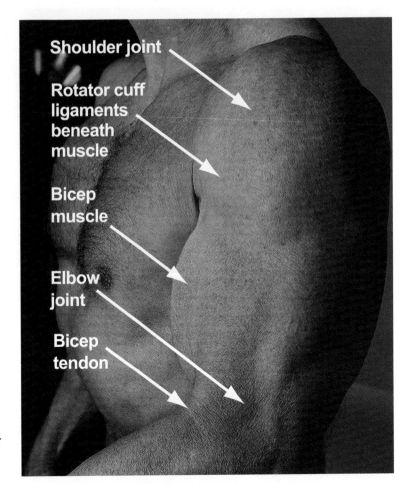

Shoulder joint

Rotator cuff ligaments beneath muscle

Bicep muscle

Elbow joint

Bicep tendon

effort. So it is imperative in a power program to strengthen the joints and connective tissues of the power chain **before** you make big gains muscle strength. Jumping into heavy weights without doing so, leads inevitably to injury, both in the weight room and on the sports field.

Following The Human Design

The Extension-Connection Cycle runs for eight weeks. It focuses on multi-joint, full-extension exercises, that train the joints and connective tissues in the complete rotational movements the muscles are designed to make. The biceps complex, for example, not only bends the arm but also rotates the forearm from full pronation (palm down, pinky out) to full supination (palm up, pinky in). All free movements of sport incorporate these rotational components.

That's why most bodybuilding curl exercises for the biceps, which are done with hands supinated and locked in one position by the bar, just don't cut it because they allow only partial non-rotational movement. They are okay for building bigger biceps, but not for building

One of the strongest men in the world, professional strongman Jimmy Pellachio (The Iron Bull) has the joint and connective tissue strength necessary to bench press the 905 lbs weight shown here. But he has also developed the flexibility and precision of rotational movement that enable him to be a black belt in karate and fine concert pianist.

biceps that will function in the movements of sport.

You make rotational joint movements in all everyday activities, but rarely under the conditions of full extension and heavy load that occur constantly on the playing field. The Extension-Connection Cycle is designed to strengthen joints and connective tissue under these extreme conditions, to protect them from the increased stresses imposed by the large increase in muscle strength you will gain from the Strength-Stabilization Cycle. You cannot use this strength effectively and safely unless you do extension-connection training first.

Extension-Connection Cycle

You do five workouts per week, done as three days on one day off, two days on one day off. You will like the days off.

You use moderate weights, 60 – 80% of 1RM. The maximum weight you can use for one repetition, is called the one-rep-max or 1RM. So if you can do a single bicep curl with 100 pounds, you would do extension-connection training using 60 – 80 pounds. You can find out what actual weights to use for your individual program from the tables in Appendix 1.

You do sets of 6 – 12 repetitions, the ideal range for increasing connective tissue thickness and strengthening joint structures, thus preparing the body for the heavier strength and power cycles.

You do three sets of each exercise. First, a light warm-up set of 10 – 12 reps, using 60% of 1RM, concentrating on form and extension. Second, a heavier set of 8 – 10 reps, using 70% of 1RM. Third is the heaviest set of 6 – 8 reps, using 80% of 1RM.

You do 6 – 8 exercises per workout. As you will see in later chapters, hormonal limits on effective weight training allow a maximum of 24 sets per workout, which limits the possible exercises in the Extension-Connection Cycle to 6 – 8 exercises per bodypart. Don't worry, when you do the best exercises, and do them properly, you will not want to do more.

You use supersets. As many of the exercises as possible are done in **opposing supersets** which make up **supercycles**. In an opposing superset, a set of one exercise, which extends a limb or rotates a joint in one direction, is followed *immediately* by a set of a second exercise, which bends the limb or rotates the joint in the opposite direction. As with the example shown in the photos overleaf, each set of bicep dumbbell curls is followed by a set of tricep kickbacks. So three supersets, each of two exercises, make up the supercycle.

You use short rest periods (30 – 60 seconds), between each superset. During this time you

stretch. So training tends to becomes a bit anaerobic by the last of the three supersets of the supercycle.

Between supercycles, **use longer rest periods (2 – 3 minutes),** to let breathing return to normal, and to allow a good proportion of creatine phosphate to regenerate in the muscles. We cover creatine phosphate in detail in a chapter ahead.

During the 8 weeks of Extension and Connection it is important not to exceed 80% of 1 RM for any weight. During this period you are teaching not only your connective tissue to become stronger but also your nervous system that controls all movement. Overload that system and, just like a computer, it will crash: that is, shut down to protect itself. From thereon in you are teaching it to crash. As masters of Tai Chi know well, **the nervous system learns best when you whisper to it.**[2]

A good example of supersets for extension and connection is a set of dumbbell bicep curls (above) followed by a set of dumbbell tricep kickbacks.

Power Principle 5: First train joints and connective tissues with the Extension-Connection Cycle.

8-Week Extension-Connection Cycle

Workouts Per Week		**5**
Exercises Per Workout		**6 - 8**
Sets Per Exercise	*Exercises done in opposing pairs as supersets, to make supercycles of 6 sets.*	**3**
Reps Per Set	Set 1	**10 - 12**
	Set 2	**8 - 10**
	Set 3	**6 - 8**
Weights	Set 1	**60%1RM**
	Set 2	**70% 1RM**
	Set 3	**80% 1RM**
Rest Periods		*30 - 60 seconds between supersets* *2 - 3 minutes between supercycles*

Spring Training

6

Stable Strength

In any free movement, the main muscles involved are called **prime movers**. The muscles that hold the joint in the desired plane of motion are called **stabilizers**. The prime movers can move the body effectively only if the stabilizers of the joints are strong enough to hold the limbs exactly as desired.[1]

Sounds complicated, but it's dead simple. Say you are sprinting. As you lift each knee forward, the prime movers — the quadriceps — perform the lift. The stabilizers, principally the **adductors** of the groin and the **abductors** of the outer side of the thigh (plus numerous other muscles of the hips and back which stabilize the pelvis), hold the thigh and knee in a straight line, parallel with the direction you want to go. If you train the quads, but neglect the adductors and abductors, then, at high power output, the leg becomes unstable. The knees wobble with each stride, because the stabilizers fail to hold them against the forces transmitted up the leg caused by the uneven ground or changing angles of footfall. Every wobble jiggles your whole body and slows you down.

We see this problem constantly, especially with athletes who have heavy upper bodies to control, such as professional footballers and basketball players. The worst problems occur with those whose leg training consists of squats done on a Smith machine, and leg presses, extensions and curls done on isolation machines. All these machines mechanically hold the body in place and prevent the stabilizers being strengthened. These athletes develop tremendous quadricep strength, but their leg stabilizers cannot take the increased stress.

rarely sprint in a straight line in their sports, so their legs are subject to greater side-to-side forces than the legs of other runners.

Over a period, such incorrect leg training **reduces** sprinting speed. Despite the much greater strength developed in the prime movers, the stabilizers become less and less able to keep the leg moving in a straight line. It's no wonder that numerous coaches still believe that weight training somehow makes athletes slower.

On the contrary, weight training makes you faster, a lot faster, but only if you do it right. Doing the Strength-Stabilization Cycle each year is a critical component of the Power Program that enables you not only to increase the strength of prime movers, but also to stabilize the joints to withstand the added stress whenever that increased strength is applied.

Strength-Stabilization Cycle

The Strength-Stabilization Cycle runs for **10 weeks**. It focuses on free weights and cable exercises that demand full participation of the stabilizers in addition to the prime movers.

You do five workouts per week — done as three days on, one day off, two days on, one day off. The days off are blissful.

You use moderate to heavy weights, 70 – 110% of 1RM.

You do sets of 3 – 10 repetitions, the ideal range for increasing strength with stabilzation.

You do three sets of each exercise. First, a warm-up set of 8 – 10 repetitions with a moderate weight (70% of 1RM). Second, a heavy set of 3 – 5 repetitions with 90 – 95% of 1RM. Depending on your vitality on the day, the second set can be done for 1 – 3 repetitions with 100 – 110% of 1RM. Third, is a set of 4 – 7 repetitions with 85% – 95% of 1RM. You can work out the actual weights to use in your personal program in Appendix 1.

You do six exercises per workout plus two light maintenance exercises. The number of different heavy exercises is limited to six per workout for two reasons. First is the strenuous nature of the work. Second is the time it takes to complete them. Remember, you can work heavy in the weight room a maximum of 60 minutes before hormonal and neural fatigue start to shut down muscle responses.[2]

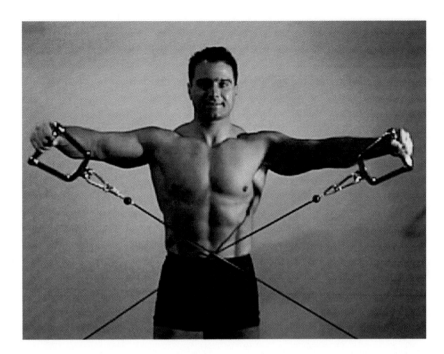

A good example of supersets for strength and stabilization is a set of cable laterals followed by a set of cable pulldowns.

You use supersets. As many exercises as possible are done in opposing supersets to make up **supercycles**. In an opposing superset, a set of one exercise which extends a limb or rotates a joint in one direction, is followed *immediately* by a set of a second exercise which contracts the same limb or rotates the joint in the opposite direction. Each set of cable laterals, for example, is followed by a set of cable pulldowns. So three supersets, each of two exercises, make up the supercycle.

You use short rest periods between superset pairs of exercises (about 60 seconds). During this time you stretch. **You use long rest periods between supercycles (3 minutes)** to allow regeneration of a large proportion of creatine phosphate in the muscle.

Power Principle 6: After extension and connection training, train stabilizers and prime movers with the Strength-Stabilization Cycle.

10-Week Strength-Stabilization Cycle

Workouts Per Week		5
Exercises Per Workout		*6 heavy plus 2 light*
Sets Per Exercise	*Exercises done in opposing pairs as supersets, to make supercycles of 6 sets.*	3
Reps Per Set	Set 1	*8 - 10*
	Set 2	*3 - 5*
	Set 3	*4 - 7*
Weights	Set 1	*70%1RM*
	Set 2	*90 - 110% 1RM*
	Set 3	*85 - 95% 1RM*
Rest Periods		*60 seconds between supersets* *3 minutes between supercycles*

7

Power Cycle

I've seen it happen a gazillion times. Young, fit athletes think they are invincible and go straight for the power. They jump into heavy, whole-body exercises such as deadlifts and high pulls, which involve many muscle chains simultaneously, and arm and shoulder joints and their connective tissues at full extension. Then, after a few weeks, they are gob-smacked when their lower back or rotator cuff or some other weak link gives way under the strain. From a quarter century of using weights with over 10,000 athletes, I can tell you that no one, no matter how fit and strong, should do whole-body weight exercises without first training for three to six months for extension, connection and stabilization.

Before **ever** starting our Power Cycle, prepare your body faithfully by completing the Extension-Connection Cycle and the Strength-Stabilization Cycle. You have to complete these preparation cycles **every year**. Otherwise you will end up both overtrained and injured. Once prepared, however, the Power Cycle will quickly bring you to a power peak, right before your competitive season — a peak that will last almost all season long.

The Power Cycle runs for **seven weeks**. It focuses on bringing together all the weight work you have done during the previous 18 weeks. It links strengthened joints and connective tissues to strengthened prime movers and stabilizers, in a network of complementary muscle chains that permit smooth, efficient transfer of power from the ground, or any fixed point of limb connection. To achieve this goal, you need to do **whole-body movements** which involve multiple muscle chains simultaneously.[1] The best weight exercises, such as high pulls, deadlifts and squats, are covered in later chapters.

You do only three workouts per week — one day on, one day off, with an extra day off at the end of each week. You need a day off between each workout to allow for recovery. You will relish recovery days.

You use heavy weights, 80 – 125% of 1RM. Such weights are very challenging and should not be done casually. Focus, concentration, form and posture are paramount. Before working out always warm up your whole body with light aerobic exercise. When working heavy, our rule in the gym is: **Never touch a weight till you've broken a sweat.**

You do sets of 1 – 6 repetitions, the ideal range for power. Also, you do light warm-up sets in the movement of each exercise to set your posture and form and prepare the particular muscles involved. These warm-up sets are not counted for the workout, but are essential preparation.

UP YOUR MASS

BARBELL

JOKA

Mike
keep up
word

World record
1,025 Squat
725 Bench
Total 2,460

You do each exercise for four or five sets, depending on your vitality on the day. After a light warm-up in the movement, the first set is 5 – 6 reps with 80 – 85% of 1RM. Second is a heavier set of 2 – 4 reps with 95% of 1RM. Third is a heavy set of 1 – 3 reps with 95 – 105% of 1RM. Fourth is the heaviest set of 1 – 2 reps with 100 – 125% of 1RM. (The fourth set is optional, depending on how good you

My friend champion powerlifter Anthony Clark — That's one big package of power!

are feeling on the day.) Fifth is a set of 1 – 3 reps with 100% of 1RM. You can look up the actual weights to use in Appendix 1.

You do only four exercises per workout. Unlike the preceding two cycles, exercises are no longer done in supercycles, because multiple muscle chains are involved in each.

You use long rest periods (3 minutes) between sets and between exercises to allow for recovery of strength. During these periods, stretch lightly. Research shows that rest periods of about 3 minutes between sets of heavy exercise result in greater strength increase than short rest periods (less than 1 minute).[2] Because of these long rest periods, your time in the gym may stretch beyond the ideal 60 minutes, but the rests and stretching allow you to extend this time a little without deficit. The Power Cycle is summarized overleaf.

Power Peaks

After seven weeks on the Power Cycle, you should be at a peak for the start of your competitive season which you should have set your calendar to be one week away. Taper off for that week, with *light* weight work, covering the whole body, using the weights and exercises of the Extension-Connection Cycle. Do not do power exercises.

Now that you know the programming of the 25-week Power Program, you are ready to slot into it the best exercises for athletes, and, to learn to do them in the most effective way. Not a simple task, because many of the weight training exercises used today grew out of competitive bodybuilding. It bears repeating that competitors in bodybuilding are concerned with the size and shape of their muscles, to exhibit them on stage. They do not have to use their bodies in sport, so they pay little or no attention to developing functional muscle. Consequently, many bodybuilding routines create muscular bodies that look good, but cannot perform on the playing field. For athletes, functional muscle is paramount. If you want to build muscle that performs superbly in any situation, the following chapters give you all the tools you need.

> ## Power Principle 7: After extension, connection, strength and stabilization training, train with the Power Cycle for power.

7-Week Power Cycle

Workouts Per Week		**3**
Exercises Per Workout		**4**
Sets Per Exercise		**4 - 5**
Reps Per Set	Set 1	**5 - 6**
	Set 2	**2 - 4**
	Set 3	**1 - 3**
	Set 4	**1 - 2**
	Set 5	**1 - 3**
Weights	Set 1	**80 - 85% 1RM**
	Set 2	**95% 1RM**
	Set 3	**95 - 105 % 1RM**
	Set 4	**100 - 125% 1RM**
	Set 5	**100% 1RM**
Rest Periods		**3 minutes**

8

The Power Equation

For 26 years, we have measured the power of numerous professional footballers, from the Green Bay Packers, the Padres and the Giants, to the All Blacks rugby footballers of New Zealand. They are big boys. But their power is often suboptimal for their mass.

Some footballers fail to develop optimal power, because old beliefs still influence them to do everything possible to put on weight, both muscle mass and an overcoat of bodyfat. They have the mistaken idea that the extra mass confers great power because, once it is moving fast, their mass times their velocity blasts them through opposing defenses.

Trouble is, these guys don't believe they are subject to the laws of physics. All force in the universe conforms to Einstein's equation $E=MC^2$. Put simply that means: force equals mass multiplied by velocity squared.[1]

To take an example, if you have a mass of say 100 units and a velocity of say only 50 units, then E (energy or force) = 100 (mass) multiplied by 50 X 50 (velocity). The mass component of the power is worth 100, but the velocity component is worth 2,500. That's why a high-velocity rifle can fire a light rubber bullet through a one-inch board. **Speed is the biggie for power.**

Like big bodybuilders that they have copied in their training, some professional athletes carry enough mass to knock down a barn. But, they are not strong enough to get it moving at a real fast speed. Their power is limited by the very muscle they worked so hard to gain.

Shawn Fitzpatrick (right), a great balance of mass and speed, seen here captaining the All Blacks rugby team, out manoeuvering the usually unbeatable David Campesi of Australia.

Case In Point

Here's an example using actual athletes from our files. Case 1 is a professional footballer who trains in the conventional bodybuilding way for mass. At 6' 4", he weighs 120 kilograms (264 lbs) and carries 18% bodyfat, that is, 21.6 kilograms (47.5 lbs). So his lean mass is 98 kilograms (216 lbs). With that mass, he can bench press 405 and squat 530, so he's no slouch in the strength department. But, hindered by excess mass, his fastest 40-meter dash is only 5.6 seconds, or 7.14 meters per second. We will take that as the measure of velocity.

The maximum power Case 1 can generate in hitting an opponent is $E=MC^2$, that is his total mass multiplied by the square of the speed he can move it. For running that is:

120 kg bodyweight times 7.14 meters-per-second velocity^2 = 120 X 7.14 X 7.14 = 6119 units of power.

Of course, his slow speed off the mark means that faster opponents rarely let him accelerate long enough to reach that maximum power.

Case 2

Now take Case 2, a footballer who trains for power rather than mass. Also at 6' 4", he weighs 105 kilograms (231 lbs). So he is 15 kilograms (33 lbs) lighter than Case 1, a big deficit in traditional beliefs about football. But he is only 10% bodyfat (10.5 kg, 23.5 lbs). So he carries 94.5 kilograms (208 lbs) of lean mass, that is 3.5 kilograms (8 lbs) *less* lean mass than Case 1.

The important point is, Case 2 is stronger than Case 1. Though he has less muscle mass, Case 2 can bench 420 and squat 560. So his strength per pound of muscle is higher than that of Case 1. His body composition is also leaner, with little dead weight of fat to carry. Stronger muscles and less bodyfat enable him to achieve a 40-meter dash time of 4.5 seconds (8.9 meters per second).

So the maximum power Case 2 can generate ($E=MC^2$) is:

105 kilograms bodyweight times 8.9 meters per sec velocity^2 = 105 X 8.9 X 8.9 = 8313 units of power.

That is 1194 more units of power than Case 1. Though Case 2 has less total mass, he is 20% more powerful, moves faster and hits harder. He beats Case 1 every time.

What I didn't tell you is that both cases are the same guy. Case 1 was when he first came to the Colgan Institute for a power program. Case 2 is 12 months later.

In the past, large, over-fat, slow athletes could score in football and other sports because of their sheer mass. Those days are over. Now the elite all train for power. A few weeks ago, I was watching the Pan Am Games, held this year in Winnipeg, Canada. Right now, as I am writing this, I'm watching the 1999 World Track and Field Championships in Seville, Spain. Twenty years ago, half the athletes competing at these meets in shot put, discus and hammer were pudgy, relying too much on mass for their power. Today, pudgies wouldn't even make the prelims, no matter how big they are. All the top athletes know well that strength without excess mass is the key to speed. And speed is the key to power.

Jonah Lomu, hailed as the most powerful rugby player on Earth, has an ideal combination of mass and speed. Trained in Power Program principles by Lee Parore, Jonah is seen here leaving France in the dust at the 1999 World Cup.

Power Principle 8: Train for maximum strength per pound of muscle, not for mass.

9

Train The Chain

Individual muscles of bodybuilders can be unbelievably strong. In the isolation movement of a leg curl machine, for example, I have watched a certain 300-lb professional, with calves like house bricks and hamstrings that might hold a suspension bridge, do 10 reps with the whole weight stack, **with one leg**, chatting to me the while. But asked to sprint up a 60-second hill, he declined purple-faced after one try, protesting: "I don't want to rick my back." He has tremendously strong muscles, but weak links between them, so his body doesn't work well when he has to exert all of it at once.

Athletic activity requires both strong muscles and strong links between muscle groups. As an athlete, you need your calves to have power links right up your leg to the hamstrings, gluteals and lumbar spine. You also need to be able to contract every muscle fully at the multiple angles of limb placement and wide ranges of eccentric torque that occur in the free movements of sport. You need to be able to carry out these movements at maximum muscle contraction, without fear of injury holding you back. You cannot achieve that goal by weight training with machines that isolate your muscles.[1]

Even if you don't get injured in your sport as a result of strengthening isolated muscles, the strength you gain under a typical bodybuilding program is of little use. The transfer of power in free movement occurs only through a linked chain of muscle groups. If any muscle, or any link of connective tissue in the chain remains weak, the power is dissipated.

I saw a dramatic example of this problem in a Strongman contest a while ago. Lou Ferrigno, of Incredible Hulk and Hercules fame, was beaten by smaller men in lifting a weight overhead.

He complained that his waist was too small to lift heavy loads above his head. In fact, the waists of some Olympic weightlifters are even smaller, and they lift much heavier weights than anyone in the Strongman brigade.

Though he is a very powerful man, on that day, Ferrigno was an example of bodybuilding's failure to train muscle chains. In his case, it was the chain from the calves through the hamstrings, gluteals and lower back, up the latissimus, through the trapezius and upper back to the rotator cuffs, that permits the step-by-step transfer of power necessary to hoist heavy weights aloft. The principles herein teach you how to train that chain.

It's not just the muscles and connective tissues you have to link. It's also the integrated sequential firing of the central nervous system.[1] You have to practice the skill movements of your sport many thousands of times in order to link them into smooth sequences of automatic neural outputs. Eventually, you can perform them smoothly, rapidly and powerfully, without thinking about it. You have to practice in the same way to link muscle chains into automatic sequences. Super-trainer Paul Chek has shown us all, that without these sequences, the strongest muscles, trained in isolation, don't do diddly.[2]

Rotating Power

The most common example of weak links caused by incorrect weight training is the rotator cuff — the complex of muscles and tendons that stabilizes your shoulder. The shoulder joint is a shallow cup of soft tissue, designed to allow the largest range of movement of any joint in your body. Unless it is held together more strongly than the muscles that pull on it, you better stick to fru-fru aerobics for exercise.

Master Trainer Paul Chek has developed myriad Swiss ball exercises to train muscle chains.

When you ask most bodybuilders about shoulders, they wax lyrical about deltoids, the much admired three-headed cannonball of muscle that caps the shoulder joint. Ask guys at the gym what they do for their external rotators, and 90% give you a blank look. Many don't even know where they are. Yet, unless you train power into the four muscles and their tendons that stabilize the ball-and-socket joint of the shoulder, strong deltoids are a liability.

These four muscles — the **infraspinatus**, the **supraspinatus**, the **subscapularis** and the **teres minor** — are shown in the figures.

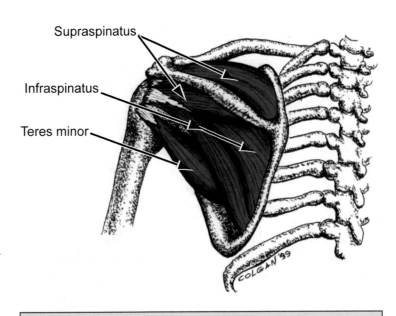

Shoulder from the back, showing three of the rotator cuff muscles.

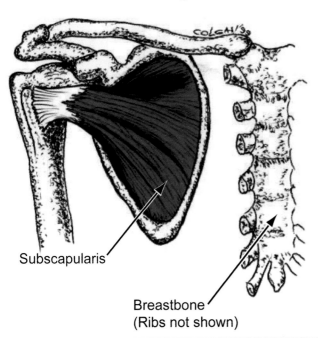

Shoulder from the front, showing the subscapularis muscle of the rotator cuff.

These muscles are small, not visible from the front, hardly even visible in a mirror from the back, so are rarely trained in bodybuilding. Yet they are essential for raising your arm to throw a ball or javelin, pushing from the front or side, and pulling from front, side or overhead. Swimming, baseball, basketball, football, judo, karate, tennis, gymnastics and many other sports all depend on these babies to transfer power from the chest and back, through the shoulder girdle, to the arms.

The external rotators are so important, and such a frequent source of shoulder injury, that I cover them in detail in Chapter 19.

If you have had shoulder problems, or if you want to avoid them, you should follow that chapter to the letter.

The rotator cuff is part of 22 major muscle chains we have identified at the Colgan Institute that are essential for sprinting, vertical and long jumping, lifting overhead, pushing, pulling, throwing, hitting, lateral acceleration and gymnastic movements. Over the last 26 years of measuring athletes, we have isolated the most common weak links in the chains. We designed the **Power Program** to focus especially on strengthening these links.

Power Principle 9: Strengthen whole muscle groups in concert. Train the chain.

Muscle Fatigue
Condition caused by eating
the same shellfish night
after night.

10

Free Movement

Gyms are awash with isolation machines, each one adorned with strange and wishful tales advocating its use. Gym owners love them because they are safe to use, they require little supervision, and you can get two machines into the same space taken by one person working with free weights or cables. If you are an athlete seeking power, leave them for the wannabees.

Except during rehabilitation, where particular weakened injured muscles require restoration, machines that train muscles in isolation cannot improve your power. Even Arthur Jones, king of the Nautilus empire that started it all, finally realized that their utility lay in rehab. These machines are not designed to produce functional bodies, but simply to enlarge and strengthen individual muscles.

For this purpose, many isolation machines work well. But their very design is anathema to athletes. The restraining straps and pads, the restricted arcs and planes of motion, and the fixed intensities of resistance for each position of arc, introduce two big causes of athletic injury. First, their design prevents these machines from strengthening the muscle in the multiple rotational planes of action, multiple angles of loading, and multiple intensities of resistance in any position that occur all the time in the free movements of sport. The muscles remain weak in all but the particular movement of the machine. Second, the design of isolation machines prevents them from strengthening the stabilizing and coordinating muscles and connective tissues. Hence, the muscle chains involved cannot operate properly in any free movement, because the joints through which they transfer their power remain unstable.

Machines Cause Injuries

Remember, all athletic activity requires **free-movement power**. So machines with fixed movements are not only useless for training athletes, they are downright dangerous. It is both useless and dangerous, for example, for a gymnast to strengthen his triceps on a machine, in the hope it will improve performance by keeping his arms straight on the pommel horse. Simply maintaining arm position on the pommel horse during free movement, requires the coordinated action of 48 muscles of the arms, shoulders, chest and back, plus all their connective tissues. To strengthen the triceps more than other parts of this system, puts all the rest at risk.

Exercise genius Paul Chek training abdominal stabilizers on the Swiss ball.

In his recent book, Arnold Schwarzenegger advises that even bodybuilders should do no more than 30 – 40% of their training on isolation machines. He cites his fellow bodybuilding champion and chiropractor, Franco Columbo, stating that these devices cause numerous injuries and are ineffecive for muscle growth.[1]

Top powerlifting coach Louie Simmons, who has trained some of the strongest guys in the world tells his clients that if a gym has more machines than free weights, think again before even going through the door.

Yet I see athletes everywhere using weight machines. If they are so bad, why are gyms not buried in mountains of lawsuits? Because using the machines *in the gym* is very safe. Injuries rarely occur *in the gym*. But when you take the unbalanced and unstable body — trained with these machines — to the playing field and expect it to perform in free movement, the whole system goes to hell in a handbasket. It's hard to prove to a court of laymen that injuries during sport are caused by previous training with machines in the gym, but that's where many of them originate.

The master at demonstrating how stable free movement is the basis of athletic power, is physiotherapist and top trainer Paul Chek, who practices in San Diego, California. Chek emphasizes how the sports field is an unstable environment, in which athletes cannot apply their strength safely and accurately, unless all the stabilizing muscles of the joints have been trained in conjunction with the prime movers. Chek advocates the rehabilitation device, the Swiss ball, as the ultimate unstable platform. In a series of excellent videos, he has raised Swiss ball exercise almost to an art form for athletic training.

Run Wobbly To Run Straight

Not all free movement exercises are good power training. A great example is runners who train primarily on flat roads, rubber running tracks and treadmills. Unless you are sprinting, smooth, even surfaces put little stress on the stabilizing muscles of running motion. So these runners tend to have unstable joints.

When they come to my training camps on Salt Spring Island in British Columbia, San Diego and in Queenstown, New Zealand, these "asphalt addicts" have to run rough mountain trails, where the uneven ground wobbles their ankles, knees and hips every stride. We can clock them on the treadmill running comfortably at a 10 mph, 6:00 minutes per mile pace. But on a mountain trail, they are dying at a 7:00-minute pace. After a few days, they often groan of sore ankles, knees or lower back.

Some coaches fail to emphasize that running only on smooth surfaces, with all the focus on speed or distance, is only half the way to learn to run. It just doesn't train the stabilizers essential to enable the body to run in a straight line. Instead, the athlete learns to fake it, making constant corrections to unstable joints, by using little swaying movements of the hips

Training stabilizers by running trails with triathlon champion Julie Moss.

Thanks to the Colgan Institute. I'm now running faster and feeling better. Best wishes, Regina Jacobs

Olympic runner Regina Jacobs seen here beating fellow champion Patti Sue Plummer.

and upper body. Every one of those side-to-side movements takes motion away from the forward direction, increases the distance you have to cover, and slows you down.

When Regina Jacobs came to me for a program seven years ago, we videotaped her running and tested her muscles, and discovered that she had an upper body sway. The major cause in her case was weak transversus, obliques and rectus abdominis muscles (weak for her very strong legs). These weaknesses forced her to compensate by swaying to absorb the unstable transfer of energy from the legs to the upper body.

After a few months on my program, she returned to the gym to show me she could do the whole set of advanced abdominal exercises shown in Chapter 18, laughing all the while. Then she broke her American record — again!

You can't see the improvement of the transversus or obliques, except for a flatter belly. But the rectus… Regina's fellow athletes call her "Six-Pack." She's still going like a train. In 1999 she broke the American indoor 3000 meters record, and in 2000 qualified for the Olympics.

We often get calls from coaches asking exactly what we did that made such a quick improvement in their runner's performance. They want to know how our magic supplements or other esoteric aspects of our program took only six weeks to accomplish what would take them many months. Well, it all works together, but improvements via nutrition or most other things we do usually take months to show.[3] A major component of the quick jump in running performance is our focus, both in the gym and on the trails, on training the stabilizing muscles of running so that the prime movers can run a straight line.

Free Weights For Free Movement

A few machines are useful when exercises on them are combined with free-movement exercises to train the whole muscle system. The **leg extension machine** is OK for warm-ups when done lightly with single legs, and when sets are alternated in supersets with the **leg curl machine**. That way the quadriceps are trained sequentially with their major antagonists, the hamstrings.

But do not think that these machinesprovide leg training. You need at least six free-movement exercises in your leg program. You need the **front and back lunges** and the **diagonal and plié lunges** to strengthen the leg and hip stabilizers, especially muscles of the groin and the connective tissues of the knee and lower leg. You also need the **squat** and the **deadlift** to link quadriceps to abdominals and psoas, and groin and hamstrings to gluteus and major muscles of the back. Without these free-weight exercises, training legs with most leg extension and leg curl machines, leg presses, hacks and Smith machines is a big cause of knee, groin, iliotibial band and lower back injuries on the playing field.

The only forms of weight training that permit free movements similar to the movements you use in sport, are free weights and weighted cables. They are also the only forms of weight training that train the stabilizing and coordinating muscles and connective tissues that link the muscle chains all over your body and stabilize your joints. They are all you need.

You gotta squat!
Franco Cavaleri shows the
correct form.

Power Principle 10: Use free-movement exercises with free weights and cables. Avoid isolation machines.

"I thought you said the problem was with your knee?"

Power Reps

Your muscles produce their maximum contractile force when moving the largest weight they can in a single effort. That's what the sport of powerlifting is all about. Increasing that maximum force requires not only growth of the muscle, but also development of its neural connections to the brain and spinal cord.

This brain-muscle system grows defensively. That is, it grows stronger primarily to protect itself. So the greatest increases in strength occur in response to overloads that threaten the muscle's integrity.[1]

Studies show that the greater the momentary force produced by a muscle, the quicker it develops strength.[2] Thus, the largest weight you can lift, the **one-repetition maximum (1RM)**, is the most effective means of stimulating the brain-muscle system to grow stronger. But it is also the most dangerous. A program consisting solely of multiple sets of 1RM lifts for each exercise would produce only a mass of injuries.

At the other end of the scale, programs consisting of high repetitions with light weights are very safe. Problem is, they produce only low contractile force, so they have hardly any effect on muscle growth or strength.[3]

Every gym has their high-reps/low-weights contingent, often encouraged by the trainers for safety reasons. Watch them. Their strength and bodyshape hardly change year after year after year. They would probably get better results applying the same energy to gardening or housework. Hell! If high-rep, low-intensity weight training produced great strength or muscle growth, ditch-diggers, bricklayers and carpenters would all be built like the Terminator.

Clearly, the range of repetitions that produces maximum strength without injury, lies somewhere between 1RM sets and high-rep sets. I'm looking at a pile of more than 100 studies on my desk, all done in the last 20 years, that have used a wide variety of training regimens to pinpoint the ideal number of reps. Overall, these studies confirm earlier work summarized by Dr J Atha in 1984, showing that you have to use weights heavy enough to stop you by the end of the sixth rep.[4]

The Energy/Strength Equation

At the Colgan Institute, we focus on the ideal number of reps from a different perspective. We start with the biochemistry of energy. If you are an athlete in good shape and rested, your muscles can store enough of the primary energy molecule, **adenosine triphosphate (ATP)**, for about five seconds of maximum work.[5]

Stored ATP is the only fuel that instantly produces energy. Therefore it is the only fuel with which the muscle can make maximum contractions. It's no accident that football players judge their speed by the 40-yard dash, which takes about five seconds, and not 60 yards or 80 yards.

In a 40-yard dash, or any maximum muscle contraction that takes about five seconds, you use all your stored ATP. Your body then has to switch to a less efficient means of energy production, called the **adenosine-triphosphate/creatine phosphate (ATP-CP) shuttle**. **Creatine phosphate** in the muscle donates its phosphate molecule to regenerate ATP. This chemical process takes time. Thus the energy supplied to the muscles is less than the instant energy provided by stored ATP.

The possible contractile force of the muscles is reduced accordingly, by about 10%, and so is performance. Hence, a 80-yard dash would not be representative of a football player's top speed in a sport where short sprints are paramount, because for the last 30 yards or so he is relying on the reduced energy supply of the ATP-CP shuttle.

After your ATP is all used (in about five seconds of maximum contractions), muscles in good shape have a store of creatine phosphate enough for about another five to six seconds of ***near*** maximum work. That makes 10 – 11 seconds in all.

It's no accident that the human sprint is set at 100 meters, or about 10 seconds. Ten seconds uses all your ATP and your stored creatine phosphate. After that, your muscles have to start converting glycogen to ATP, a much slower process that reduces muscle force dramatically. Even at 10 seconds, and even if you are Donovan Bailey or Maurice Green, you spend the last

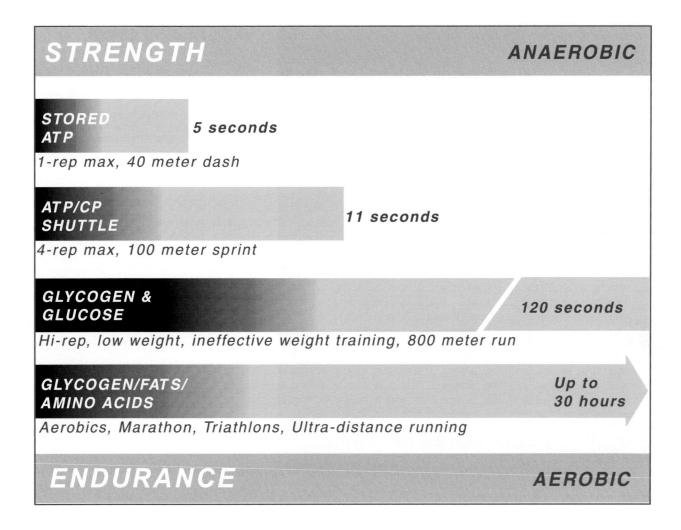

half of the 100-meter sprint fighting against slowing down, because your body has to rely on the less than maximum energy of the ATP-CP shuttle.[5]

Maurice Green beat Bruny Surin by a nose in the 100 meters at the 1999 World Track and Field Championships in Seville, Spain. The videotapes show that Surin was moving faster than Green at halfway and was well ahead. Surin lost because he slowed down more than Green in the last 30 meters. Green probably had a tad more creatine phosphate to play with.

From the above illustration of the basic biochemistry of energy, you can see that 10 – 11 seconds is all you've got to play with for a set of exercises, when you are working as hard as you can (about 90 – 95% of maximum muscle contraction). That's enough time to do 3 – 5 reps, depending on the particular movement and the speed at which you do it. The biochemistry of energy indicates that the ideal range of reps for maximum generation of muscle force, and therefore maximum growth of strength, is 3 – 5 reps.

Strength trainer Charles Poliquin advocates 3 – 6 reps as ideal for maximum strength gain.

Reps And Strength

Bill Kraemer of Penn State University recently reviewed studies that measured the gains in strength for different numbers of reps. He came to the same conclusion that we did from the biochemistry. Maximum strength gain occurs with sets of up to 6 reps.[6]

Top strength coaches also cite the same range. Charles Poliquin, for example, with his wealth of knowledge of strength training applied to the working athlete on a day-to-day basis, advocates 3 – 6 reps.[7] Thus, the chemistry of energy, the research on reps and strength, and the practical application in strength training of athletes, all indicate that, for maximum strength gains, ***sets beyond 6 reps are mostly a waste of time***.

In contrast, most weight training programs emphasize higher numbers, usually 8 – 15 reps. At this range, the muscle cannot contract maximally on even a single rep. They talk a lot of hokum about "going for the burn" or squeezing out the last rep with a supreme effort when the muscle is failing. These techniques do work to increase muscle mass, but they do diddly for strength, because the muscle is working at too low a contractile intensity to stimulate the neural and muscular components of strength growth.

A muscle fails at 7 reps or more for three main reasons. First, as the set extends beyond 10 – 11 seconds, energy production switches from ATP and creatine phosphate, to the slower process of glycogen conversion, which at best delivers only 75% of maximum energy.[5] Second, the build-up of lactic acid has lowered the pH of the muscle into the acid range (the burn), thereby interfering with the chemistry of muscle contraction.[5]

Third, many fast-twitch power fibers have fatigued by the fifth or sixth rep and have dropped out of the game.[4] If muscle fibers are no longer contracting, there is no way to make them grow stronger. So, no matter how much you strain, that supreme effort on the last few reps of a 10-rep set does next to nothing to stimulate the brain-muscle system to increase your strength.

If you only want to grow muscle for show, rather than strength for performance, stay with the bodybuilding rep range. You will get some strength, but mostly you will increase the size of muscle fibers and their sheaths, and the vascularity of the muscle. You can increase the blood content of the muscle by up to 25%. With more blood flowing through it, the muscle becomes a lot larger, but not a lot stronger. Studies show clearly that ranges of 8 – 15 reps cause maximum growth of muscle mass but only moderate growth of strength.[1,8,9]

Reps And Endurance

Some folk argue that the 8 – 15 rep range increases endurance, which they claim does not happen with the 3 – 6 rep range. They are dead wrong. The most effective way to gain endurance requires much higher reps than 8 – 15, and is best achieved by practicing the actual movements you need for your sport.

Olympian Jeff Galloway, king of endurance trainers, has taught more people to run marathons than anyone else on Earth.

A long-distance runner, for example, will gain 100 times the endurance possible with weight training, simply by running — using his muscles for ***thousands of reps*** of the same movement. For endurance, you should follow experts like Olympian Jeff Galloway, who has taught more people to run marathons than anyone else on Earth.[10]

The bodybuilding range of 8 – 15 reps doesn't work for endurance in the weight room either. Whenever we test the endurance of a muscle strengthened with low reps and heavy weights, it beats the hell out of the endurance of a muscle trained the bodybuilding way.

At my seminars, some athletes find this evidence difficult to understand until they see the science of it. First, the power-trained muscle has less mass to move for its strength. So it uses less energy for any given movement. Consequently, it can continue to repeat movements for less total energy cost than the bodybuilding-trained muscle. Second, when performing at a lower weight level, the power-trained muscle uses a smaller percentage of its maximum strength to do the work. The lower the percentage of strength used in a movement, the more reps you can do. Power trained muscles win every time.

Low Reps And Heavy

To avoid injury you have to approach low-rep heavy sets slowly, with eight weeks of the higher rep Extension-Connection Cycle to protect you. When you do get there, the Strength-Stabilization and Power Cycles of the Power Program may feel too quick. You will get little of the pump or the burn experienced when grinding out higher rep sets. You don't leave the gym exhausted or even tight or sore. But your strength, the first requirement of athletic power, will grow out of sight.

If low reps still seem too quick, think about it Larry Scott's way: "Make every rep a set." Concentrate on each rep as if it is 10. As we proceed, you will see that a power rep is not merely flopping the weight up and down. It involves at least four different stages, each done with specific timing, speed and intensity. Get these right and you will never go back to conventional weight training.

Power Principle 11: Go low reps and heavy to failure, or go home.

Fast-Twitch

Muscle fibers come in numerous different types. For power, the important distinction is between **Type 1, slow-twitch**, red fibers and **Type 2, fast-twitch**, white fibers. These are all you have to worry about.

Slow-twitch fibers are red because they have a large number of capillaries, thus a very good blood supply. They also contain more mitochondria to produce energy, and higher levels of endurance enzymes than fast-twitch fibers. But, as their name implies, slow-twitch fibers are slow to react, so they cannot produce great power. Remember, from Chapter 8, speed is always the biggie for power.

If you give slow-twitch fibers a continuing supply of glycogen and fat for fuel, and oxygen to "burn it" for energy, they will continue to produce low-force muscle contractions for hours.[1] **Consider slow-twitch fibers the endurance components of your muscles.**

Fast-twitch fibers are just the opposite. They are white because they have only a meager blood supply. They contain more contractile proteins than slow-twitch. They also contain more glycolytic enzymes for production of energy in the absence of oxygen, and more creatine phosphate to quickly regenerate adenosine triphosphate (ATP), your primary energy molecule. Thus they react swiftly and produce maximum force, but for only a short time.[1] **Consider fast-twitch fibers the power components of your muscles.**

World mountain bike champion Rishi Grewall has the massive power-trained thighs necessary for sprinting uphill over rough terrain.

Power Measurement

Recent direct measures of athletic power confirm the power function of fast-twitch fibers. Researchers at Faculté Medecine LyonSud in France, did a series of studies using heavy braking resistance on the cycle ergometer. Then they biopsied the vastus lateralis of the quadriceps. They found that the proportion of fast-twitch fibers was highly correlated with sprint speed and squat jump performance.[2]

A further study by Linossier et al at the Physiological Laboratory of Saint Etienne Medical School in France, compared heavy sprint training against low resistance sprints on the cycle ergometer (popularly called "spinning" in the US). The spinning had little effect on muscle power.

In contrast, sprint training against heavy braking resistance caused conversion of substantial numbers of muscle fibers to fast-twitch. These changes in muscle fiber composition, measured by biopsy of the vastus lateralis of the quadriceps, remained after a 7-week detraining period.[3] Such studies are representative of considerable recent literature, indicating that, if you want power, you better train for fast-twitch growth.

Low Reps For Fast-Twitch

Sub-maximal exercise, such as a 10-rep barbell curl with a weight you can do for 10 reps, uses mainly slow-twitch fibers. The few fast-twitch fibers that are recruited at the beginning of the set, fatigue and drop out of the contraction long before you reach the tenth rep. Hence, they are not affected by the last few difficult reps of the set, and growth of strength is minimal.[2]

In contrast, maximum intensity exercise, such as a 5-rep barbell curl to failure with a heavy weight, recruits many fast-twitch fibers. And they are still firing at near maximum at the end of the set, so growth of strength is optimized.

Fast-twitch fibers also grow stronger with heavy exercise more quickly and easily than slow-twitch fibers.[1] So for the greatest growth of strength — the first component of athletic power — weight programs must be designed to stimulate fast-twitch.

Dr Colgan with Olympic sprinter Leroy Burrell. As with all successful sprinters, Leroy's muscles have a very high proportion of fast-twitch fibers.

Dr Colgan with Grandmaster William Cheung, master of Wing Chung and a teacher of Bruce Lee. In keeping with his blinding speed, Grandmaster Cheung has a very high proportion of fast-twitch fibers.

These physiological differences in muscle fibers fit nicely with the biochemical evidence discussed in Chapter 11, where I showed you that maximal muscle contraction is limited to the 10 – 11 seconds that the muscle can produce near maximal energy. Consequently, the number of reps that maximally stimulates growth of fast-twitch fibers is 10 – 11 seconds worth, about 3 – 5 reps.

Of course, you can't do this low number of reps without first training the muscle with a medium weight through its full range of movement with the Extension-Connection Cycle. To work heavy without doing so, is to court injury. But, after eight weeks of extension and connection, and a good warm-up set, the weight should be loaded so that muscle failure occurs by the end of the fifth rep.

It bears repeating that in sets of more than 6 reps, one big reason the muscle fails is that most of the fast-twitch fibers have ceased to fire.[1-3] That is, they are no longer being used, so are not affected at all by struggling to do the last reps.

Even sillier is adding partial or assisted reps at the ends of such sets, or drop sets in which you get a training partner to take off weights from the bar, so you can go for the "burn" and continue to squeeze out a few more reps at lower and lower intensity. These are bodybuilding techniques designed to increase muscle mass. They do diddly for strength.

The silliness becomes obvious if you consider a weight with which you can do 50 reps before failure. The intensity of muscle contraction is so low that only bubble-brains believe such light resistance increases strength.

What about the pump you get from high reps? The muscle stuffs itself with lactic acid and blood, and grows bigger and harder. Bodybuilders love the "pump," but it is only a temporary defensive mechanism that does little to increase muscle power. Within 30 minutes or so, the muscles deflate again as they clear the lactic acid, and the blood flow to them declines.

Muscles do get bigger from pumping forms of exercise. Slow-twitch fibers increase in thickness and the muscle also increases capillary density to supply more blood to slow-twitch fibers. Over a period of high-rep and pumping exercises, these effects can increase muscle size by 25 – 50%.

But these bodybuilding techniques have another effect, opposite to power training, an effect that is decidedly detrimental to athletes. Some of your precious fast-twitch fibers convert to slow-twitch.[1,4-6] Also, satellite muscle fibers are brought into the muscle and develop into new slow-twitch fibers. So you build a muscle with a higher level and greater weight of slow-twitch fibers and blood — making it larger and heavier. Your fast-twitch fibers then have a harder job trying to move these large, heavy muscles with the speed required for top sports performance. Leave them for the beach boys. You need maximum fast-twitch power.

Power Principle 12: Train for fast-twitch fiber growth.

Quadriceps
Muscle on front of thigh
that turns into a
prehistoric beast on
leg day.

Swimming champion Vern Moen took a Colgan Institute program to help him improve his fast-twitch performance.

13

Essential Eccentrics

For any exercise, the **concentric** contraction is that half of a repetition during which the muscle is *shortening* under load. The **eccentric** contraction is that half of a repetition during which the muscle is *lengthening* under load. It's easy to work out. Just think, is the exercised muscle shortening or lengthening?

In standing dumbbell curls, for example, the concentric contraction shortens the biceps and raises the dumbbell to the neck. The eccentric contraction lengthens the biceps and returns the dumbbell to the thigh. For the bench press, the eccentric contraction occurs when you lower the weight to the chest, and your pectorals lengthen out towards your armpits. For the squat, the eccentric contraction occurs when you are going down, thus lengthening the quadriceps and gluteus.

Eccentrics are vital for athletes seeking power, because muscles grow stronger primarily to defend themselves. Just like an elastic band, the more a muscle lengthens under load, the smaller it becomes in cross-sectional area. Thus the load per square inch of cross-section becomes progressively larger. Since the early '80s, numerous scientists have shown that when a muscle is in eccentric contraction, it is most vulnerable to the microscopic damage that signals the brain to re-grow it stronger.[1]

As the illustration shows, vulnerability to micro-damage occurs mainly because of the way muscle is constructed. Each muscle is made of bundles of muscle fibers called **fasciculi**. Each muscle fiber is made of about 1,000 microscopic filaments called **myofibrils**. Now we're really getting small! Each myofibril is a chain of sub-microscopic segments called **sarcomeres**, which shorten or lengthen to make the muscle work. When a muscle lengthens under load, the sarcomeres do not lengthen uniformly. Consequently, some parts of the myofibril, and other myofibrils adjacent and attached to it, are stressed more than others.[2,3] Some sarcomeres fail under the strain, and signal your brain to re-grow them stronger. *Myofibrillar damage that occurs under heavy eccentric load is the major way in which the contractile fibers of your muscles increase their strength.*

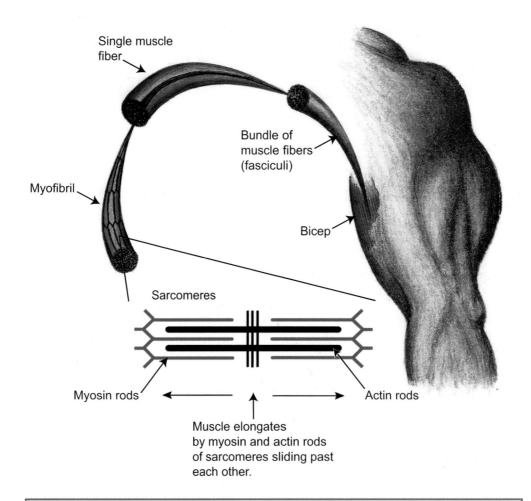

Single muscle fiber

Bundle of muscle fibers (fasciculi)

Myofibril

Bicep

Sarcomeres

Myosin rods

Actin rods

Muscle elongates by myosin and actin rods of sarcomeres sliding past each other.

Damage to the sarcomeres of the myofibrils occurs because of the uneven sliding of actin and myosin rods that occurs mainly with heavy eccentric loads.

Concentric Codswallop

Now you know another big reason why many conventional weight training strategies are useless for gaining power. First, myofibrillar damage has nothing to do with exhaustion. Forcing out the last couple of reps of repeated 10 – 12 rep sets does little for strength, because a weight with which you can do ten reps is too light to cause the requisite damage.

The popular ploy of going for the burn doesn't cause myofibrillar damage either, because it requires you to use weights that are light enough to do the high reps necessary to raise muscle acidity to the point of pain. The burn is simply an accumulation of lactic acid and other metabolites of muscle use. It does nothing to increase contractile strength.

The slow repetition strategy, slow up and slow down, is almost as bad. Weights that you can lift for eight reps or more in slow concentric contractions are too light to pose much risk to the muscle on the eccentric phase, no matter how slowly you let them down. Unless you use heavy weights, you haven't got a prayer for power.

The above strategies do make muscles bigger, both by increasing water content and because the body tries to defend itself against acidity by rushing more blood to the area. Thus, you get "the pump" beloved of posers and strutters. And, over a period of time, the muscle grows more **capillaries** (fine blood vessels) and thickens its membranes and slow-twitch fibers, so you do get size. But you get little power.

Shades Of The Circus

Most of the concentric codswallop arose from a focus on the old carnival strongman act of getting the weight up there. You still see it in the gym every day. "Look at me, I got it up!" Then the bozo drops the bar with a thump just to make sure everyone knows. It's not the way to athletic power.

To explain without getting into a mountain of biochemistry, I will oversimplify a bit. When the muscle is shortening under load (concentric), its cross-sectional area increases — it gets bulkier. Thus, the force per square inch across the muscle area progressively declines. So, as you lift a weight concentrically, there is progressively less threat to the integrity of the sarcomeres, progressively less risk to the myofibrils. The microscopic damage required for muscles to grow is minimal.[2]

Research with athletes backs up this physiological explanation. In the early '90s, a series of collaborative studies by Dudley in the US and Tesch in Sweden showed that concentric contraction training yields only small gains in strength.[4-9] In a representative example of this research, Dudley examined progressive heavy resistance training (6 rep sets) for leg extension and leg press lifts, using four groups of subjects. Over 19 weeks, one group did only concentric contractions, a second group did double concentric contractions, a third did concentric plus eccentric contractions, and a fourth group did no training. All groups were tested for both concentric and eccentric strength before and after the program.

As you might expect, the No Training group showed no change in strength. The two Concentric Only groups showed an average strength gain over the two lifts of 15%. The Concentric/Eccentric group showed a huge average strength gain of 28%.[6] So even if you train low reps and heavy, you still have to focus on the eccentric contraction to get optimum results. Whenever you see athletes grunting to get a weight up, then letting it flop down again, you know they are missing the most effective bit of the rep.

Instead, you should lift the weight concentrically as quickly as possible (maintaining good form), then lower it slowly, fighting all the way.

A good counting tempo for each rep is:
Concentric:
1-little-elephant, up.
Eccentric:
1-little-elephant,
2-humungous-elephants,
3-f___!!#/bleeping-*
elephants, down!

How Muscles Grow

The importance of eccentrics becomes even clearer when we consider how muscles grow. Old beliefs in physiology still litter college text books, asserting that the number of muscle fibers you have is genetically determined and cannot change. They assert that muscles grow only by **hypertrophy**, (thickening of existing fibers). We know now this notion is dead wrong.

Although muscles do grow primarily by hypertrophy, growth also occurs by at least two other mechanisms. The first is **splitting** of fibers to form two separate fibers. The second is **hyperplasia**, recruitment of satellite stem cells in the muscle to grow new fibers. Splitting of muscle fibers occurs readily with any heavy weight training,[10,11] but growth of new muscle fibers requires special stimulation.

The satellite stem cells from which muscles can grow new fibers were first found by Mauro in 1960.[12] Essentially, these cells form the muscle's reserve in case of traumatic injury. They usually develop into muscle fibers only to re-grow a badly damaged muscle.[13] Recent work, however, shows that high levels of eccentric contraction stress can activate satellite cells into growth.[14,15]

In a representative study, Darr and Schultz showed that a single bout of steep downhill treadmill running (18% grade) for 105 minutes,

Doug Benbow worked hard on muscle hyperplasia as well as muscle hypertrophy to gain his athletic physique.

dramatically activated satellite cells in the leg muscles of rats. Even 24 hours later, new satellite cells were still being recruited to grow into functional muscle fibers.[14]

The possible degree of strength increase by growth of new muscle fibers is unknown. But animal studies and autopsy examination of muscles of human accident victims, in which researchers counted the fibers precisely, suggests it is at least 10%.[16-18] This growth occurs only with extreme stress on the muscle, and is unlikely to occur with usual bodybuilding training.[8,18,19]

For you, the potential increase in muscle fibers by hyperplasia offers a 10% edge. But it will happen only if you stress heavy eccentrics in your training. It's a big edge. Give me any two athletes of equal ability. If I make one of them 10% stronger, he will beat the other one every time.

Eccentric-Grown Muscle Lasts

As I discussed in Chapter 1, you cannot train heavy all year long. To do so produces overtaining, neural fatigue and injury.[20] You have to periodize, using a maximum of about 25 weeks of each year for power training. The rest of the year is for competition, so you have to build strength that, with a minimum maintenance program, will last all year.

Eccentrics can give you just those results. We have recorded many cases at the Colgan Institute in which strength gained by eccentric power training continues long after the gains of usual bodybuilding fade away. But we don't have to rely only on single cases. In 1991, Dudley and colleagues showed that athletes trained by stressing eccentric contractions over 19 weeks, maintained their strength increases over a 4-week de-training period. A control group using concentric-only training lost most of their gains.[6]

Hather and colleagues did a similar experiment over 10 weeks training. After a 4-week de-training period, the group using concentric training lost almost all their increase in muscle cross-sectional area. The group that used eccentrics maintained their new muscle.[7] To maintain your gains, become an eccentric in weight training.

Power Principle 13: Use slow eccentrics all the time.

Negatives Are King

As I explained in Chapter 11, low reps with heavy weights are the keystone for gaining strength. And Chapter 13 showed you that the eccentric contraction is the most important half of each rep. But there's one more step if you want optimum strength. Real weight training gyms, affectionately called "iron pits," have always used heavy free weights for low reps. And a lot of them know all about eccentrics. But some still fail to take full advantage of the science of weight training, because they focus on using weights that can be handled concentrically. They do it 80% right and 80% of the benefits.

Making this claim in a lecture at a well known iron pit in Venice, California, I escaped with my life only after giving hot and heavy evidence. So I better do a bit of the same here. In the early '80s, researchers reasoned that, if intensity of eccentric contraction is the key to rapid strength increase, then using a weight heavier than the 1-rep maximum (1RM) should be the fastest way to build strength. Doing reps in this way, with weights of more than 100% of what can be handled concentrically, has come to be known as **negatives**.

Research Supports Negatives

The idea proved correct, but early studies used previously untrained subjects and ran for only a few weeks. Just about any sort of weight training works with novices, so the findings were not accepted by many trainers.[1-3] More recent research, however, shows that heavy negatives can increase strength of fast-twitch fibers in experienced weight trainers up to 10 times more than concentric-only training.[4] Yes, 10 times!

Ted Arcidi, world record breaker in the bench press, knows the power of negatives.

Most studies don't show quite such spectacular results, but negatives are still a big advantage. Hakkinen and Komi have done some of the most meticulous research, so we tend to go with their evidence. A typical example of their studies trained experienced powerlifters in squat and bench press for 12 weeks. One group used only weights they could handle concentrically, the usual sort of training you see in most gyms, even a lot of iron pits. Two other groups stressed eccentric contractions and negatives, using 80 – 100% of the 1RM weight they could handle, for sets of 1 – 6 reps, and 100 – 130% of their 1RM for sets of 1 – 3 reps.

Over 12 weeks of training, doing three sessions per week, all three groups improved their 1RM squat and bench press. The group using conventional concentric loads improved an average of 20%. The groups stressing eccentrics and negatives improved 28%. That's an enormous edge, especially for folk already well-trained and near the top of the weight game.

To better establish the degree of superiority of negatives, Hakkinen and Komi examined Olympic weightlifters, all of them elite athletes, whose previous performance records were well documented. One group made no change to their usual training, which used concentric loads both concentrically and eccentrically. A second group did 25% of their eccentric contractions as negatives, using loads of 100 – 130% of their 1RM.

Over 12 weeks, the group doing their usual training improved 7% in the snatch and 6% in the clean-and-jerk. The group using negatives improved 10% in the snatch and 13% in the clean-and-jerk, nearly double the gain.[5] That's the difference between a gold medal and also ran. As the best growth stimulus for strength, heavy negatives reign supreme.

The Calves Connection

Calves are the neatest example I know of the power of negatives. Ever wondered why calf muscles are so resistant to training? Simple really. Your calves are in continuous use while you are standing. They contain a high proportion of tough, slow-twitch muscle fibers that are subjected to high eccentric loads every day in braking your body against gravity and motion. The easiest example to understand is running downhill, or even walking down stairs. The eccentric braking load on the calves far exceeds the concentric load required to push the body forward.

In conventional weight training, calf work consists of lifting weights you can handle concentrically then lowering them. It has little effect. Calves fatigue and burn with such effort, making you think that something must be happening. But you hardly ever damage them to stimulate growth, because the calf fibers resist eccentric loads every day that are much greater than loads they can handle concentrically.

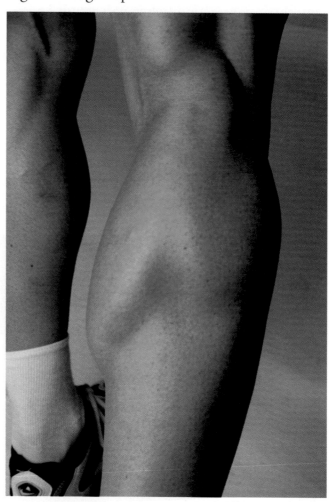

Calves need heavy eccentric stress in order to grow.

The bodybuilder who can lift what seems an incredible 1000 pounds for 10 reps to exhaustion on the shoulder calf machine, hardly stresses his calves at all because the eccentric load is too small. If you are one of the thousands who has worked calves to distraction, and they still look like chicken legs, you know exactly what I mean. Mountain runners on the other hand are constantly whacking their calves with big eccentric downhill braking stresses. Every mountain runner we have worked with over the last 25 years has monster calves.

Now you know exactly how to fix the problem. Providing you don't have dicky knees, you will get more calf growth from short, steep, downhill sprints than you will ever get with conventional training in the gym. If you can't get out there to do sprints, then try this. On the seated calf machine, load up for a 6 – 8 rep maximum set. On each rep, at the top of the concentric contraction (when you are up on your toes), take away one leg and do the eccentric with the other. Do three progressively heavier sets with each leg. Then do the same on the standing calf or, preferably, the donkey calf machine. These extremely heavy negatives will grow your calf strength like crazy.

Too Much Of A Good Thing

Calves are an exception. Most other muscles in your body can't stand such heavy overloads. Coaches and athletes have faxed and e-mailed me like crazy about new studies reporting that heavy negatives conferred no advantage. The reason is simple to see. In their zeal for results, the researchers were thrashing the muscles to insensibility.

A representative example of these studies, by Godard et al,[6] trained the quadriceps of previously untrained men and women for 10 weeks. For one group, they had the subjects use 80% of their 1RM in usual bodybuilding style. The second group used 80% of their 1RM for the concentric contraction, and 140% of their 1RM for the eccentric contraction. Both groups did one set of 8 – 12 reps per session. Both groups increased dramatically in concentric strength, but there was no difference between them.

Heavy eccentrics helped John Hansen build his Mr Universe physique.

This study had three design errors. First it used previously untrained subjects. Worse, it used the wrong range of reps. Worst of all it used negatives that were ***too heavy***. Except for calves, we have found that when negatives exceed 120 – 130% of 1RM, your brain shuts down most of the muscle response, probably because of a signal of imminent muscle injury. There's no way that the subjects using 140% of 1RM for negatives in the above study could possibly maintain a maximal eccentric contraction for even a couple of reps, let alone 8 – 12. The only reason they could follow the protocol at all was that their responses were controlled by an isokinetic machine. They were just going through the motions.

You can demonstrate this muscle shut-down for yourself using a pull-up on the bar. Say you can do a 1RM pull-up with 100 pounds tied around your waist. Get up there on a stool with 120 pounds. That is 120% of your 1RM. Now do negatives. You may get 3 – 5 reps, fighting all the way down. Now rest 5 minutes, then increase the weight to 140 pounds, that is 140% of your 1RM. Not only will you fail to fight the weight down, but you will find your muscles suddenly lose strength and you drop like a stone. The brain shuts down the muscles at the threat of injury from the excessive overload.

Evidence supporting our findings comes from a new study by Bishop et al,[7] which measured the myoelectrical activity of the biceps during concentric and eccentric contractions. The electrical activity of the muscle declined dramatically when the eccentric load was increased from 100% to 150% of the 1RM.

When a muscle shuts down, it does diddly for growth. So, when using negatives, stay within the range of 100 – 125% of your 1RM. That's the **precision zone** for power.

Power Principle 14: Use precision zone negatives in every power workout.

"Of course bribes are better than drugs in sport.
Bribes don't tilt the playing field."

How Many Sets?

The debate over sets still waxes as furious as it did when I first got into the power game 26 years ago. Still fudging the scientific evidence (who wants science hobbling a good argument!) the multi-set wallahs continue to hurl insults at the 1-set brigade. Super trainer Charles Poliquin calls Mike Mentzer's 1-set exercise program "the rantings of a lunatic."[1] The indomitable Mike's replies are best left unprinted. When I began, it was Bob Hoffman and the Olympic weightlifting community, versus the man they called "Weedy Weider," as Joe Weider's clever bodybuilding promotions gradually stole their market.

These raves continue with such ferocity, they remind me of the prearranged antics of professional wrestling — Tweedledum in trashcan lid and cooking pot, whacking Tweedledee in pudding basin and rolling pin. It keeps fans streaming through the pay booths, but has nothing to do with athletic power.

Let's get it straight. The ideal number of sets is not determined by the size of the musclehead or the wit of his invective, or any magic formula. It is controlled by many constraints on the workout, including periodization cycle, hormonal reactions, number of reps per set, speed of each rep, number of exercises, recovery between sets, and bodypart being trained.

Short Sharp Workouts

As I show in my forthcoming book, **Colgan Sports Nutrition**,[2] your anabolic hormones give you only about 60 minutes to complete a heavy weight workout. Beyond that, on any decent program, catabolism begins to overtake anabolism, and weight training becomes counterproductive. One hour might seem a short time to folk used to spending two or three hours on a bodybuilding routine. But if you want power, short and sharp is the way to go.

It's simple to work out how many sets you can fit into that crucial workout hour. After an optimal workout, you should leave the gym having trained to failure the maximum number of fibers of the muscles being trained, both the prime movers and their stabilizers. From Chapter 11, you know already that the ideal number of reps for power training, that is, for gaining maximum strength per pound of muscle mass, is 1 – 6, with the sixth rep being the failing effort. From Chapters 13 and 14, you know that each rep that accentuates eccentric contractions and uses negatives, can take several seconds to complete. So a set of 6 reps takes about 15 – 20 seconds. And because of the physiological limits on energy production outlined in Chapter 11, only the first half of that 20 seconds is really effective. Then you have to rest.

Lovely Jina Buchert shows the sort of body you can acheive with short sharp power workouts.

How Long To Rest Between Sets

After each set, you have to allow for recovery of muscle fibers. It's useless for power training to pause for a few seconds or even a minute, the usual practice in many bodybuilding routines. As you know from Chapter 12, most of the fast-twitch fibers you are trying to grow, will still be shut down and unable to respond.

How long these fibers are shut down depends on multiple factors, such as intensity of effort and condition of the athlete. We've developed a good rule of thumb based on the chemistry of fatigued muscle. You will recall from Chapter 11 that adenosine triphosphate (ATP) and creatine phosphate (CP) in the muscle allow about 11 seconds of near maximum anaerobic work. That is, you can perform near maximum contractions with very little need for oxygen, the ideal situation to recruit and stress your fast-twitch muscle fibers. After that, the fast-twitch fibers fatigue and drop out of the exercise, leaving the work to the slow-twitch fibers, which can use the much slower process of converting glycogen and fat into energy in the presence of oxygen.

Since the research of Greenhaff and colleagues in the early '90s, we know that it takes about two minutes for 50% of creatine phosphate (CP) in the muscle to regenerate, and about four minutes for 90% to regenerate.[3] Regeneration of CP is a good measure of the energy storage

After every power set you have to rest for four minutes to allow regeneration of creatine phosphate and ATP in the muscles, and to release the muscles from neural inhibition.

Supersets which use opposing muscles, such as a set of bicep curls immediately followed by a set of tricep kickbacks, enable both muscle groups to work harder.

that gives the fast-twitch fibers the potential to fire again at near maximum. So the ideal rest between sets, after which you can recruit most of the fast-twitch fibers again, is approximately four minutes.

Combining the exercise and recovery times, including set up and take down of weights as part of the recovery, each set takes about five minutes. That's only 12 sets per hour, with a lot of time sitting around between sets. You use some of the time for stretching, but you still need to get the work in before your hormonal response to exercise starts to decline. **Supersets** are the way to do it.

Supersets Every Time

It's not necessary to spend most of your time in the gym sitting around waiting on your chemistry. During recovery from a set you can do a different exercise which recruits different muscle fibers. This strategy is called **supersets**. Some bodybuilding routines arbitrarily specify all sorts of weird supersets, such as squats supersetted with pullovers, or curls supersetted with sets of abs. There is a better way.

If you can devise supersets in which the muscle in the first set is opposed by the muscle in the second set, such as the bicep curl opposed by the tricep kickback, you gain several advantages. Muscles oppose each other by a process known as **reciprocal inhibition,** to keep joints from becoming spastic. The triceps, for example, makes tiny continual contractions to straighten your arm to oppose the tiny continual contractions of the biceps that try to bend it. When you exhaust a muscle, it gives you a small window of about a minute or so, during which reciprocal inhibition is recovering its function. If you exercise the opposing muscle during this recovery period, it can contract just a little bit harder than otherwise.

So, whenever you exercise opposing muscles in sequential supersets, the fibers of both are able to contract more strongly than usual. Remember, it's the intensity of eccentric contraction that forces growth, so these supersets give you a nice little edge.

Also, you can use the exercise period of one of the opposing pairs of muscles as part of the recovery period for the other. So you don't waste a lot of gym time sitting around. Instead of just 12 single sets, you can get 20 – 24 sets into the crucial anabolic hour. How you divide them up into different exercises deserves the next chapter to itself.

Power Principle 15: Use superset pairs of opposing exercises for a total of 20 – 24 sets, taking not more than one hour in the gym.

Laps
Dehydrated runners who fall and slurp furiously from puddles during a marathon.

"I used to think persistence was the key to sports success: then I met Danny."

Note that I called the bodypart division "nominal." You are always working on your power posture. And the power of every exercise flows from your core. To help make these physical and neural connections, you work different parts of the core specifically on back, chest and leg days.

Your goal as an athlete is to link all the muscle chains in your body into one integrated unit. To train the chains, the **Power Program** also contains many linking exercises, with a bodypart acting merely as the main focus for a particular day.

Steve Rockburn used a Colgan Program to knit together this integrated package which won him Mr Québec Natural 2000.

Power Principle 16: Train each bodypart only once per week.

Stamina
Speech impediment
brought on by
overtraining.

Franco Cavaleri developed principles of training similar to those of the Power Program before ever meeting Dr Colgan. Here he is at the height of his bodybuilding career in form to win the North American Professional Championship.

How Many Exercises?

Elite athletes in top condition (the top 1%) can do short weight workouts twice a day during the 25-week power training phase of their annual periodization program. So they have about 40 sets to divide up into different exercises. But for most of us, a single, one-hour, 24-set weight workout per day is all the body can stand. Sure, you can will yourself to continue, or even go back to the gym again on the same day, but I guarantee that if you do, the **Power Program** will quickly run you into injury or overtraining. Either can sideline you for months. Instead, you should consider 24 sets per day your maximum, and learn to divide them up between the most effective exercises.

What works best depends a lot on the sport you do. Powerlifting, for example, requires athletes to practice particular movements in the gym that they also use in competition. So their weight training centers around these movements, with a greater number of sets per exercise, and therefore fewer exercises per workout. Take the chest as an example. Some powerlifters use only three different exercises on chest day, doing each for 6 – 8 heavy sets. If you are a gymnast, however, you need more general training on chest day; a wide range of movements connecting the whole chest and upper body, with full joint extension, especially for the shoulder rotators. You may need 8 – 10 different exercises, permitting only two or three sets of each. Golf or tennis players need to focus more of their chest workout on internal and external rotators of the shoulders, and the chain of connections through the abdominals and rotators of the trunk. Six exercises, at 3 – 4 sets each, can see them well through chest day.

The wide range of differences in the free movements of different sports, demand different numbers of exercises to accommodate them. And in our individual programs for athletes that's the way we do it. Here I can give you only a rule of thumb that is a good compromise for about 90% of sports. **In order to train the major muscle chains and stabilizers involved in most sports, athletes need to do 6 – 8 of the most effective different exercises per workout.**

Full Range of Motion

Effective exercises are hard to find. Many exercises that appear to recruit the whole muscle, fail miserably because of human anatomy. Separating the gold from the dross is no easy task. Take the standing barbell bicep curl, especially when done with an easycurl bar. You see it every day in gyms all across America. Countless books and charts on gym walls extol its virtues as a bicep exercise. It is next to useless for arm training.

As shown in the illustration, the biceps complex consists of two muscle heads that originate in the shoulder girdle and span the upper arm to insert into the lower arm at the elbow. A third muscle, the brachialis, which lies under the biceps, originates on the humerus bone of the upper arm and inserts into the elbow. The barbell curl recruits only some of the fibers of the biceps and few of the brachialis.

There's a whole slew of physiological reasons why the barbell curl doesn't work, but I have room to mention only a couple. A good part of the function of the biceps is to supinate (turn up) the palm of the hand. Consequently, to

Shoulder joint

Bicep tendons

Elbow joint

Biceps

Brachialis

Biceps complex consists of the two-headed biceps plus the brachialis.

recruit many of the biceps fibers, you have to begin a curl motion with your palm down (pronated), then turn it as far up as possible.

Try this yourself. Put one hand on your bicep. Now make an arm curl motion, tensing the biceps but keeping your hand supinated all the way, just as it is held by the bar in the photo. Now start again, but this time make an arm curl with full biceps motion from full pronation to full supination. Feel how much more the bicep muscle group is activated.

A second reason for the inefficiency of the barbell curl is that the brachialis is hardly activated. The stronger biceps override it, because you cannot help throwing your shoulders into the motion, no matter how erect you stand.

A third reason is that the stabilizers of the arm during bending are not properly activated, because the arms are locked together and stabilized by the bar. There are few occasions in sport where you can rely on such mechanical stabilization.

We do include barbell curls in our programs, but as a heavy, full-body integration exercise to tie together muscle chains of the arms, shoulders, back and legs.

The barbell bicep curl is a poor exercise for arms. It contracts only part of the biceps complex and does so through a very restricted range of motion.

Only The Best

There are literally hundreds of free weight and cable exercises for each major bodypart. Bill Pearl's book, **Keys to the Inner Universe**,[1] describes more than a thousand. We have spent two decades examining the mechanics of most of them. One reason our power program is so successful, is precise selection of only those exercises that produce maximum power on the playing field.

Michael Colgan in the multiple angles and planes of motion of a plié lunge.

As we have seen in earlier chapters, the weight you use, the number of reps, and the way you do each rep, all influence the number of muscle fibers recruited in a particular exercise. From the bicep example above, you can see that the angles through which the exercise moves your limbs are equally important. Remember, your goal in the gym is to train as many muscle fibers as possible. Muscle fibers that are not recruited to perform an exercise cannot increase their strength. It is vital, therefore, to use only the best exercises for each bodypart.

Planes of Motion, Gravity & Grip

Before you can choose exercises wisely, you have to know about three other variables which determine muscle fiber recruitment:

1. The planes of motion of the exercise.

2. The orientation of your body with respect to gravity.

3. The placement of hands and feet.

You can feel these three variables in action with numerous exercises, but although the experience may convince you personally, what folk "feel" is too unreliable for science. Science is the art of measurement which gave you everything in modern life, from the fillings in your teeth to the digital watch you wear, the car you drive, and the high tech sports shoes that support your feet. If you can't measure it, forget it.

Measuring muscle fiber recruitment during exercise is difficult, because athletes have a peculiar reluctance towards multiple large needles being stuck into their bodyparts for hours at a time. Instead, we have to use electromyographic (EMG) activity of the muscle, recorded through stick-on electrodes.

Each muscle fiber is connected to a nerve which fires whenever that fiber, or other fibers connected to the same nerve, are activated in a muscle contraction. The nerve and the fibers connected to it are called a **motor unit**. The greater the number of motor units activated by an exercise, the higher the EMG activity. So the EMG provides a fair measure of muscle fiber recruitment.

Even an ineffective exercise such as the lat pulldown, shown here by lovely Dawn Blacklidge, activates millions of muscle fibers of arms, shoulders and back.

When you measure muscle fiber recruitment with the EMG, results often show that conventional beliefs about particular exercises are dead wrong. A recent study by Barnett and colleagues provides a good example. They measured EMG activity in chest and shoulder muscles and compared the flat bench press with the incline and decline bench presses. They also used various different spacings of the hands.[2] That is, they measured the same exercise movement with the three different variables noted above, different planes of movement, different orientations of the body with respect to gravity, and different limb placements.

Results showed that the mid-chest (the sternoclavicular head of the pectoralis) is activated most by the flat bench press, no matter what hand spacing is used. The upper chest (the clavicular head of the pectoralis) is activated a bit more during the incline bench with a narrow grip, than during the flat bench, but not a lot, contrary to conventional beliefs that the incline bench is essential to train the upper chest. The flat bench also activated the long head of the triceps more than either incline or decline benches, especially with a narrow grip. The decline bench and wide grips proved to be the poorest muscle activators.

Now you know why all those guys who love decline benches don't show great benefits. It continues to be a popular exercise, because bodily orientation with respect to gravity allows you to use more weight, giving the illusion that you are stronger. As we found in our own analysis at the Colgan Institute, the flat bench press is definitely best. You will not find the decline bench or wide grips in our programs.

We use only the best, as the next seven chapters will show you. Each exercise is designated for its primary use for Extension-Connection, Strength-Stabilization, Power or Link Cycles.

Power Principle 17: Do 6 – 8 of the best exercises per workout.

Second Wind
Running behind a fartlek.
See p.28

Abdominals: Power Core

Endless abdominal machines, crunch boards, sit-up devices and tortuous torso routines promise flat bellies and chiseled abs. Hardly a one of them works worth a damn, mainly because their makers show little understanding of human anatomy.

Spread on my desk, I have 22 articles on abs taken from recent issues of muscle and fitness magazines. None of them correctly identifies abdominal musculature, and only two show any exercises that will improve abdominal power. It's a sad commentary on the influence of bodybuilding, which focuses on improving the appearance of only one of the abdominal muscles, the *rectus abdominus*, popularly called the "six-pack," but which is actually an eight-pack.

Under this musclehead media influence, millions of misguided folk endure endless hours at sit-ups, crunches, leg lifts, Roman chairs and ab machines. The net result of all this agony is a minor increase in ab strength and a minimal reduction in the girth of the waistline. You would get better abs with less effort chopping firewood.

If you want athletic power, don't waste your time with conventional ab flapdoodle. Consider what you need in the midsection. Remember, it is your body's core, your power center. First, your abdominal muscles have to hold your organs firmly, so that power can be transferred smoothly up and down your body. Second, you have to train the muscles that flex the trunk from side-to-side and that rotate it about the spine. Third, you have to train the muscles that flex the trunk forward to bring the rib cage towards the pelvis. Fourth, you have to

Dean Miller is a fine example of a bodybuilder who knows how to train abdominals properly. What a tight gut!

train the muscles that extend the trunk to bend the back backwards and move the rib cage away from the pelvis.

Unless all these muscles are strong, you will never be able to use your full power, because you will never be able to transfer it from the point of leverage where the feet grip the ground, through the pelvis and trunk to the upper body. It all starts with a tight gut.

Tight Gut

By tight I do not mean a sucked in gut, but rather a natural inward curve of the abdominal wall when the muscles are relaxed. Why is the inward curve important? Because without firm support, all your soft squashable organs and intestines flop around inside, dissipating your power. A loose gut is like a sealed rubber tube, loosely filled with little rubber balls. If I take a mallet and whack the top of the tube, it squashes and bulges. Very little of the power of the mallet blow is transferred out the bottom. But if the tube is tightly filled and firm as a fence post, almost all the power is transferred.

I helped boxer Bobby Czyz in his training to become a three-time world champion. He trained his abs right and could punch like a sledgehammer. All boxing coaches know that haymaker punches come from a solid, flat-footed stance, giving maximum leverage. But some are still caught by old notions about ab training. They work the abs with sit-ups and medicine balls to train resistance to body punches and to train endurance. But they fail to train them for power, because they are not fully aware of the vital role a tight gut plays in power transfer.

I can state this boldly, because numerous coaches — not only in boxing, but also in javelin, shot-put, discus, golf, martial arts, every sport in which punching, hitting or throwing are paramount — have applauded the abdominal program at our training camps, because it increases power so rapidly in their athletes.

The right information is finally getting out there. Michael Johnson said recently,

> *I used to be a good 400 meter runner. Then I discovered the weight room. Now I'm a great 400 meter runner.*

I just saw Johnson run 43.18 to break Butch Reynold's 11-year-old world record in the 400 meters, at the 1999 World Track and Field Championships in Seville, Spain. Here he is at the finish. Talk about a tight gut! His body was a fence post from top to bottom, with arms and legs transferring power like a fine Swiss watch.

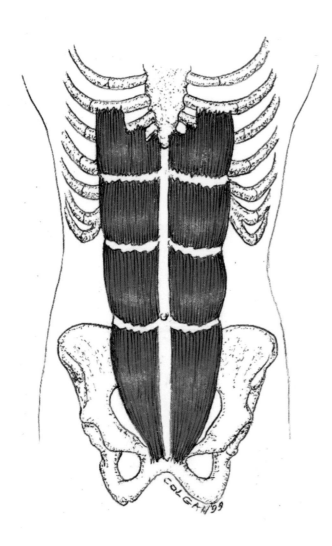

The rectus abdominus ("eight-pack") runs from the fifth, sixth and seventh ribs to the pubic bone. It curls the back to move the ribs towards the pelvis. In doing so, the eight-pack shortens and thickens the waist, never makes it flatter.

Not The Eight-Pack

The first big surprise to many folk at my seminars, is to learn that the eight-pack muscle (*rectus abdominus*) has nothing to do with a flat stomach or a tight gut. As shown in the illustration, the eight-pack is a long thin muscle whose fibers run vertically down the body from the breastbone and fifth, sixth and seventh ribs, to the top of the pubic bone. The eight sought after bumps poke out through a grid of flat tendons that run down the center and across the muscle at intervals.

The function of the eight-pack is to flex the trunk so that your rib cage moves towards your pelvis. In doing so, it causes the stomach to bulge. The eight-pack **never** causes the stomach to become flatter. There's no mechanism by which the eight-pack can flatten your gut: its fibers run the wrong way.[1]

Haven't you ever wondered why some bodybuilders have incredibly defined abs but, when relaxed, they stick out like a beer belly. That's what ab training with sit-ups, crunches and Roman chairs will do for you.

Still not convinced? Try this. Lie on your back and put one hand on your gut. Now do any type of crunch or sit-up you like. You will feel the stomach bulge immediately as the eight-pack shortens and thickens. Do those exercises repeatedly and your gut will stick out permanently.

Transversus Power

The main muscle that holds your gut flat and tight is the **transversus**, a thin sheet of muscle to the sides of the eight-pack that joins into the connective tissue behind it. As shown in the illustration, the transversus is your body's natural corset. Its fibers run across the gut, join into the back sheath of the eight-pack and wrap around the sides of the body, attaching all along the rib cage, around the top of the pelvis and into the back muscles.

The transversus is the main muscle that pulls the gut in and holds your organs firm. But despite this clearly defined physiological action, the transversus is hardly ever trained in conventional ab routines, probably because you can't see it in a mirror.

You use the transversus whenever you suck in your gut. Because of its attachment to your diaphragm, it also lifts the rib-cage, moving it away from the pelvis, thereby lengthening and slimming the waist, exactly opposite to the action of the eight-pack. For a trim waistline, training your transversus to a natural inward curve is the only way to go.

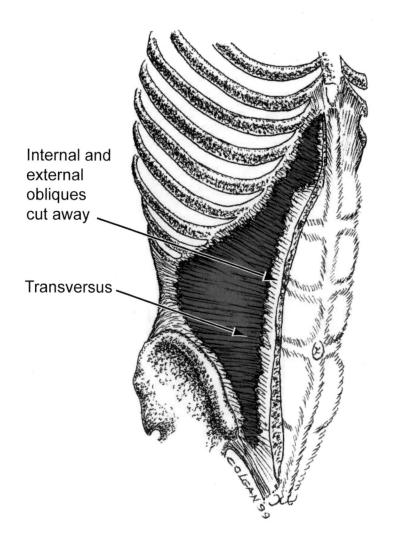

Internal and external obliques cut away

Transversus

The transversus is your body's natural corset. Its fibers travel horizontally. It is the main muscle that flattens your stomach and holds your organs firm.

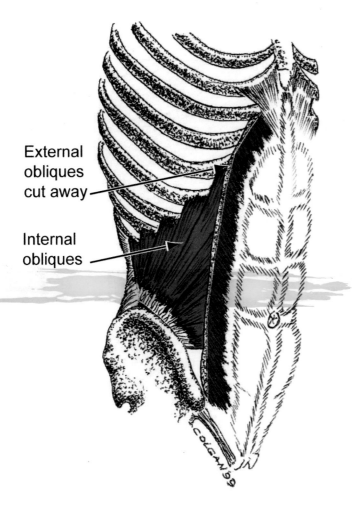

External
obliques
cut away

Internal
obliques

Internal Obliques: Stability

The transversus is assisted by the main stabilizers of the trunk, the **internal oblique** muscles. As the illustration shows, the diagonal fibers of the internal obliques fan out from the pelvis to the ribs and the back side of the eight-pack to provide a criss-cross layer of support over the horizontal fibers of the transversus.

By this stage of the book you know the importance of stabilizing muscles. Unless you have stability you cannot control the transfer of power. Yet, because they are invisible in a mirror, the internal obliques are rarely trained in bodybuilding routines. Athletic coaches, however, do realize their value, and use side-to-side routines with medicine balls to get at them. The **Power Program** achieves strong internal (and external) obliques with the woodchop and reverse woodchop cable exercises shown ahead.

A strong transversus and strong internal obliques are important for athletes for another reason as well as stabilizing your core and holding it firm. They reduce pressure on the vertebral discs of your spine by up to 50%, especially when you pull the gut up and in when lifting. Weight lifting belts and those weird back supports, used by truck drivers and warehouse staff reduce vertebral pressure by only about 20%. Natural muscle wins every time.

> *The* internal obliques *are the main stabilizers of the trunk. Strong internal obliques also assist the transversus to reduce pressure on the discs of your back.*

External Obliques: Rotation

The final outer layer of muscle, which *is* visible, consists of the **external oblique** muscles. As the illustration shows, fibers of the external obliques run on the opposite diagonal to the internal obliques, from the front of the pelvis and eight-pack back to the ribs. They provide a further criss-cross layer of support for the gut.

The external obliques also rotate your trunk and bend it sideways, and help hold in the lower part of the abs. All are important functions for athletes. But obliques are often shunned in conventional ab training, because bodybuilding exercises make their lower fibers show like love handles, and make the waist wider.

Most idiotic of conventional ab training routines are the hundreds of standing or bent over trunk twists done with a broom handle, or worse, a barbell on the shoulders, in vain attempts to make the external obliques smaller. The net result of vigorous ballistic twisting is to stretch these muscles where they attach to the pelvis, and make them sag out even further. *Never* do these trunk-twisting exercises because, once you have over-stretched the external obliques, the sags are there to stay. Correct internal oblique exercises, the cable woodchops shown ahead, rotate the trunk against resistance and keep the muscles where they should be — tight on the gut to hold it in place.

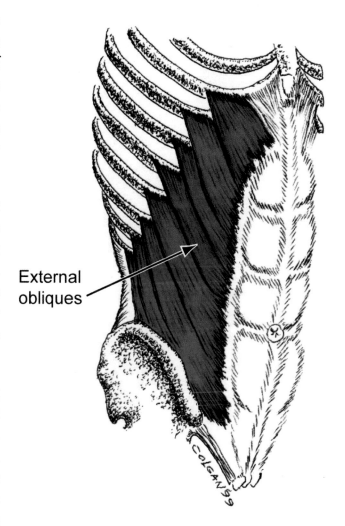

External obliques

Fibres of the external obliques run on the opposite diagonal of the internal obliques. They rotate the trunk and bend it side-to-side.

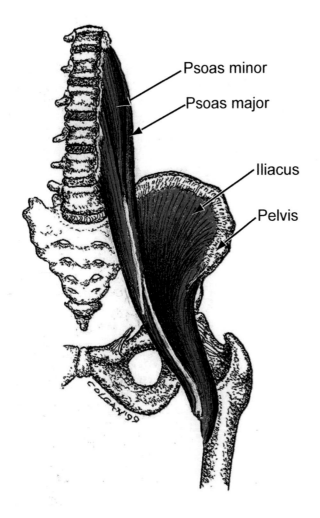

Psoas minor

Psoas major

Iliacus

Pelvis

The iliopsoas complex moves the knees towards the trunk.

Eight-Pack Or Psoas

Once you get the transversus, internal obliques and external obliques under control, then you can consider the eight-pack for its important athletic function in moving the breastbone towards the pubic bone. But even this simple movement is screwed up by most conventional ab training. Sit-ups, including those with bent knees, lying straight leg raises and Roman chairs, and lying or sitting ab machines that constrain the feet or legs, primarily exercise the **psoas muscles**.

The psoas run from the top of the femur (thigh bone) through the pelvis to connect to the lumbar vertebrae. They act to move the knees towards the trunk. That's why some conventional ab exercises give you a sore lower back.

The psoas become very strong whenever you arch your back to increase their leverage, and will override the eight-pack, which is weak in any arched-back position. Arched back means belly out, not the way you want to be for sport, or for life. Arched back with psoas under load also puts a shearing load on the lumbar spine, a big no-no for athletes.

Our rule is, bum in and round the back whenever you work your abs.

The Pelvic Floor

The floor of your pelvis, which supports your organs and intestines, is made of muscles. These muscles are pushed down by compression of the organs whenever you increase intra-abdominal pressure. So whenever you pull up on the transversus to tighten the gut, you should also pull up on the **pelvic floor** muscles to hold up your guts.

Martial artists have always recognized the importance of internal pelvic exercises to build a strong power center. Many athletes, however, find it difficult to lift the pelvic floor, because it is neglected by all but the most sophisticated trainers.

Here we are concerned only with the main supporting muscles, the **sphincter ani**, the **levator ani** and the **coccygeus**. Together with a mesh of connective tissues, they form a muscular hammock, slung across the gap in the pelvis. Studies show that lifting weights, and other activities that increase intra-abdominal pressure, try to push your guts out through this hammock.[1,2] The stronger you can make it to resist the pressure, the stronger your core.

To do it, pull the anus up and in, an instant ***before*** exertion which increases intra-abdominal pressure. That way the pelvic floor muscles are subjected to eccentric contraction during the exertion, the best way to strengthen them.

Women are usually familiar with the pelvic floor because of the Kegel exercises taught to expectant mothers. But many male athletes have little awareness. To improve awareness, repeat this sequence during odd times, such as sitting in traffic. Pull up and in on the levator muscles. Karate master Masatoshi Nakayama says, "Make the distance between the naval and the anus as short as possible." Hold for five seconds. Relax five seconds. Now do five one-second pumping lifts. Relax five seconds. Within a few weeks you will be able to hold up the pelvic floor for at least a minute.

Paul Chek doing his variation of the crunch, one that really works, the Swiss ball curl-up – with a 180 lb dumbbell!

Strong Lower Back

The last component of a powerful core is to strengthen the back muscles shown in the diagram, the **iliocostalis**, the **longissimus**, the **serratus posterior** and the **multifidi**. The transversus and obliques pull on the lower back whenever you tighten them. In the event of overload, it's usually the back that gives way. We tackle the problem with three exercises. First is the **back extension curl-up** on the back extension bench. Most folk you see using the back extension bench move up and down with a straight back, and even go into hyperextension — not a good idea. Instead, we teach athletes to uncurl their back, vertebra by vertebra, from a tightly curled position to the horizontal.

Our second back exercise is the **reverse back extension**, in which the legs hang down and are brought up to the horizontal. This exercise used to be a power secret of powerlifters and weightlifters, who constructed their own benches to do the job. The guy who taught us all about it is top powerlifting coach Louie Simmons. Now I see commercial reverse extension benches being advertised. About time!

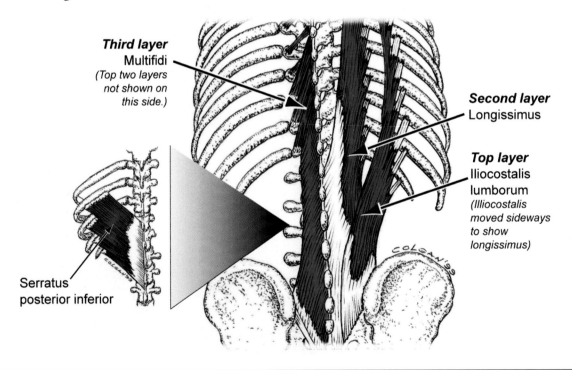

Third layer
Multifidi
(Top two layers not shown on this side.)

Second layer
Longissimus

Top layer
Iliocostalis lumborum
(Illiocostalis moved sideways to show longissimus)

Serratus posterior inferior

Major muscles of the back occur in three main layers which extend from the pelvis all the way to the neck. In addition, the serratus posterior inferior, which runs from the pelvis to the lower four ribs, causes athletes a lot of trouble.

The third and most powerful exercise for the lower back is the deadlift. But this full-body power exercise requires such precise technique in order to be safe and effective we don't cover it here. I describe the deadlift in detail in Chapter 24 on legs.

The Best 10 Abdominal Exercises

For every ab exercise, center yourself first by pulling up and in on both the transversus and the pelvic floor. Retain this up and in posture even when breathing. Inhale on each concentric contraction and, just before each slow eccentric contraction, exhale forcibly by squeezing in more on the transversus and pelvic floor. Initially this action will be very strenuous. Without tightening the gut, you might do 50 reps of a movement such as hanging and kicking the knees to the chest. With power exercise you will be lucky to make eight reps.

Because many athletes have weak abdominals, our series of five hanging exercises is listed here from easy to hard. Initially you may be able to do only the first one or two. As you progress, you should reverse the order, doing the hardest abdominal exercises first. Do all seven hanging and back extension exercises without weights until you can do them for each set of eight reps. Then add strap-on soft weights to increase difficulty.

Alternate each sets of the hanging exercises in supersets, with one then the second, of the two back extension exercises than follow then.

Don't use those wimpy hanging straps to stay on the bar. The hand strength you need for sports is hard to come by. You will develop it only by taking every opportunity to use your bare hands. And don't use gloves. Gloves inhibit the kinesthetic feedback from your palm which signals the stabilizing muscles of the arms to contract. Bare hands are the way to go for all weight training.

Power Principle 18: Build abs and back for a core as firm as a fence post.

Hanging Knee Kick

- Hang on bar with back rounded and toes pointing forwards.
- Pull up on transversus and pelvic floor.
- Inhale.
- Kick knees up to chin.
- Hold and exhale, keeping transversus and pelvic floor tight.
- Slowly lower legs to start position.

These two exercises are primarily for Extension-Connection Cycles.

Hanging Half Leg Raise

- Hang on bar with back rounded and toes pointing forwards.
- Pull up on transversus and pelvic floor.
- Inhale.
- Raise straight legs up to horizontal so they make a 90° angle with the body.
- Hold and exhale forcibly, keeping transversus and pelvic floor tight.
- Slowly lower straight legs to start position.

Hanging Full Leg Raise

- Hang on bar with back rounded and toes pointing forwards.
- Pull up on transversus and pelvic floor.
- Inhale.
- Raise straight legs up to touch bar between hands.
- Exhale forcibly, tightening transversus and pelvic floor.
- Slowly lower legs to start position.

These two exercises are primarily for Strength-Stabilization Cycles.

Horizontal Scissors

- Hang on bar with back rounded and toes pointing forwards.
- Pull up on transversus and pelvic floor.
- Inhale.
- Raise straight legs up to touch bar between hands.
- Keep transversus and pelvic floor tight.
- Exhale while you scissor legs out to sides.

Hanging Vertical Scissors

- Hang on bar with back rounded and toes pointing forwards.
- Pull up on transversus and pelvic floor.
- Inhale.
- Raise straight legs to touch bar between hands.
- Exhale and tighten transversus and pelvic floor.
- Keep one leg at bar and lower other straight leg to below horizontal.
- Reverse legs with a scissor movement while inhaling.
- Keep transversus and pelvic floor tight throughout exercise.

This exercise is for Power Cycles.

Reverse Back Extension

- Lie face down on extension bench with legs hanging vertically and apart.
- Grasp bench and rest chest on pad.
- Pull on bench to lengthen back.
- Pull up on transversus and pelvic floor.
- Inhale.
- Raise straight legs to horizontal while pushing on bench.
- Slowly lower straight legs to vertical while pulling on bench and exhaling

This exercise is for Strength-Stabilization and Power Cycles.

Developed by top powerlifting coach Louie Simmons, the Reverse Back Extension is one of the most effective lower back and core exercises.

Back Extension Curl-up

- Lie face down on extension bench, with pelvic bones protruding over edge.
- Clasp hands to chest, or preferably behind neck.
- Push straight out with elbows, making back as long as possible.
- Pull up on transversus and pelvic floor.
- Inhale.
- Lower trunk and curl back tightly.
- Slowly uncurl trunk one vertbra at a time, starting from the lower back until you reach start position. Exhale while uncurling.

In the conventional back extension, the back is kept straight so the exercise is restricted to the lumbar spine. In contrast the Back Extension Curl-up trains the whole length of the spinal muscles vertebra by vertebra from pelvis to neck.

This exercise is primarily for Extension-Connection Cycles.

Cable Woodchop

- Hold rope and stand as shown.
- Pull up on transversus and pelvic floor.
- Inhale.
- Accelerate rope forward and diagonally down and rotate trunk, as if chopping a log on the opposite side of the body from the cable.
- Allow rope and body to return slowly to start while exhaling.

The Cable Woodchop and Reverse Cable Woodchop was developed to strengthen the tranversus, internal obliques, external obliques and spinal muscles of the core. These two exercises done in supersets are very effective.

This exercise is for Strength-Stabilization, Power and Link Cycles.

Reverse Cable Woodchop

- Hold rope and stand as shown.
- Pull up on transversus and pelvic floor.
- Inhale
- Accelerate rope up at a diagonal and rotate trunk as if trying to throw rope back over the shoulder opposite from the cable.
- Allow rope and body to return slowly to start while exhaling.

The Cable Woodchops are also excellent training to connect muscle chains all the way from the toes to the upstretched arms.

This exercise is for Strength-Stabilization, Power and Link Cycles.

Swiss Ball Curl-up

- Lie back on the Swiss ball with feet constrained.
- Pull up on transversus and pelvic floor.
- Inhale.
- Curl up your torso, starting with the head and shoulders, curling your back as much as possible to bring your breastbone towards your pubic bone, until your back is just above the horizontal.
- Return slowly to start position while exhaling.

The Swiss Ball Curl-up was developed by exercise genius Paul Chek. Unlike bench or floor crunches, the spherical surface of the Swiss ball allows you to extend the rectus abdominus fully by a supported hyper-extension of the spine.

Keep the psoas out of it. If you curl any higher than shown, your psoas starts to take over the movement to try to bring your knees to your chest. You activate the psoas as soon as you start to bend at the hips. Your abdominals may be very weak at first in this movement, but in a while you will be able to do it holding a dumbbell on your chest.

Merlot
Ancient wizard. Patron
saint of masters athletes.

This exercise is for Strength-Stabilization Cycles.

Shoulder Power

The shoulder is the most mobile joint in your body. To achieve such mobility, the top end of the humerus bone of the upper arm is held in a shallow cup of flesh, called the rotator cuff, composed of ligaments, tendons and four small muscles. Unlike the hip, there is no bony socket to help stabilize the joint. Consequently, unless the muscles and other tissues that hold it together are strong, the violent movements of sport can easily separate or dislocate your shoulder, or crucify any of the multiple connective tissues that compose it and feed into and out of it.

Usual shoulder routines don't do a lot to help, becaue they focus on the big, showy deltoid muscles. And bodybuilding exercises, such as bench pressing with a wide grip and flat dumbbell flyes done with straight arms, are almost a guarantee of rotator cuff problems.

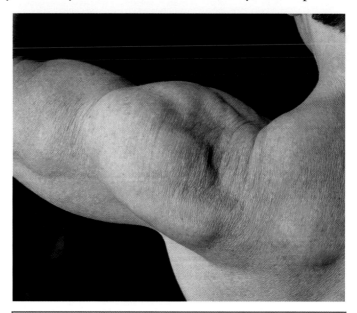

Here is a shoulder developed for athletic power. It looks similar to a shoulder developed by bodybuilding, but is vastly superior in function.

This loony exercise, shown here for demonstration only, holds the arms internally rotated with palms pronated. It is a major cause of rotator cuff injuries. Don't do it.

Then there's the bubble-head exercise, the upright row, shown above. Because the shoulder is internally rotated, with the hands locked in pronation (palms down) by the bar, at the top of the movement the head of the humerus is moved forward. In this position it pinches the tendon of the long head of the biceps and also whacks the shoulder **bursa** (a sac-like cushion filled with fluid), squashing it into the acromium of the scapula. A few weeks of such exercise may give you bigger shoulders, but they are useless for anything but sideshow, because you also have an inflamed bicep tendon and the beginnings of bursitis. If you want chronically painful, non-functional shoulders, do this exercise every day.

I could name another dozen common weight training exercises that produce shoulder problems. In fact, the whole gamut of shoulder routines in the half dozen weight training books now overflowing my trashcan, are an invitation to shoulder injury. Notable exceptions, remaining on my desk are Charles Poliquin's **The Poliquin Principles,**[1] Paul Chek's work,and the writings of Bill Kraemer and Steve Fleck.[2] Together with Janet Travell and David and Lois Simon's brilliant work on shoulder anatomy and function,[3] and our 26 years of work with athletes at the Colgan Institute, we have figured out what you need to do.

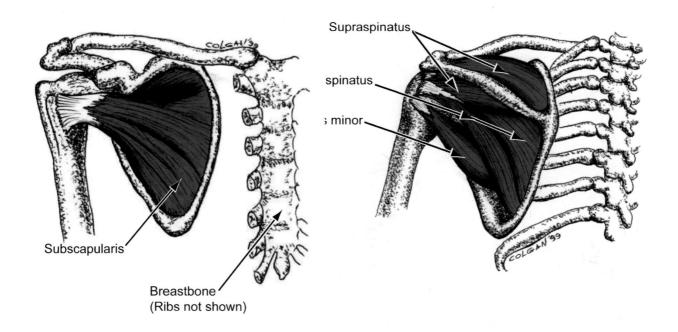

Supraspinatus

spinatus

; minor

Subscapularis

Breastbone
(Ribs not shown)

Shoulder from the front (left) and back (right) showing the four muscles of the rotator cuff. Get these four strong first if you want powerful shoulders.

Stability, Stability, Stability!

As an athlete, your first requirement is to stabilize the shoulder in its whole range of motion. You can see from the illustration that the rotator cuff is stabilized by four muscles: the **infraspinatus**, the **supraspinatus**, the **subscapularis** and the **teres minor**.

These muscles are trained best with what we call external and internal rotations. Cables are the way to do it because of the continuing resistance at all points of the movement. You can use dumbbells, but they fail at the beginning and end of the movement because they rely on the straight down pull of gravity for their resistance.

Power Principle 19: Stabilize the shoulder throughout its full range of movement.

External Rotation - Bottom To Top

- Hold low cable handle at thigh as shown.
- Inhale and pull up on transversus and pelvic floor.
- Raise straight arm rapidly at an angle in line with the cable.
- Lower straight arm slowly to start position while exhaling.

Superset external rotations with the opposite internal rotation motion. Oppose external rotations – bottom to top with internal rotations – top to bottom.

These two exercises are for Extension-Connection and Strength-Stabilization Cycles.

Internal Rotation - Top To Bottom

- Hold high cable handle as shown.
- Inhale and pull up on transversus and pelvic floor.
- Pull straight arm rapidly down and at an angle in line with the cable.
- Raise straight arm slowly to start position while exhaling.

External Rotation - Top To Bottom

- Hold high cable handle as shown.
- Inhale and pull up on transversus and pelvic floor.
- Lower straight arm rapidly at an angle in line with the cable.
- Raise straight arm slowly to start position while exhaling.

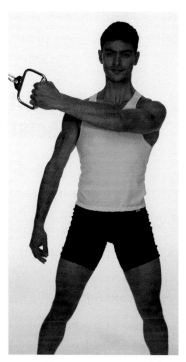

Oppose external rotations – top to bottom in supersets with internal rotations – bottom to top.

These exercises are for Extension-Connection and Strength-Stabilization Cycles.

Internal Rotation - Bottom To Top

- Hold low cable handle as shown.
- Inhale and pull up on transversus and pelvic floor.
- Pull straight arm rapidly up and at an angle in line with the cable.
- Lower straight arm slowly to start position while exhaling.

Folk whose shoulders are already sore should find a plane of motion for external and internal rotations in which they can move without pain. A good plane of motion for many shoulder tweaks is horizontal with a bent arm.

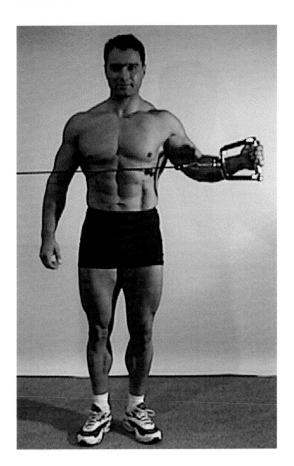

Bent-Arm Horizontal External Rotation

- Hold cable with bent arm across chest (like the finish position of the internal rotation shown below, but with the cable on the other side of the body).
- Inhale and pull up on transversus and pelvic floor.
- Extend bent arm rapidly out to side as shown.
- Return bent arm slowly across chest to start position while exhaling.

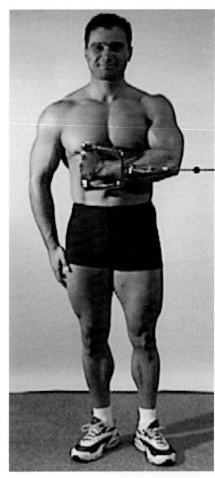

> **This exercise is for rehabilatation.**

Bent Arm Horizontal Internal Rotation

- Start with bent arm out to side (like the finish position of the external rotation shown above, but with the cable extending on the other side of the body).
- Inhale and pull up on transversus and pelvic floor.
- Bring bent arm rapidly across chest as shown.
- Return bent arm slowly out to side while exhaling.

Shoulder Flexion And Extension

In addition to rotation, the rotator cuff also assists the deltoids in flexing and extending the shoulder, and in raising it. The best exercise for raising the shoulder and for the lateral head of the deltoid is the lateral cable raise. Second best is the lateral dumbbell raise.

Lateral Cable Raise

• Start with low cables held as shown.
• Inhale and pull up on transversus and pelvic floor.
• Raise straight arms rapidly up to shoulder level.
• Lower arms slowly to start position while exhaling.

This exercise is for Extension-Connection and Strength-Stabilization Cycles.

Using dumbbells for the lateral raise is not quite as good as using cables because they rely on gravity for resistance. So there is little resistance at the start of the movement.

Lateral Dumbbell Raise

- Start with dumbbells held as shown, with arms slightly bent.
- Inhale and pull up on transversus and pelvic floor.
- Raise slightly bent arms rapidly to shoulder level.
- Lower arms slowly to start position while exhaling.

> **This exercise is for Extension-Connection and Strength-Stabilization Cycles.**

Cable and dumbbell laterals are well opposed by cable lateral pull-downs which you will find work the shoulders heavily despite their direction of travel. Cable pushdowns also help tie the shoulders to chest and back.

Cable Lateral Pull-down

- Stand as shown, holding double cables with arms straight, palms down.
- Inhale and pull up on transversus and pelvic floor.
- Pull straight arms rapidly down to sides.
- Do not lean forward to engage chest muscles.
- Allow arms to return slowly to start.

This exercise primarily is for Extension-Connection Cycles.

The best exercise for flexing the shoulder, and for the front head of the deltoid, is front dumbbell raises with the hand partly supinated. Oppose this motion in supersets with the front cable pull-down.

Front Dumbbell Raise

- Hold dumbbells at sides as shown.
- Inhale and pull up on transversus and pelvic floor.
- Raise straight right arm rapidly, keeping palm turned in as shown.
- Lower to start while exhaling.
- Alternate arms.

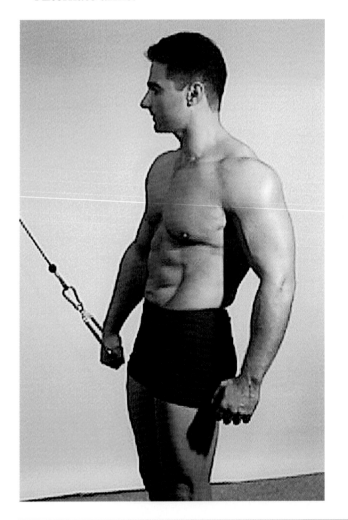

These two exercises are for Extension-Connection Cycles.

Front Cable Pull-down

- Hold cable with straight arm extended at shoulder height.
- Inhale and pull up on transversus and pelvic floor.
- Lower straight arm rapidly to thigh.
- Raise arm slowly while exhaling.

Stabilize Your Scapula

If you refer back to the rotator cuff illustration you will see that the four stabilizing muscles of the cuff all attach to the **scapula** (shoulder blade). So rotator cuff stability is also dependent on scapula stability.

Remember from Chapter 9 how the body works in muscle chains. To stabilize the shoulder, you also have to go one step further down the chain to the muscles that stabilize the scapula. They are a complicated lot, linking the scapula to five other major muscle chains. These links enable you to raise the scapula, to rotate it up and down and sideways, move it in and out across the ribs and to lower it against resistance. To simplify a bit, I will note only the nine major muscles involved. First in order to lift your scapula, you use the back muscles, the **levator scapulae**, the **upper trapezius**, the **rhomboid major** and the **rhomboid minor**. The best exercise is the rotation dumbbell shrug also covered in Chapter 21, as part of back training.

Dumbbell Shrug

- Hold dumbbells as shown.
- Inhale and pull up on transversus and pelvic floor.
- Shrug shoulders up.
- Rotate shoulders back and lower to start position while exhaling.

This exercise is for Strength-Stabilization Cycles.

In sports, lifting your scapula hardly ever occurs without some degree of upward rotation. Stabilization of the scapula in this movement utilizes your upper and lower **trapezius**, and also your **serratus anterior**. The best exercise is Larry Scott's variation of the overhead dumbbell press, which is also one of the best exercises for the deltoids.

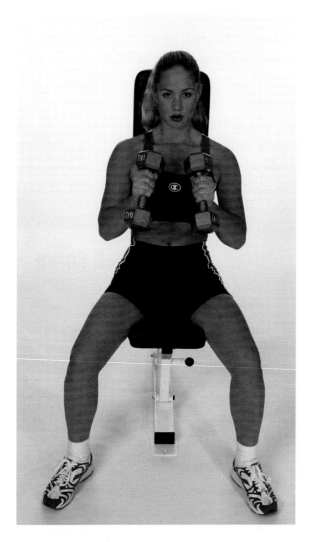 

Scott Dumbbell Press

- Hold dumbbells as a farmer holds his suspenders.
- Inhale and pull up on transversus and pelvic floor.
- Raise arms rapidly by rotating elbows back to the position shown above.
- Do not straighten arms.
- Lower arms slowly to start position while exhaling.

This exercise is for Strength-Stabilization Cycles.

To lower the scapula and rotate it downward against a load, you use your latissiumus dorsi, pectoralis major, pectoralis minor and subclavius, as well as varying degrees of eccentric contraction and relaxation of all the muscles that raise the scapula. The best exercise is the Larry Scott's pull-up and pull-down with contraction and extension of the scapulae. We cover these beauties more fully in Chapter 21 on the back.

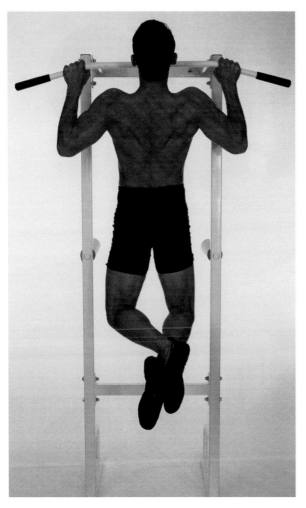 

Scott Scapular Pull-up

- Pull up on transversus and pelvic floor.
- Inhale.
- Squeeze shoulder blades as close together as possible.
- Pull up to touch chin to bar.
- Extend shoulder blades as far apart as possible.
- Lower slowly while exhaling.

This exercise is for Strength-Stabilization Cycles.

Moving the scapula out across the ribs involves the **pectoralis complex** and the **serratus anterior**. The best exercises are the flat bench press and the bent-arm pullover. We cover these exercises more fully in Chapter 22 on the chest.

Flat Bench Press

- Press back flat on bench.
- Inhale.
- Pull up on transversus and pelvic floor.
- Unrack bar and lower in a straight line to sternum.
- Accelerate bar off sternum in a curve back towards chin.
- Press out straight above tip of nose while exhaling.

This exercise is primarily for Power Cycles.

Four other good exercises for the shoulder are:

Lying Rear Delt

- Lie as shown.
- Pull up on transversus and pelvic floor.
- Inhale.
- Raise arm rapidly to just above horizontal.
- Lower slowly to start position while exhaling.

This exercise is for Extension-Connection Cycles.

The Lying Rear Delt trains the muscles of the rotator cuff and the rear deltoid and its connections to the upper back muscle chains.

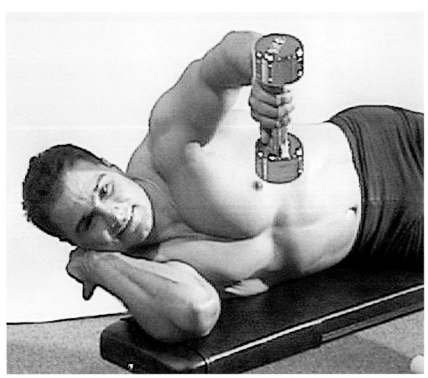

Lying Dumbbell Internal Rotation

- Lie as shown.
- Pull up on transversus and pelvic floor.
- Inhale.
- Raise bent arm rapidly to vertical.
- Lower slowly to start while exhaling.

> **This exercise is for Extension-Connection Cycles.**

Primarily a rehabilitation exercise for shoulder tweaks, the Lying Dumbbell Internal Rotation trains muscle chains connecting shoulder to chest.

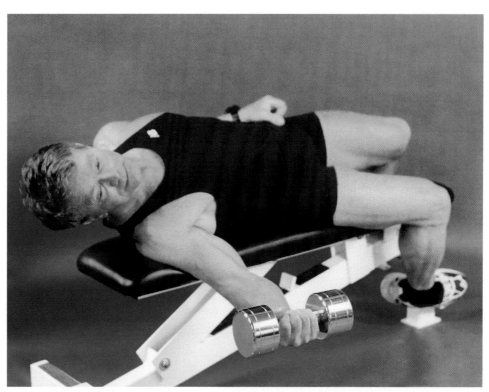

Labrada Rear Delt

- Kneel as shown about two feet from cables.
- Pull up on transversus and pelvic floor.
- Inhale.
- Raise straight arm rapidly up to position shown.
- Release arm slowly to start while exhaling.

> **This exercise is for Extension-Connection Cycles.**

Lying Cable Pullover

- Lie as shown, with rope in both hands.
- Pull up on transversus and pelvic floor.
- Inhale.
- Raise arms rapidly to above head, as shown.
- Lower arms slowly to start while exhaling.

This exercise is for Extension-Connection and Strength-Stabilization Cycles.

Arm Power

We will focus on just four muscles of the arm: the two-headed **biceps,** the **brachialis**, the **brachioradialis** and the three-headed **triceps**. Those are the only arm bits you really need to know.

Conventional weight training also includes specific exercises to develop the multiple small muscles of the forearm. Don't bother. Unless you have a particular weakness in a wrist that requires rehabilitation, wrist curls, wrist roller devices, hand springs, rubber squeegees and other such foolery are just a waste of gym time.

Better than all the forearm and hand exercises is always to use bare hands and squeeze your grip tightly whenever you lift. The kinesthetic feedback from your bare palm causes the muscles of the forearm to contract strongly. Exercise habitually with a tight grip for optimal forearm power.

Biceps

As the illustration on the next page shows, the short inner head of the **biceps** lies next to the chest, and originates in the coracoid process of the **scapula** (shoulder blade). The long head originates on the glenoid tubercle of the scapula. Both heads fuse together at the bottom into one tendon which attaches to the **radius** bone of the forearm. With this arrangement, the biceps works to bend your arm, flex your shoulder and rotate your forearm to supinate (turn up) the palm. Notice that the biceps spans both shoulder and elbow joints. It does not attach to the upper arm bone (**humerus**) at all, an important anatomical feature to note when designing arm exercises. Biceps are best trained with dumbbell exercises that move the bending elbow through its full range of motion from pronation to supination, and do not lock the hands together with a bar.

Brachialis

The **brachialis** is a single joint muscle that originates on the humerus bone and attaches to the top of the **ulna** bone of the forearm. The brachialis works to bend your elbow. It is best trained with dumbbell and cable exercises that limit shoulder movement and hence limit biceps involvment, such as seated overhead curls and kneeling overhead curls shown ahead.

Brachioradialis

Not often covered in weight training books, the **brachioradialis** muscle originates on the lower humerus and attaches to the radius bone. For athletes it is important as a stabilizer and flexor of the elbow joint and rotator of the forearm. It returns the forearm to a neutral position from either pronation or supination.[1,2] It is best trained by dumbbell and cable triceps exercises which move the palm between supination and pronation.

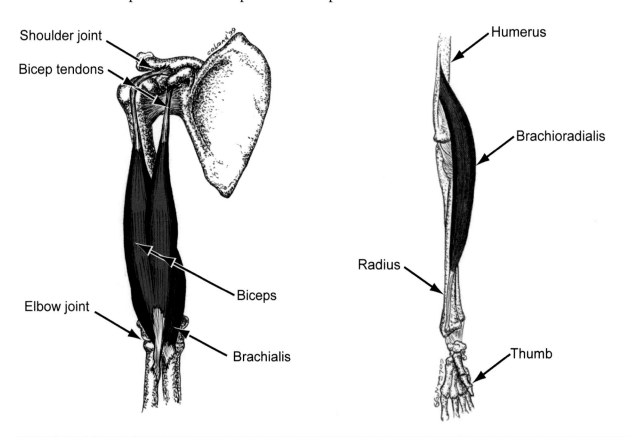

The biceps complex, which flexes (bends) the elbow, and rotates the forearm consists of the biceps, the brachialis and the brachioradialis.

Triceps

The long head of the three-headed **triceps** muscle originates at the tip of the scapula of the shoulder. It spans the shoulder joint. With this shoulder attachment it works to help the latissimus and teres muscles to extend and to adduct (move arm sideways away from body) the arm at the shoulder. The long head is best trained by cable and dumbbell exercises that move the palm from supination to pronation.

The medial and lateral heads of the triceps do not span the shoulder joint and have no effect on its movement. They originate on the back of the humerus. So these two heads are trained best with movements that do not involve the shoulder, such as the overhead cable and kneeling cable tricep exercises shown ahead.

All three heads of the triceps fuse together into a common tendon which attaches to the ulna at the forearm. Together they extend (straighten) the arm at the elbow.

The long head of the three-headed triceps helps the teres and latissimus extend the shoulder. The long, medial and lateral heads together extend the arm at the elbow.

The short **anconeus** muscle connects from the humerus to the ulna to strengthen the joint and assist the triceps in extension of the arm at the elbow.

Power Principle 20: Train biceps and triceps together in opposing supersets.

16 Top Arm Exercises

The twisting Dumbbell Curl trains the bicep complex, connective tissues and stabilizes in the full motion of bending the arm from full pronation to full supination.

This exercise is primarily for Extension-Connection Cycles.

Standing Twisting Dumbbell Curl

• Stand as shown.
• Pull up on transversus and pelvic floor.
• Inhale.
• Curl dumbbell rapidly from full pronation (pinky out) to full supination (pinky pointing to chin) at shoulder.
• Lower slowly while exhaling.
• Alternate arms.

Single Cable Pushdown

- Stand as shown with hand fully supinated.
- Pull up on transversus and pelvic floor.
- Inhale.
- Extend arm down rapidly while pronating palm.
- Open hand at extreme straight arm position and push down on area of palm between thumb and index finger.
- Raise arm slowly while supinating palm and exhaling.

The Single Cable Push down trains the tricep, connective tisue and stabilizes in the full motion of straightening the arm from the full supination to full pronation.

This exercise is primarily for Extension-Connection Cycles.

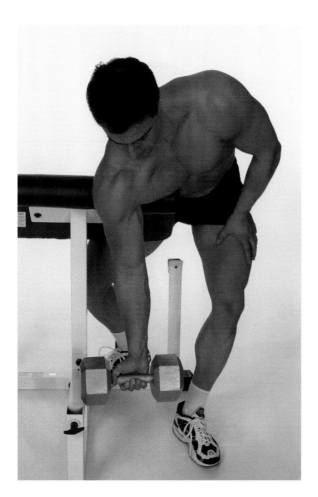

Dumbbell Preacher Curl

- Hold dumbbell on preacher bench as shown. (Most benches will have a vertical pad to support upper arm.)
- Pull up on transversus and pelvic floor.
- Inhale.
- Curl dumbbell rapidly while supinating palm fully.
- Lower slowly while exhaling.

By limiting shoulder motion, the Dumbbell Preacher Curl emphasizes involvement of the brachialis and brachioradialis.

> **This exercise is for Extension-Connection and Strength-Stabilization Cycles.**

Spider Bench Dumbbell Curl

- Lie on spider bench as shown.
- Pull up on transversus and pelvic floor.
- Inhale.
- Allow arm to hang in relaxed position.
- Curl dumbbell rapidly starting with the wrist while supinating palm fully.
- Lower slowly while exhaling.

Better than the preacher bench, Larry Scott's Spider Bench limits shoulder involvement while training the brachialis and brachioradialis and stabilizers.

This exercise is for Extension-Connection and Strength-Stabilization Cycles.

Triceps Kickback

- Kneel on bench as shown with palm supinated and elbow at hip.
- Pull up on transversus and pelvic floor.
- Inhale.
- Extend arm rapidly while pronating fully.
- Keep elbow at hip.
- Return slowly to start while exhaling.

The Colgan Institute form of the Tricep Kickback trains the tricep from full supination to full contraction at pronation.

This exercise is for Extension-Connection and Strength-Stabilization Cycles.

Overhead Rope Curl

- Sit holding high cable as shown.
- Pull up on transversus and pelvic floor.
- Inhale.
- Curl rapidly to behind neck.
- Return slowly to start while exhaling.

The Overhead Rope Curl limits shoulder involvement to stress training of the brachialis.

This exercise is for Extension-Connection and Strength-Stabilization Cycles.

Overhead Rope Triceps

- Stand holding rope as shown with upper arms at ears.
- Pull up on transversus and pelvic floor.
- Inhale.
- Extend arms rapidly above head while pronating palms.
- Return slowly to start while exhaling.

The Overhead Rope Triceps limits shoulder involvement to stress training of the lateral and medial heads of the triceps.

This exercise is for Extension-Connection and Strength-Stabilization Cycles.

Kneeling Rope Curl

- Kneel holding low rope with head below bench level as shown.
- Pull up on transversus and pelvic floor.
- Inhale.
- Curl rope rapidly to behind neck.
- Return slowly to start while exhaling.

The Kneeling Rope Curl limits shoulder involvement to train the brachialis and brachioradialis.

This exercise is for Strength-Stabilization Cycles.

Scott Kneeling Rope Triceps

- Kneel holding low rope with head below bench level as shown.
- Pull up on transversus and pelvic floor.
- Inhale.
- Extend arms rapidly keeping head low and elbows on bench.
- Return slowly to start position while exhaling.

Larry Scott's Kneeling Rope Tricep is excellent for training the medial and lateral heads of the triceps.

This exercise is for Strength- Stabilization Cycles.

Refined by John Parrillo, the Drag Dumbbell Curl stresses the upper bicep and is excellent for tying the biceps to the shoulder chain.

This exercise is for Strength-Stabilization Cycles.

Drag Dumbbell Curl

- Stand with dumbbells as shown.
- Pull up on transversus and pelvic floor.
- Inhale.
- Curl dumbbells rapidly keeping them close to ribs and pushing elbows back.
- Return slowly to start while exhaling.

Rope Triceps Pushdown

- Stand holding high cable as shown.
- Pull up on transversus and pelvic floor.
- Inhale.
- Lower palms rapidly to thighs keeping body straight.
- Return slowly to start while exhaling.

The conventional Triceps Pushdown usually done with a bar, trains all three heads of the triceps. But it is best done with a rope, which also trains the stabilizers and connective tissues and allows rotation of the arm.

This exercise is for Strength-Stabilization Cycles.

Seated Hammer Dumbbell Curl

- Sit with dumbbell in hammer position as shown.
- Pull up on transversus and pelvic floor.
- Inhale.
- Curl rapidly while maintaining hammer position.
- Lower slowly to start while exhaling.

The Hammer Dumbbell Curl stresses training of the brachioradialis and elbow stabilizers.

This exercise is for Strength-Stabilization Cycles.

Skullcrushers

- Lie on bench with barbell held in a close grip as shown.
- Pull up on transversus and pelvic floor.
- Inhale.
- Lower barbell slowly to forehead by bending forearms only to touch knuckles to forehead.
- Return rapidly to start while exhaling.

Skullcrushers are best done with dumbbells to train arm and shoulder stabilizers along with triceps but dumbbells are dangerous in this exercise, hence, the name skullcrushers.

This exercise is for Strength-Stabilization Cycles.

Arnold Concentration Curl

- Stand as shown with dumbbell hanging loosely.
- Pull up on transversus and pelvic floor.
- Inhale.
- Curl dumbbell rapidly while supinating palm.
- Swing hip across as shown to keep elbow pointing at floor.
- Return slowly to start while exhaling.

Arnold Schwarzenegger's form of the Concentration Curl is excellent for training the bicep complex and arm stabilizers along with connective tissues.

This exercise is for Strength-Stabilization Cycles.

Cable Concentration Triceps

- Stand supporting body on knee and holding cable with palm supinated as shown.
- Pull up on transversus and pelvic floor.
- Inhale.
- Extend arm rapidly by moving forearm while pronating palm.
- Return slowly to start while exhaling.

Done in supersets, with the Arnold Concentration Curl, the Cable Concentration Triceps trains all three heads of the triceps plus stabilizers and connective tissues.

This exercise is for Extension-Connection and Strength-Stabilization Cycles.

Barbell Curl

- Stand as shown, holding barbell.
- Pull up on transversus and pelvic floor.
- Inhale.
- Curl barbell to chest.
- Return slowly to start while exhaling.

The Barbell Curl is not an efficient exercise for training arms but is a great integration exercise when done with heavy weights for arms, shoulders, back, core and legs.

This exercise is for Strength-Stabilization Cycles.

Now those are arms! Not just a muscleman, Ted Arcidi is also a fine actor. Here he is as the bad guy in the popular TV series Law and Order.

Back: Power Lift

Six of every ten athletes we test have weak lower backs. Most of them suffer back and leg pain and reduced function. Yet it's an easy two-step to build and maintain a strong back. First, you have to know what muscles you are trying to train. Second, you have to know how to avoid the bad exercises and how to do the good exercises exactly right.

It All Starts With Posture

When our primate ancestors evolved to stand up, they put a kink in the lower spine, stretched their quads and hamstrings, and shortened the connective tissues of the back. We gradually evolved this way to a natural erect posture. Problem is, modern culture has most of us sitting for extended periods. Habitually seated posture shortens the hip flexors. We grow short quads and psoas muscles from habitually bent thighs, and short hamstrings from habitually bent knees. We also over-stretch the back muscles, tendons and ligaments, from habitually rounding our backs to bend over desks, benches and computer terminals, so we also develop stooped shoulders and a stuck out head.

No, no, not you, never. But take a look around. The average seated posture in the coffeehouse resembles a consumptive chimpanzee. The chimp is excused because he doesn't have the structure to sit or stand erect. Humans are the only animals with the musculature capable of balancing the head and torso over the hips.[1] That's the way we function best. If you want to excel as an athlete, re-read Chapter 3 and resolve to put as much postural distance as possible between you and your primate cousins.

Good Morning — Goodbye Charlie! This is one of the dill-brain stiff-legged exercises that most damages the lower back.

Some weight-lifting books seem to be unaware of human postural problems. They advocate stiff-legged lifts, such as the stiff-legged deadlift, the stiff-legged bent-over row and the "good morning" (bowing from the waist with a barbell on your shoulders). A recent review of 287 people with herniated discs concluded that stiff-legged lifting was the number one cause.[2] Simple to avoid. **Never** lock your knees when lifting weights.

Next Comes Flexibility

The usual daily grind gets us another way too. We hardly ever rotate or side-bend the spine. Watch older folk. Most of them have lost their spinal rotation. In order to look 90° to one side or the other, they have to turn their whole body. Move like that on the playing field and you're a dead duck.

So, before you even think of strengthening your back, go back to Chapter 4 and resolve to make the Vital 15 stretches a pre-workout sacred ritual.

Trapezius First

The back is such a big part of your musculature we have to divide it into sections. As we go along I will note other body parts that are synergistic to give you a better idea of muscle chains. We start with the **trapezius**.

Studies have examined the action of the trapezius in at least 14 sports including swimming, golf, baseball, tennis, basketball and other throwing sports. In almost all cases the middle and lower trap fibers fire more strongly than the upper fibers.[3] Conventional weight training, however, stresses only the upper fibers, because bodybuilders like those two big hunks of muscle to show on either side of the neck. As an athlete you want the whole tamalé, with most emphasis on the middle and lower traps.

We have already looked at the upper traps under shoulders in Chapter 19. That's where it stops in most books on weight training. But, as you can see from the drawing, your trapezius is actually a twin pair of muscles with three divisions, and much bigger than most folk think. They travel all the way down the spine to the start of the lower back, all across the back of the scapula (shoulder blade) to the shoulder joints, and forward to attach along half of the clavicle (collar bone). The fibers of the upper, middle and lower trapezius have different attachments, travel in different directions, and have different functions. They therefore require different exercises to train them.

Numerous bodybuilding books advocate a straight up and down shrug as the best, and often only, exercise for the trap. They are dead wrong! Both

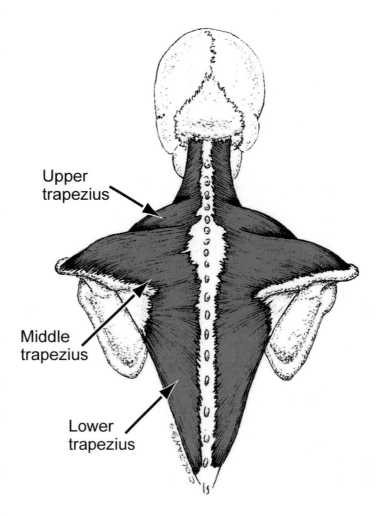

Upper trapezius

Middle trapezius

Lower trapezius

The trapezius is a three-part muscle with upper, middle and lower divisions, each with different attachments and different functions.

the anatomy of this muscle, and numerous studies of its function, show that most of the neck and shoulder fibers of the trapezius are not designed to exert a direct upward pull on the clavicle or the scapula.[4] To activate even the upper trap requires a rotational movement. This is achieved best by rolling the shoulders up, then back and down.

Together with the **sternocleidomastoid**, the long muscle that runs from the hollow of the neck back to the ear that makes female necks so gorgeous, the upper trap also flexes the neck from side to side and assists rotation of the head. Training to strengthen these functions is essential for athletes who try to knock each other's heads off, such as boxers, wrestlers, martial artists, footballers and rugby players. The best exercises are wrestler's bridges and head side lifts, and rotational lifts with a head strap.

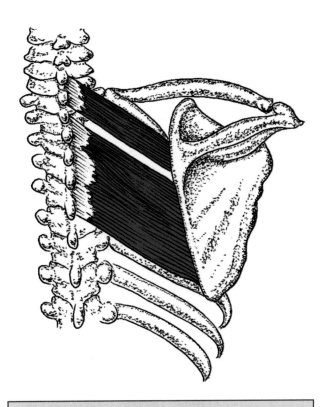

Shown from the back of the body, the rhomboids help the trapezius pull in the scapula towards the mid-line of the back.

Middle Trapezius

The middle fibers of the trap run almost horizontally across the body to the tip of the shoulder and attach along the top edge of the scapula. As with the upper trap, studies show that elevation of the scapula with rotation of the shoulder in either direction fires these fibers strongly.[5] The upper and middle trap are also activated strongly along with the deltoids and rotator cuff muscles in all shoulder exercises that raise and rotate the arm.[6]

Together with the **rhomboids**, the middle trap also helps draw the scapula towards the midline of the back.[7] It is therefore trained well by exercises that draw in the shoulder blades. Best are the Scott scapular pull-up and pull-down, T-bar row, jockey row, and the Colgan diagonal pull-down. All these exercises are pictured and described ahead.

Lower Trapezius

The lower trap fibers run from the inner half of the scapula diagonally down to attach to the spine. They function to hold down the scapula, acting as a stabilizer for other muscles such as the **serratus** to rotate the outer scapula. They are best trained by rotational back exercises such as the Scott scapular pull-up and pull-down.

The middle and lower traps are directly antagonistic to the pectoralis major and, to some extent, the pectoralis minor.[5] So supersets which oppose exercises for traps and pecs are the way to go for building optimal power in both.

Latissimus

As the figure shows for one side of the body, the **latissimus dorsi** is a big pair of muscles. They run all the way from the sacrum (tailbone), pelvis, lumbar vertebrae, lower six thoracic vertebrae, and lower four ribs, to the humerus of the upper arm. There they attach, intermingled with the attachment of the **teres major**.[8]

Together with the teres major, the lat works primarily to pull the arm down and in at the shoulder, and to hold down the whole shoulder girdle. It also affects both posture and movement of the trunk and pelvis via its lower spine, pelvis and rib attachments.

The lat is not well activated in conventional weight training with wide grip pull-downs either to the chest or to the back of the neck, because a wide grip only exercises part of the muscle and only through the middle part of its range of motion.

Wide grip lat bars were developed to place the line of pull directly in line with the muscle fiber direction of the outer portion of the lat. Lots of wide bar lat work develops the outer lat to that thick batwing flap seen in big bodybuilders. Lats developed in this way do not have a lot of power. Don't believe me? Ask one of those big boys to do a few chins with his bodyweight in plates around his waist. Leave wide lat bars for the posers.

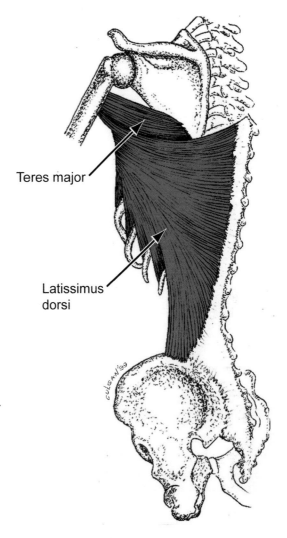

Teres major

Latissimus dorsi

The latissimus *pulls the arm down and in at the shoulder, holds down the shoulder girdle, and helps stabilize and rotate the spine.*

The teres major *is a separate muscle at the top, which helps pull in the shoulder.*

Conventional pull-down exercises are also very poor for other reasons. The behind-the-neck position with hands pronated, constricts the shoulder joint. And the pull-down-to-chest position with hands pronated, stresses the lower back. The latissimus is best activated by exercises that fully extend the arm and hip to stretch the muscle and then fully contract them. The best of the best are Larry Scott's single cable row and scapular pull-up and pull-down shown later in the chapter.

Teres Major

The **teres major** (shown in the latissimus illustration on the previous page) assists the lat in adducting (pulling in) the shoulder. It shows as that separate lump under your arm above the lat. The teres major runs from the humerus to the scapula. It helps pull your arm down and in.

Together with the latissimus, rhomboids and middle trapezius, the teres is strongly trained with the Colgan diagonal cable pull down (shown ahead). In addition, these muscles are all trained well with the jockey row, the supported T-bar row, the kneeling dumbbell row, and the seated row to the neck. All are shown ahead.

Chin-up For Power

Probably the best single move for the whole upper back is the chin or pull-up. In his book **The Poliquin Principles**, top trainer Charles Poliquin devotes a whole chapter to this premium exercise. And Larry Scott's scapular pull-ups are legendary for back development. Adopting Poliquin's definition, a chin is done with the palms supinated (facing you), or semi-supinated (palms facing each other). A pull-up is done with palms pronated (facing away from you).

Here's a simple test of upper back strength. Do twenty full chins, with a shoulder width grip and palms facing you. None of these half chins with your legs kicking to get you up. A chin is counted as full only if your chin gets high enough, so that you can touch it to the bar, and you then lower yourself to full arms length. If you can't do it, you need to get a back.

Don't use bodybuilding straps either. Opponents on the sports field will not wait while you wind a strap around them. Always use your bare hands. Hand strength is hard to get: take every opportunity you cans to develop it.

I know some big football boys, very powerful at pushing because of lots of pressing and power sled exercises, who wonder why they can't pull. The chinning bar shows right away.

Spinal Muscles

Now we come to the most important group of back muscles for athletes, the spinal muscles that hold up your spine and hold your back together. Unless you get these babies strong, all the showy muscles that cover them are next to useless in any backbending action more strenuous than pulling up your pants.

As the drawing on the next page shows, your spinal muscles consist of three main layers. The two outer layers consist of the long fibers of the **erector spinae** which run from the base of your skull, down the whole length of your spine to connect to the pelvis. The major muscles are the **iliocostalis** which lies on top of the **longissimus**. They extend (hold up) and stabilize your spine.

The inner layer consists mainly of short diagonal fibers. The major muscles shown in the drawing are the **multifidi** and the **rotatores.** As you can see they attach to every one of your vertebrae. They adjust and rotate the spine, making possible all the fine postural movements we take for granted.

Can you guess which football star this is?

He has no trouble with 20 weighted chins nor with pulling opponents' arms off.

Another of the multiple muscles of the back is the **serratus posterior inferior.** As the drawing shows, this little troublemaker for the mid-back, runs from the lower four ribs to the last two thoracic vertebrae and the first two lumbar vertebrae. It helps stabilize and rotate **your spine.**[9]

You should also know the **quadratus lumborum,** shown overleaf, which runs from the 12th rib and top four lumbar vertebrae to the pelvis. It is the major stabilizer of the spine on the pelvis.[10] Without a reasonably functioning quadratus lumborum you could not even walk.

Although these spinal muscles perform the vital functions of stabilizing your spine, keeping it connected together and helping rotate it, they are rarely noted in books on conventional weight training. Why? Because they lie underneath the big back muscles, the trapezius and the latissimus, so you can't see them. Yet, if the spinal muscles are weak your back is weak. You have nothing to pull against when you exert the big muscles. No surprise then that a lot of bodybuilders, and those athletes who copy them in their training, have dicky backs.

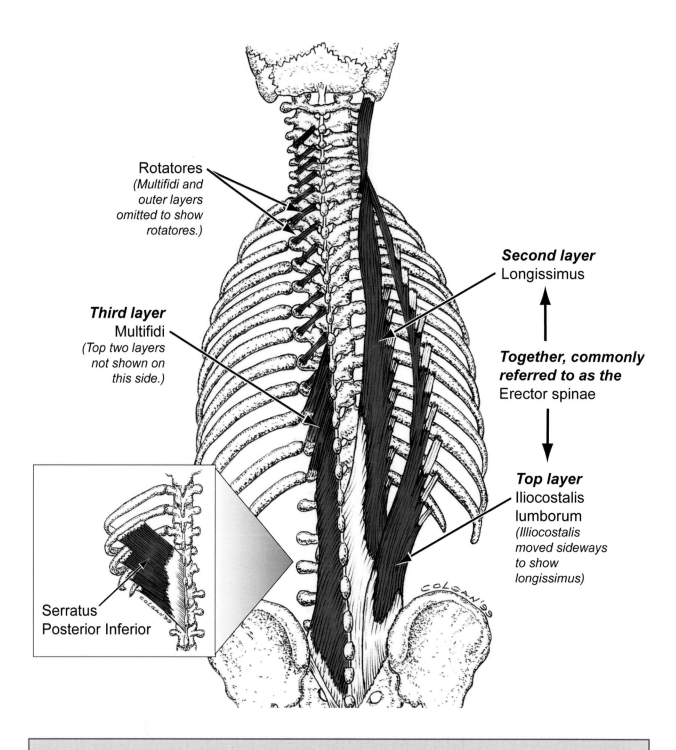

Rotatores
*(Multifidi and
outer layers
omitted to show
rotatores.)*

Second layer
Longissimus

Third layer
Multifidi
*(Top two layers
not shown on
this side.)*

**Together, commonly
referred to as the**
Erector spinae

Top layer
Iliocostalis
lumborum
*(Illiocostalis
moved sideways
to show
longissimus)*

Serratus
Posterior Inferior

*Major Spinal Muscles. The muscles which support the spine and hold it together
occur in three main overlapping layers.*

The spinal muscles are well trained by the deadlift and the chin, plus Larry Scott's various rows, pull ups and pull downs. Because of its big leg component we cover the deadlift in Chapter 23 on legs. For a strong spine you should add the back extension roll-up, reverse back extension and woodchops covered under core training in Chapter 18.

Shown from the front of the body, the quadratus lumborum runs from the 12th rib and top four lumbar vertebrae to the pelvis. It is the major stabilizer of the spine on the pelvis.

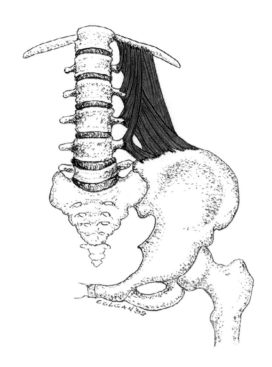

Power Principle 21: Train back strength from inside to outside.

Ripped.
Athlete who tried to lose the
last of his fat by roping himself
behind a truck going to Florida.

15 Top Back Exercises

Shrug

- Hold dumbbells as shown.
- Inhale and pull up on transversus and pelvic floor.
- Shrug shoulders up.
- Rotate shoulders back and lower to start position while exhaling.

Rotational motion of the shoulders in the Shrug is essential to train the middle trapezius, muscle fibers that are more important to athletes than the upper trapezius.

> **This exercise is for Strength-Stabilization Cycles.**

Pronated Pull-up

- Hang on bar as shown.
- Pull up on transversus and pelvic floor.
- Inhale.
- Pull up rapidly to touch chin to bar.
- Lower body slowly to start while exhaling.

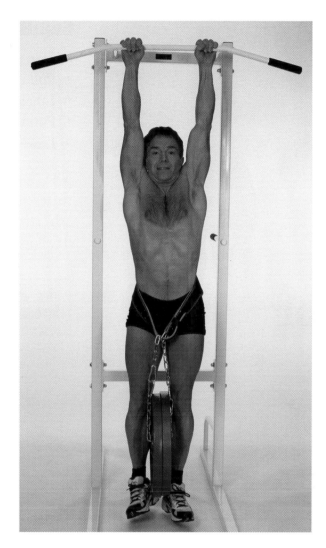

This form of the conventional Pull-up is an excellent exercise to start building back power by tying together muscle chains of arms, shoulders and back. Initially, you may not be able to use weight around the waist. But in a year or so, you will be doing sets with a big plate or two.

> **This exercise is for Strength-Stabilization and Power Cycles.**

Supinated Chin (palms facing you)

• Hang on bar as shown.
• Pull up on transversus and pelvic floor.
• Inhale.
• Pull up rapidly to touch chin to bar.
• Lower slowly while exhaling.

The Supinated Chin is the easiest position from which to learn to pull up to a bar. It relies a great deal on arm strength and is not as effective as pull-ups for back development.

> **This exercise is for Extension-Connection and Strength-Stabilization Cycles.**

Semi-supinated Chin (palms facing each other)

• Hang on bar as shown.
• Pull up on transversus and pelvic floor.
• Inhale.
• Pull up rapidly to touch chin to bar.
• Lower slowly while exhaling.

The second easiest positon for pulling up to a bar, the Semi-Supinated Chin has more back involvement than the Chin. It is also the safest of the chins and pull-ups because the shoulders remain constrained.

> **This exercise is for Strength-Stabilization Cycles.**

Scott Scapular Pull-up

- Hang on bar with palms pronated.
- Pull up on transversus and pelvic floor.
- Inhale.
- Squeeze shoulder blades together, hold them that way and pull up rapidly.
- At top of movement throw shoulders out as wide as possible.
- Lower slowly keeping shoulders wide, while exhaling.

The Scapular Pull-up developed by Larry Scott is the single most effective exercise for back development.

This exercise is for Strength-Stabilization Cycles.

Scott Scapular Pull-down

- Sit at pull-down with handled bar as shown.
- Pull up on transversus and pelvic floor.
- Inhale.
- Squeeze shoulder blades together and pull bar down rapidly, bringing hands to shoulders.
- Rotate shoulders to throw shoulder blades out as wide as possible and return bar slowly to start while exhaling.

Not quite as good as the Scapular Pull-up, the Scapular Pull-down is much easier to do and is the exercise for starting back development. Use a bar with loose handles on chains, as shown, to train back and shoulder stabilizers as well as the prime movers, the latissimus, teres and trapezius.

This exercise is for Extension-Connection and Strength-Stabilization Cycles.

Layback Chin To Chest

- Hang on bar with V-handle as shown.
- Pull up on transversus and pelvic floor.
- Inhale.
- Lay back and pull up rapidly to bring chest to V-bar.
- Lower slowly while exhaling.

The layback chin is very effective for fibers of the lower trapezius and most fibers of the latissimus.

> **This exercise is for Extension-Connection and Strength-Stabilization Cycles.**

Hanging Stretch

Simply hanging relaxed from a bar is a excellent stretch for the whole body that you can do during back exercises.

> **This stretch can be done any time during workouts.**

Diagonal Pull-down

- Hold high cables and kneel as shown.
- Pull up on transversus and pelvic floor.
- Inhale.
- Pull elbows into sides keeping palms facing forwards.
- Lean forward to engage back muscles.
- Return cables slowly to start while exhaling.

The Diagonal Pull-down is one of the very few exercises that gets the teres rhomboids and other muscles of the upper back. Note the teres major showing contracting under the arms. It is also excellent for tying shoulders and back together.

This exercise is for Extension-Connection and Strength-Stabilization Cycles.

Jockey Row

- Hold low cable and stand as shown.
- Pull up on transversus and pelvic floor.
- Inhale.
- Pull handle into chest while keeping body low in a jockey position.
- Return handle slowly to start while exhaling.

The Jockey Row was developed by the legendary Vince Gironda, who knew more than a thing or two about weight training. It exercises the whole upper back.

This exercise is for Extension-Connection and Strength-Stabilization Cycles.

Scott Single Cable Row

- Stand holding low cable as shown with elbow pressed against knee for stability and hip back as far as possible to stretch latissimus.
- Pull up on transversus and pelvic floor.
- Inhale.
- Pull handle rapidly into lower ribs and simultaneously move hip forward and push shoulder down to contract lat fully.
- Return slowly to start position while exhaling.

This Larry Scott beauty allows the biggest range of motion for the latissimus.

This exercise is for Extension-Connection and Strength-Stabilization Cycles.

Seated Row To Neck

- Sit at cable row as shown.
- Pull up on transversus and pelvic floor.
- Inhale.
- Pull handle rapidly to upper chest while raising shoulders.
- Rotate shoulders back and down to bring hands to belly.
- Return slowly to start position while exhaling.

This rotational form of the seated row is far more effective than the conventional form for upper and mid-back development.

This exercise is for Extension- Connection and Strength-Stabilization Cycles.

T-bar Row

- Hold T-bar row as shown.
- Pull up on transversus and pelvic floor.
- Inhale.
- Pull T-bar rapidly up as high as possible.
- Lower slowly to start while exhaling.

Unlike the conventional T-bar apparatus for mid back training, the Colgan Institute form of the supported T-bar Row, using loose handles, also permits rotational movement and stabilizer training of the scapula and the middle of the back.

This exercise is for Strength-Stabilization Cycles.

Kneeling Dumbbell Row

- Kneel as shown holding dumbbell with hand fully pronated and forward in a position like sawing wood.
- Pull up on transversus and pelvic floor.
- Inhale.
- Lower dumbbell rapidly to lower ribs while semi-supinating hand.
- Return slowly to start position while exhaling.

The Colgan Institute form of the Kneeling Dumbbell Row fully extends the latissimus by pronating the palm and extending the arm forward in a sort of a rotational sawing wood motion.

This exercise is for Extension-Connection Cycles.

Cable Reverse Wood Chop

- Hold low rope cable as shown and stand forward of cable machine.
- Pull up on transversus and pelvic floor.
- Inhale.
- Chop diagonally upwards rapidly while rotating spine.
- Lower slowly to start position while exhaling.

Covered in Chapter 18, on core training, the Reverse Woodchop also trains back strength in rotational movements of the spinal muscles. It is excellent for tying together muscle chains from the feet throught core to hands.

This exercise is for Strength-Stabilization and Power Cycles.

Deadlift

- Place feet parallel, shoulder width apart.
- Hold bar tightly with slightly wider than shoulder width grip.
- Maintain normal inward curve of lower back throughout deadlift.
- Pull up on transversus and pelvic floor, and engage tongue lock.
- Inhale.
- Track knees over second toe throughout deadlift.
- Keep head level and eyes on horizon.
- Keep muscles tight as you lift.
- Accelerate bar by pulling it towards your shins. Lift by straightening your legs.
- Stick out your chest but keep your head level, chin in.
- Exhale slowly on the way up, keeping core tight.
- Finish lift with knees bent 15°, normal inward curve in lower back, and bar supported by upper body muscles.

The Deadlift is **the** #1 power exercise for athletes.

> **This exercise is for Power Cycles but should be practised with light weights as warm-up during Strength-Stabilization Cycles.**

No, no, doc. I can get advice from anyone.
From you, I want a miracle.

Chest: Power Push

We will focus on only the four chest muscles most important for athletic power. They are the **pectoralis major**, the **pectoralis minor**, the **serratus anterior**, and the set of smaller muscles called the **intercostals**. You have a lot more small chest muscles, but space prevents me covering them here. The exercises we use ensure they are trained along with the big boys.

Pectoralis Major

Though it is a favorite of bodybuilders, the **pectoralis major** is rarely shown correctly in muscle magazines. It's a mystery why, because the anatomy and physiology have not changed since I taught it in the '70s, and were first correctly described way back in 1919.[1] If you are going to develop a program to train the pectoralis properly, you have to know how it works.

As the illustration overleaf shows, the pectoralis major has four separate divisions, in layers that overlap like fanned out playing cards. On top, there is the **clavicular division**, which runs from the top of the humerus of the arm to the clavicle (collarbone). Next layer is the **sternal division**, which runs from the humerus to the sternum (breastbone). Third is the **costal division**, which runs from the humerus to the cartilages of the second to seventh ribs. Fourth is the **abdominal division**, which runs from the humerus to connective tissues of the abdominals, both the rectus abdominus and external obliques.[2]

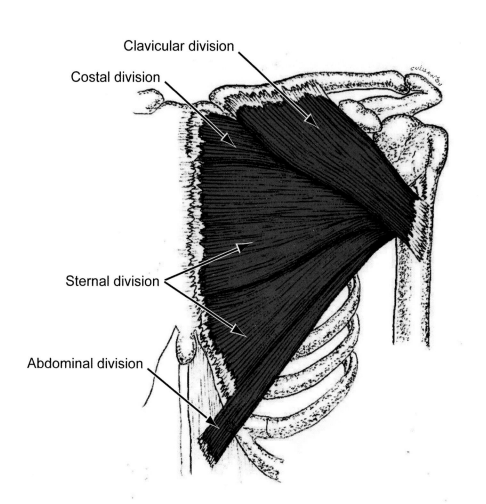

Clavicular division

Costal division

Sternal division

Abdominal division

The pectoralis major has four separate divisions, the clavicular, costal, sternal and abdominal. Each division connects to different points on the body and needs different movements to train it.

Because they connect to these widely differing points on the body, each division of the pectoralis major needs different movements to train it. Overall, the muscle acts to adduct the arm (pull it towards the midline of the body). The best exercises to strengthen this action are the internal rotations covered under Shoulders in Chapter 19.

The pectoralis major also rotates the humerus at the shoulder and flexes the humerus (pulls it forward). Good exercises to strengthen this action are the flat dumbbell bench press, incline dumbbell bench press, and bent-arm dumbbell flyes. The flat and incline barbell bench presses are also useful as overall power exercises to tie all these movements together.

With the arm stuck out, the costal division of the pectoralis works to pull the humerus backward. A good exercise for this action is the front, straight-arm cable pull-down. Finally, the abdominal division pulls the arm down and forward. The best exercises for this action are the bent-arm dumbbell pull-over, and front straight-arm pull-down.

> *The pectoralis minor stabilizes the scapula (holding it close to the back) and acts to pull the shoulder down and forward.*

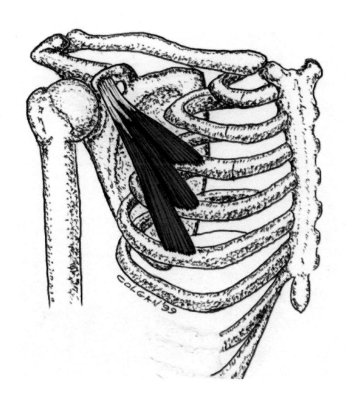

Pectoralis Minor

All the arm movements controlled by the pectoralis major can occur strongly only if the rotator cuff is both strong and stable. The exercises that will give you rotator cuff strength and stability are covered in Chapter 19. In that chapter, I also discuss the necessity for stabilizing the scapula, because all the rotator cuff muscles attach to it. The internal rotation exercises and overhead press in Chapter 19 do part of the job to link these muscle chains. Chest exercises do most of the rest.

As the illustration shows, the **pectoralis minor** lies underneath the pectoralis major. It originates on the third to fifth ribs and inserts on the coracoid process of the scapula. Not being visible, the pectoralis minor is ignored in many bodybuilding programs. But for athletes, it is important as a stabilizer of the scapula, holding it close to the back. It also acts to pull the shoulder down and forward. The best exercises for the pectoralis minor are front straight-arm pull-down, bent-arm pull-over, and flat twisting dumbbell bench press.

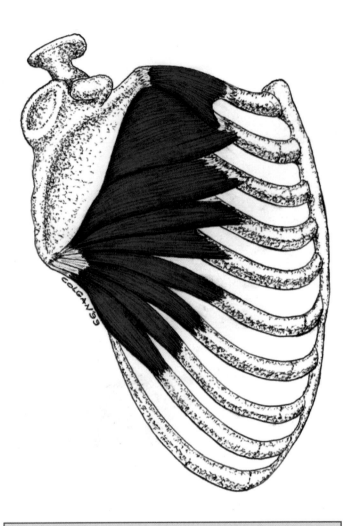

The serratus anterior (commonly known as the "boxer's muscle") is a fan-like series of overlapping sections that run fom the scapula to the ribs. It stabilizes the scapula as a fixed point from which to move the arm.

Serratus Anterior

The serratus anterior covers the side of the upper chest. It originates on the first eight ribs and runs back to insert on the middle edge of the scapula. Called "the boxer's muscle," the serratus is the most important stabilizer of the scapula, anchoring it to the back. This stabilizing action allows other muscles to use the scapula as a fixed bone from which to move the arm.

The serratus is vital to any athletic action of pushing or punching, or forward throwing. Best chest exercises for this muscle are the flat and incline dumbbell bench presses and internal rotations.

The Intercostals

The narrow intercostal muscles connect and fill the space between each rib and stabilize the chest wall. They are evident only in very lean athletes. All the chest exercises given involve these muscles.

As you can see, the chest needs a wider range of exercises than most other. Now we have sketched the anatomy of the chest muscles necessary to understand how to train them, we can get to it.

The Barbell Bench Press

The bench press is far and away the most popular chest exercise. It is also extensively but mistakenly used as a measure of athletic power. As we will see in Chapter 25, it only measures pushing strength from a supported back, a position that rarely occurs in sports. For athletes, the bench is an exercise for integration of arms, chest and shoulders, nothing more.

Opposite to most weight exercises, the lift starts with the eccentric contraction. The prime movers of the chest and shoulders lengthen under the load as you lower the bar. Then comes the concentric contraction as you push it up again.

Some of the worst errors in benching are: lifting the hips and buttocks off the bench which leads to back injuries, bouncing the barbell off the chest which leads to chest injuries and too wide a handgrip which leads to shoulder injuries. So keep a flat back, don't bounce the bar and hold a medium grip.

Rick Weill was the first man in history to lift triple his bodyweight in the bench. At 180 lbs he broke the world record with 551 lbs. Rick says:"Powerlifters most often use a medium grip because it incorporates all the upper body muscles." Here's world champion bench presser Ted Arcidi demonstrating the right grip.

World champion bench presser Ted Arcidi demonstrates the correct medium width grip.

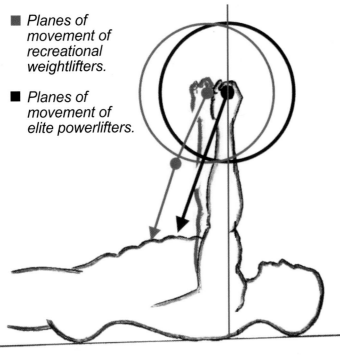

■ *Planes of movement of recreational weightlifters.*

■ *Planes of movement of elite powerlifters.*

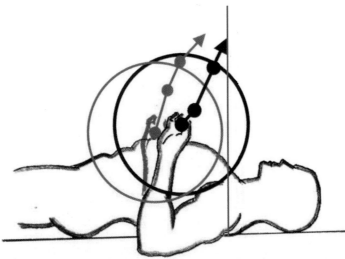

These drawings compare the bench technique of elite powerlifters (black) with the inefficient and hazardous technique of recreational weight lifters (red).[3]

Bench Like An Expert

One of the best studies done to discover the most efficient form for the bench was done by Nels Madson and Tom McLaughlin at Auburn University in Alabama. They studied the bench presses of 19 national and world class powerlifters filmed during competition, and compared them with the filmed bench presses of 13 recreational weightlifters.[3] The differences were dramatic.

The illustration, drawn from the Madson study, shows champion bench technique in black and amateur bench technique in red. You can see that the recreational weightlifters:

• Started with the bar far out of balance, well forward of the vertical.

• Lowered the bar in an inefficient arc.

• Lowered the bar too quickly (out of control).

• Lowered the bar to a point too far down the chest and out of control so that it whacked the chest.

• Raised the bar in an inefficient arc ***away from*** the shoulders, making the lift a lot harder.

• Finished at a point still way out of balance.

In contrast the elite powerlifters:

- Started the lift with the bar balanced on the vertical formed by the arms.

- Lowered it slowly under control in almost a straight line to stop at the sternum.

- Lifted the bar initially at a 60° angle ***towards*** the shoulders. That is the ***opposite*** arc of travel from the arc used by the recreational lifters.

- Pressed the bar out to almost a balanced vertical position.

The correct arc of travel when pushing the bar up deserves stressing. Because many studies of the bench press involve only recreational weight lifters, the common recommendation is for the inefficient arc found with the recreational lifters above.[4] Don't do it!

Though the elite were handling 80% more weight than the recreational lifters, they required only 43% more force to do it. If you want strength in the bench press, learn to do it the expert way.

Power Principle 22: Train the chest with wide-range precision.

Fatburner:
Flamethrowing device
guaranteed to reduce
bodyfat to zero.

12 Top Chest Exercises

Barbell Bench Press

- Balance bar on arms.
- Pull up on transversus and pelvic floor.
- Inhale.
- Lower bar slowly to stop at sternum just below sternal head of pectoralis.
- Accelerate bar at 60° towards shoulders.
- Press out while exhaling

The Barbell Bench Press is a great exercise for integrating muscle chains of chest, arms and shoulders. But it is a poor measure of athletic power and does little for stabilizers and connective tissues.

This exercise is for Power Cycles but should be practised with light weights as warm-up during Strength-Stabilization Cycles.

Flat Bench Twisting Dumbell Press

- Hold dumbbells as shown with hands semi-supinated.
- Pull up on transversus and pelvic floor to flatten back to bench.
- Inhale.
- Raise dumbbells rapidly, rotating elbows out and up while pronating palms.
- Lower slowly while exhaling.

The flat, twisting dumbbell bench press, which turns the palm from supination to pronation, is the best overall chest exercise for athletes, because it trains the chest stabilizers and connective muscle tissue better than the barbell bench. It gets both the pectoralis major and the pectoralis minor.

This exercise is for Extension-Connection Cycles.

Flat Dumbbell Flye

- Hold dumbbells as shown as if hugging a tree.
- Pull up on transversus and pelvic floor.
- Inhale.
- Keeping arms bent, lower dumbbells to sides as shown.
- Accelerate up to hugging tree position again while exhaling.

The Flat Flye ties together muscle chains of chest and shoulder. To protect shoulders, be careful to keep arms well bent as if hugging a big tree. Bring dumbbells only up to a tree hug position. Bringing dumbbells together across the chest fails to stress the chest muscles as there is no longer tension on them.

This exercise is for Strength-Stabilization Cycles.

Incline Barbell Press

- Hold barbell balanced above nose.
- Pull up on transversus and pelvic floor.
- Inhale.
- Lower bar slowly to touch upper chest.
- Accelerate bar up in an arc towards nose while exhaling.

The Incline Barbell Press is an integration exercise for muscle chains of chest, arms and shoulders.

This exercise is for Strength-Stabilization Cycles.

Scott Incline Dumbbell Press

- Hold dumbbells as shown.
- Pull up on transversus and pelvic floor.
- Inhale.
- Raise dumbbells rapidly by moving elbows back and up.
- Keep arms partially bent in top position.
- Lower slowly to start while exhaling.

Larry Scott's form of the Incline Dumbbell Press is superior to the Incline Barbell Press for the chest and shoulders because it also trains rotational movements of stabilizers and connective tissues.

This exercise is for Extension-Connection and Strength-Stabilization Cycles.

Straight-Arm Pull-down

- Hold upper cable as shown.
- Pull up on transversus and pelvic floor.
- Inhale.
- Bring arm down rapidly to thigh.
- Raise slowly to start position while exhaling.

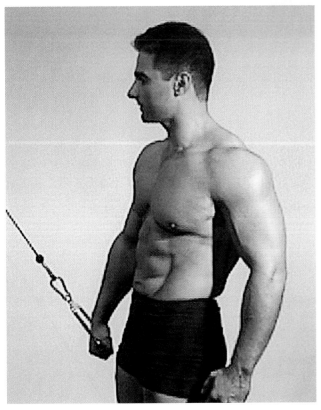

The Straight Arm Pull-down is an effective exercise for strengthening the serratus anterior muscles and the abdominal division of the pectoralis major and tying their action to the abdominal muscles of the core.

This exercise is for Extension-Connection Cycles.

Bent Arm Pullover

- Hold dumbbells as shown.
- Pull up on transversus and pelvic floor.
- Inhale.
- Lower dumbbells slowly behind head.
- Accelerate up to start position while exhaling.

The Bent Arm Pullover trains the serratus anterior and lower fibers of the pectoralis. It also helps stabilize the rotator cuff.

Using two dumbbells for this exercise is far more efficient than the bar because it trains more stabilizers and connective tissues.

This exercise is for Strength-Stabilization Cycles.

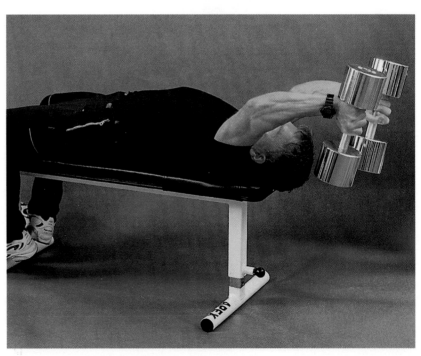

High Cable Crossover

- Hold high cables as shown with arms slightly bent in gullwing position.
- Pull up on transversus and pelvic floor.
- Inhale.
- Lower slightly bent arms rapidly to groin.
- Raise arms slowly to start while exhaling.

The High Cable Crossover especially trains the middle of the pectoralis, including its sternal and abdominal divisions.

This exercise is for Extension-Connection and Strength-Stabilization Cycles.

The Low Cable Cross trains the upper and inner pectoralis and its shoulder connections.

> **This exercise is for Extension-Connection Cycles.**

Low Cable Cross

- Hold low cables as shown with hands pronated.
- Pull up on transversus and pelvic floor.
- Inhale.
- Raise slightly bent arms rapidly forward to head level while supinating palms.
- Lower arms slowly to start position while exhaling.

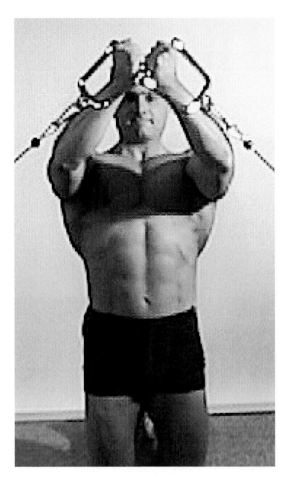

Internal Rotation - Bottom to Top

- Hold low rope cable as shown and stand forward of cable machine.
- Pull up on transversus and pelvic floor.
- Inhale.
- Raise slightly bent arm rapidly diagonally upwards.
- Lower slowly to start position while exhaling.

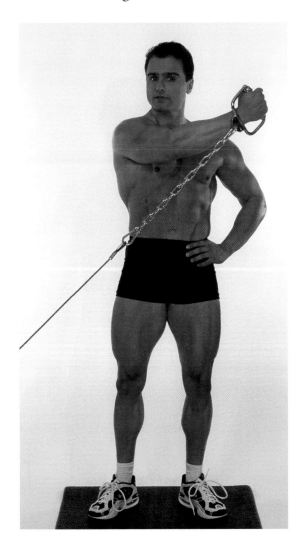

Internal Rotations, also covered in Chapter 19 under shoulders, train the whole chest including stabilizers and connective tissues of the chest, shoulders and back. For most sports, they are superior to chest exercises from a supported back position.

> **This exercise is for Extension-Connection Cycles.**

Internal Rotation - Top to Bottom

- Hold high cable handle as shown.
- Pull up on transversus and pelvic floor.
- Inhale.
- Pull straight arm down rapidly at an angle in line with the cable.
- Raise straight arm slowly to start position while exhaling.

Without internal rotations to tie chest, shoulders and back together, strength gained from supported back exercises makes your back the weak link in the chain.

This exercise is for Extension-Connection Cycles.

Weighted Push-up

- Assume push-up position with arms and body straight.
- Place weight on back. Usually you would use plates steadied by a training partner.
- Pull up on transversus and pelvic floor.
- Inhale.
- Lower straight body slowly until nose touches floor.
- Return rapidly to start position while exhaling.

This exercise is for Strength-Stabilization and Power Cycles.

The weighted push-up is an excellent strength and integration exercise for chest, shoulders, back and core.

Prostrate
Position assumed by some athletes after doing weighted pushups. For those out of shape, it becomes "enlarged prostrate".

Victoria Johnson, famous for her fitness videos and TV fitness program, Victoria's Body Shoppe, on Prime Sports Network transformed her body with Dr Colgan's counsel.

Legs: Power Base

In conjunction with a strong core to transfer force, the major source of power in the human body lies in the buttocks, hips and thighs. These are your power base. You can train other parts of the body to distraction, but you will never achieve your potential unless you develop a strong base. We start at the top of the leg and work down.

Men Are Not Quite Apes

In order to walk and run upright, you have to have a very strong muscle to hold the torso erect over the hips against the force of gravity. So humans developed a massive **gluteus maximus**, the only mammals to do so, and the only mammals capable of erect posture.[1] This evolutionary quirk freed our hands, and permitted development of our unique manual dexterity, which numerous scientists believe sparked the growth of human intelligence.[2]

It's a humbling thought that the whole of human culture developed from a bulge in the butt, but it stresses the importance of this muscle to human performance. In any standing movement, the gluteus maximus is contracting continuously to stop your upper body falling forward at the hip. To be able to contract for long periods without fatigue, it is composed mainly of Type 1, slow-twitch fibers. That's why bodybuilding techniques, which are great at growing slow-twitch fibers, grow a big butt so fast. For athletes, however, big butts are a liability, just excess weight to carry. You need a butt with maximum strength per pound of muscle mass.

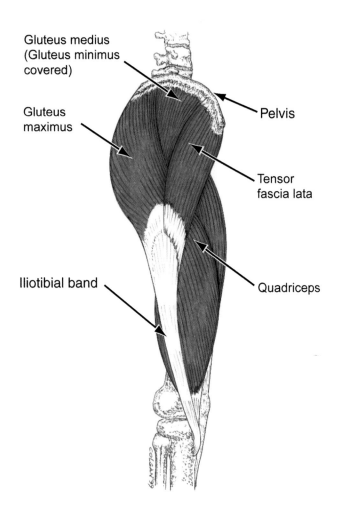

Gluteus medius
(Gluteus minimus
covered)

Gluteus
maximus

Iliotibial band

Pelvis

Tensor
fascia lata

Quadriceps

*Shown from the side of the leg,
the gluteus maximus stabilizes the
pelvis and extends (straightens) and
laterally rotates the thigh at the hip.
The gluteus medius and minimus
stabilize the pelvis and abduct and
rotate the thigh. The tensor fascia
lata assists bending the thigh.*

Gluteus Maximus

The **gluteus maximus** runs from the iliac crest, sacrum and coccyx of the pelvis, to the femur and iliotibial band. It is a major stabilizer of the pelvis, and extends (straightens) the thigh at the hip. It also rotates the thigh laterally (away from the midline of the body.

To train properly for sports, you need to tie standing and forward bending movements into lateral rotation and diagonal movements of the thigh. We do this with squats, deadlifts, diagonal lunges, diagonal to plié lunges, and abduction/rotation exercises.

Gluteus Medius And Minimus

Lying mostly underneath their big brother maximus, the **gluteus medius** and **minimus** run from the iliac crest of the pelvis to the head of the femur. They stabilize the pelvis and are your strongest abductors of the thigh (moving it laterally away from the body. They also rotate your thigh medially (towards the midline of the body). We tackle these muscles with diagonal lunges, diagonal to plié lunges and adduction/rotation exercises.

Tensor Fascia Lata

A big troublemaker for athletes, the **tensor fascia lata** runs from the iliac crest of the pelvis into the **iliotibial band** and fascia of the knee. It assists bending of the thigh at the hip and also works with the gluteus medius and piriformis.

The tensor fascia lata is notoriously a tight muscle. Anyone with a problem in this area should avoid sitting cross-legged in yoga positions, avoid leaning forward in a jack-knife position over a desk. Also avoid steep uphill running and avoid sleeping with knees drawn up. Tilt the seat back when driving too.[3] A good stretch for the tensor is given in the Vital 15 in Chapter 4.

Quadriceps

The **quadriceps** are variously cited as "knee extensors" (straightening the leg at the knee) or "hip flexors" (bending the thigh at the hip). Both these oversimplified views have spawned an endless parade of leg extension and hip flexion machines. They are next to useless for athletes.

Let's get it straight. As the drawing shows, only one of your four quads, the **rectus femoris** crosses both hip and knee joints. So it alone can work with your psoas and pectineus muscles to flex the hip.

The other three quads cross only the knee, so they cannot affect hip flexion. But whenever the four quads are

Shown from the front of the leg, the four-headed quadriceps primarily extends the knee. One head, the rectus femoris, also flexes the thigh at the hip.

extending the knee in any free movement of sport, your rectus femoris is working simultaneously to flex the hip, and is being opposed simultaneously by the gluteus maximus to control hip flexion. These movements are locked together like ying and yang and should be trained in opposition to each other.

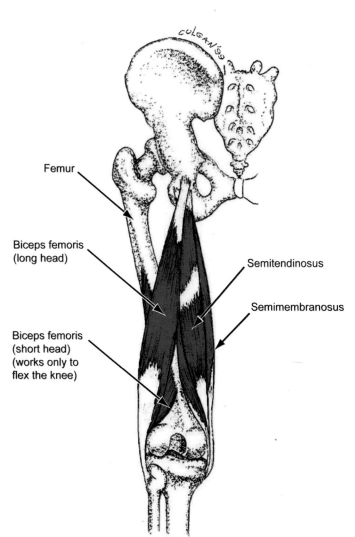

Femur

Biceps femoris
(long head)

Semitendinosus

Semimembranosus

Biceps femoris
(short head)
(works only to
flex the knee)

Shown from the back of the leg, the three major hamstrings work the gluteus maximus to hold the trunk up during standing, to keep the thigh from bending at the hip, and to bend the leg at the knee.

In the seated posture of a leg extension machine the movements get all screwed up. The hip is already bent, the gluteus maximus is largely inactivated, and there is no vertical load on the feet. The action of every muscle of the leg and hip changes radically whenever you take the vertical load off the feet.[3] As most athletes spend most of their time with vertically loaded feet, that's how you should train the legs.

The leg extension machine also holds the legs in one plane and prevents you training your leg stabilizers or leg rotators. All four quads then work simply to straighten the knee, an isolated move that **never** happens in sport. The strength gained and the neural changes learned have little transfer to the sports field.

Need more convincing? Bear with me. There's a lot more. But first we have to look at your main knee flexors, the hamstrings.

Hamstrings

The three true hamstrings are the **semimembranosus** and the **semitendinosus** on the inside of the leg, and the **biceps femoris** on the outside. They all attach to the **ischial tuberosity** (seatbone), with the two inside hamstrings running down to the side and back of the **tibia**, your main lower leg bone, to attach below the knee. The biceps femoris runs down to the **fibula**, your smaller lower leg bone on the outside of the leg.

In scientific gobble, the hamstrings are hip extensors (straightening the hip) and knee flexors (bending the knee). They work with the gluteus maximus to hold the trunk up during standing, and hold the thigh from bending at the hip, and they bend your leg at the knee. Strong hamstrings are essential for all running, jumping and forward bending movements.[4]

Being opposed to the quadriceps, the hamstrings have been the target of all sorts of seated leg curl machines. Most of them are a liability to athletes. In the posture of a seated leg curl machine, the hip is bent, largely inactivating the hip flexors and the gluteus maximus. The machine also prevents you training the leg stabilizers or leg rotators. The hamstrings then work solely to bend the knee. As with the leg extension machine, this isolation movement **never** occurs during sport. It trains the wrong neural output, and the strength gained has little transfer to the sports field.

Adductors

I hear groans about groins at least once a week. The culprit is usually one or other of the **hip adductors**, so frequently injured because they are so seldom trained in conventional weight routines.

The three main adductors of the thigh, shown in the drawing, assisted by a fourth muscle, the **gracilis** at the back of the leg, stabilize the leg, pulling it towards midline of the body. They also assist in rotation and flexion of the thigh, but the main job is stabilization.[5,6] These muscles are all highly active during running, jumping, sideways motion, skiing and horseriding. They are antagonistic to the gluteus medius, and gluteus

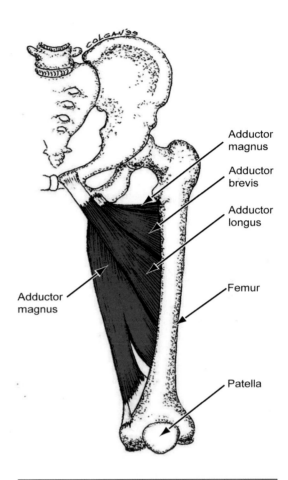

Shown from the front of the leg, the three major adductors of the thigh work with the pectineus and gracilis (not shown) to pull the femur in towards the midline of the body and to rotate it.

minimus of the outer side of the leg. So it is an advantage to train both sets of muscles in opposing supersets, using pliés with diagonal lunges, and abduction/rotation with adduction/rotation.

Athletic Moves

Compare the isolation movements of leg extension and leg curl machines with what happens on the sports field. Most of the time your legs are under load. The **gluteus maximus** is working with the **iliocostalis** and **longissimus** of the back to hold the torso upright. It is also working to extend the

Training leg muscles for athletic power is effective only if you also maintain their flexibility.

thigh and to rotate it laterally, continuously opposed by the **rectus femoris** of the quads working in conjunction with the **psoas** and **pectineus** to flex the thigh. Simultaneously, the three other **quads** are working to extend the knee while the **hamstrings** are working to bend it.

That's not even considering the stabilizers and rotators. To mention a few, the **gluteus medius** and **minimus** are working to lift the thigh sideways, while the **adductors** of the groin work to hold it in. The **piriformis** and four other short muscles in the pelvis are working to laterally rotate the thigh, opposed by the **adductors** and the **tensor fascia lata,** which medially rotate it. And the whole complex system works with a smooth precision and integration that even the robot makers of Disney have failed to match.

In order to teach your brain the right neural output to work all these muscles as a single integrated unit of power, you have to train them in the gym with movements that simulate their function on the sports field. Squats and deadlifts, cleans and high pulls, forward and backward lunges, diagonal and plié lunges. These are the babies you need for leg power. Tough exercises? Who said it was easy!

On Weight Belts

At least a dozen studies show clearly that weight belts increase intra-abdominal pressure, reduce stress on the spine and help to increase a 1RM effort. But they do *not* increase strength over sets of six repetitions so are of little benefit for power training.[7]

On the contrary weight belts weaken you. By performing part of the function your core should be performing, a weight belt acts like a crutch. There is a sound reason to use a crutch to support a broken leg until it heals, but you have to ditch it as soon as possible for the leg to regain full strength. Weight belts used to support a weak core, effectively *prevent* the core from growing stronger. Just like a crutch, used routinely, they *weaken* the bodyparts they support.

Top strength coach Charles Poliquin derides weight belts as "a fashion statement."[8] You know the scene: "Look, I'm wearing a biiiig belt, I lift heavy." There is some reason to use a belt if you are going for a new 1RM. But for all other training, they are just another piece of commercial floss to keep muscleheads emptying their wallets.

Power Base Exercises

The **Big Four** power exercises for athletes are the deadlift, the squat, the high pull and the power clean. Three others we add during the Power Cycle are the bench press, the weighted chin and the cheating barbell curl, already covered in previous chapters. You should learn the techniques for these seven during the Strength-Stabilization Cycle by using the movements as light warm-ups.

I advise you strongly to get a professional trainer to teach you the Big Four. They are the most powerful weight exercises you will do. Done with correct form they integrate all the muscle chains you have been training into one single body of power. Without correct form, they can cripple you.

A whole other category of power exercises that also require professional instruction is **plyometrics**. They are so complicated and controversial I give them a separate chapter ahead. Here we prepare your legs and back to take the strain with the squat, deadlift, clean and high pull. And, in the next chapter, I show you ten other great exercises that train not only legs , hips and back, but also give you calves of iron and knees of steel.

Power Principle 23: Use the Big Four to power your legs.

You Gotta Deadlift

The best overall power exercise is the deadlift. But you have to do it right. Despite the numerous books advocating stiff-leg deadlifts, don't do them. I have dealt with the back problems of so many weight trainers who went the stiff-legged route. A stiff-legged deadlift literally hangs the weight on the tendons, ligaments and fascia of the back, stressing them enormously. You need a 15° bend in the knees to do deadlifts correctly, with your muscles, not with your connective tissues.

You also need a whole lot of other things. Correct form for the deadlift takes about 6 – 8 weeks to learn. Get professional instruction. Otherwise you are courting back injury.

Champion powerlifter Ed Coan in action. He can deadlift 860 pounds at a bodyweight of 198. Here's a little advice from Ed on coming up from the floor:

- *Drive with the legs.*   • *Pull the weight into your body.*
- *Stick out your chest.* • *Keep your head in and your eyes at the horizon.*

12 Steps To Dynamite Deadlifts

1. Place feet parallel, shoulder width apart.
2. Hold bar tightly with slightly wider than shoulder width grip.
3. Maintain normal inward curve of lower back throughout deadlift.
4. Pull up on transversus and pelvic floor and engage tongue lock.
5. Inhale.
6. Track your knees over your second toe throughout the deadlift.
7. Keep your head level, your eyes on the horizon.
8. Keep muscles tight. Do **not** let your shoulders slump or bar hang on connective tissues of your back as you lift.
9. Accelerate bar up by pulling it towards your shins. Lift by straightening your legs.
10. Stick out your chest but keep your head level, chin in.
11. Exhale slowly on the way up, but keep core tight all the way.
12. Finish lift, with knees bent 15°, normal inward curve in lower back, and bar supported by upper body muscles **not** by connective tissues of back.

> **This exercise is for Power Cycles but should be practised with light weight as warm-up during Strength-Stabilization Cycles.**

You Gotta Squat

The squat runs a close second to the deadlift as an overall power exercise. It is essential power training for athletes. Recruiting some different muscle chains to those recruited by the deadlift, it ties together more of the work you have done in the 18 weeks of extension-connection and strength-stabilization.

You have to use correct form for the squat. This form takes an average of 6 – 8 weeks to learn. Get professional instruction. To go into heavy squats without correct form is just inviting injury to back, hips and knees.

One of the most common errors is to use a block to lift your heels. This practice causes a dangerous forward lean and increases stress on the knees. Keep your feet flat on the floor throughout the squat.[9,10,11] If you can't keep your feet flat, ***don't do squats*** until you have developed the ankle flexibility required.

Champion powerlifter Ed Coan squatting at the IPF World Championships.

A second common error is to look up while squatting and to press the neck back against the bar. Books that advocate a head up/looking up position are dead wrong. This stance puts excess strain on the connective tissues of the neck. Looking down is equally bad. It tends to round the back, the cause of many back injuries in the squat.

Don't squat in Smith machines either. It's just too much temptation to lean back against the bar, which stresses the neck and puts a big shear force on the knees. The Smith machine also supports you from side to side, effectively preventing you from training the leg stabilizers.

A third common error in the squat is to go down too fast. Some athletes try to squat quickly, because they're afraid if they go slow they will run out of energy and not be able to come up. In fact they use more energy stopping the bar after they have accelerated its descent. Studies show that elite powerlifters go down slowly to minimize the bar's acceleration. They know that a slow descent is essential to minimize the energy required to stop the bar and reverse its direction of travel.

Ed Coan, zen-like ,with even more weight, 16 plates. That's movin' heavy iron!

Fifteen Steps To Supersquats

1. Align bar evenly balanced on upper trapezius, 1 – 2 inches below the back of the neck.
2. Place feet parallel, shoulder width apart, with knees slightly bent.
3. Track knees over your second toe throughout the squat.
4. Keep back straight, maintaining normal lumbar curve throughout.
5. Align head with chin in, eyes looking forward at horizon level.
6. Pull up on transversus and pelvic floor and engage tongue lock.
7. Inhale.
8. Go down ***slowly***, under control
9. Do ***not*** lean forward.
10 Maintain a tight core throughout.
11. Squat to a depth where upper surface of thighs is parallel with floor. To go deeper puts big shear forces on the knee.[9]
12. Do ***not*** relax at the bottom of squat. Relaxing threatens back and knees. Stay tight.
13. Accelerate out of low position. Do not lean forward. Use your quadriceps to get hips under bar.
14 Lift by straightening legs.
15. Exhale slowly on the way up keeping core tight.

This exercise is for Power Cycles but should be practised with light weight as warm-up during Strength-Stabilization Cycles.

Power Clean

- Crouch with back straight and eyes looking straight ahead as shown.
- Place feet parallel, just over shoulder width apart.
- Pull up on transversus and pelvic floor.
- Inhale.
- Pull bar rapidly up to shoulder height.
- Drop under bar by bending knees and catch it on chest.
- Lower slowly to start position while exhaling.

The Power Clean kicks in where the deadlift stops, by tying together the muscle chains involved, especially those on the front of the body, in lifting resistance from waist to shoulder. It is an essential exercise for athletes.

This exercise is for Power Cycles but should be practised with light weight as warm-up during Strength-Stabilization Cycles.

High Pull

- Crouch with back straight and eyes looking straight ahead as shown.
- Place feet parallel just over shoulder width apart. Pull up on transversus and pelvic floor.
- Inhale.
- Raise bar rapidly as shown to shoulder level.
- Lower slowly to start position while exhaling.

Like the Power Clean, the High Pull moves weight to shoulder weight. But because the weight is suspended away from the body, the High Pull is better for training the muscle chains of the back.

This exercise is for Power Cycles but should be practised with light weight as warm-up during Strength-Stabilization Cycles.

Steel Knees: Iron Calves

Knee problems make up one-quarter of all sports injuries.[1] Three whopping hamstrings and a fourth smaller one cross the knee at the back to bend it. Four even bigger quadriceps hook into the patella of the knee, to extend it. Three big adductors run from the pelvis to the thigh bone (femur) to pull the leg in, and the huge gluteus medius and minimus and tensor fascia lata all hook into the iliotibial band to pull the leg out. The winky little knee joint has to be Herculean to withstand the forces of some of the biggest muscles in your body. Yet most of the athletes I see following conventional bodybuilding training for their legs, are working hard to give themselves chronic knee injuries.

Ask any dozen veteran footballers, basketball players or skiers. Half of them will be happy to show you their knee surgery scars and lament lost dreams. I've seen 20-year old talented Olympic hopefuls sidelinded **permanently** because of knee injuries on the sports field, caused by incorrect weight training in the gym.

Knees Rotate

It's often difficult for coaches and athletes to connect weight training in the gym with knee injuries that happens during sports, because the training and the injury occur remote from each other. So I will spell it out. Conventional leg training with squats, leg presses, leg extensions and leg curls, can put a lot of strength into straight flexion and extension of the knee. But the squats are often done supported by a Smith machine "for safety." And the other three exercises are all on machines that confine the leg to artificial movements that never occur on the sports field. This common leg routine provides no training for leg

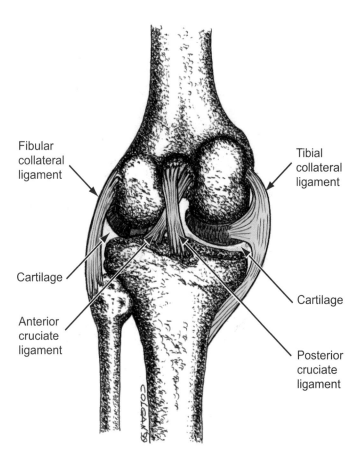

Fibular
collateral
ligament

Tibial
collateral
ligament

Cartilage

Cartilage

Anterior
cruciate
ligament

Posterior
cruciate
ligament

Right knee from the back with the bones separated a little to show the major ligaments and cartilages. In a normal knee, the femur and tibia bones fit snugly into the connective tissues to form a tight package.

stabilization or rotation. And, as we will see, various machine squats, leg presses and leg extensions also damage your back and knees.

Knees never work front-to-back in the free movements of sport. All the leg muscles noted above variously rotate the bones at the knee joint, relying mainly on the ligaments shown in the drawing, plus the little popliteus muscle, to hold it together.[2] Unless these connective tissues are trained to resist the increased rotational forces applied by weight-strengthened leg muscles, they become the weak link in the chain. Especially so, during the extreme rotational stresses experienced in sports with erratic side-to-side motion, such as football, basketball, tennis, skiing, and martial arts.

Skiing is the best example, because we attach long levers to our feet that multiply the rotational stress many times. An athlete who has used conventional weight training catches a tip, so that one ski swings out sideways, twisting the unstable knee. His strong quads and hamstrings continue to push on straight down the slope. There's a muffled explosion and excruciating pain, which is the least of his problems. The tibial colateral ligament over-stretches and tears, ripping out a chunk of the medial cartilage along with it. Goodbye Charlie! For every athlete who has successfully rehabilitated a knee ligament and cartilage injury to return to elite status, there's a dozen who never make it back beyond weekend warrior.

To help give you knees of steel, we have developed (and borrowed) stabilization and rotation exercise movements from a variety of sources that can be adapted for the weight room. The best five of these exercises are given ahead, diagonal dumbbell lunges, plié dumbbell lunges, diagonal to plié lunges, cable adduction/rotation and cable abduction/rotation.

Leg Extension Folly

Your knees also need heavy work, front-to-back. But it has to be the right heavy work. As the drawing shows, you have four main stabilizing ligaments in your knee — the **tibial** and **fibular collateral ligaments,** which prevent side-to-side distortion, and the **anterior** and **posterior cruciate ligaments,** which prevent front-to-back distortion. As long as the force applied is compressive, pushing the femur (thigh bone) down on the tibia (main lower leg bone) one down on the other, normal knees absorb it well. But the human knee is not designed to take large shear forces, that is force applied across the joint.[3]

The worst culprit is the leg extension machine, often mistakenly dubbed "safe" because it use to be used extensively for rehabilitation and for supposedly testing quadricep strength. We know now from numerous studies over the last decade or so, that leg extensions isolate the quadriceps from the hamstrings and the soleus, and produce maximal shear force at the knee by

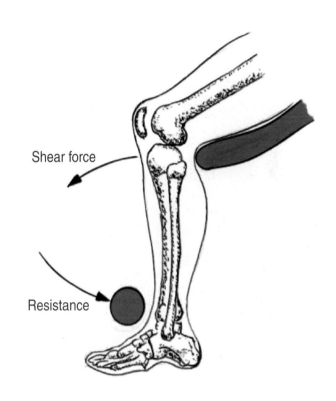

Shear force

Resistance

Many leg extension machines create a damaging shear force on the connective tissues of the knee by applying resistance at the end of the uncompressed tibia. The damage often does not show until subjected to large rotational forces on the playing field.

Single leg extensions are OK for warm-ups and for rehabilitation when done with light weights. But heavy weights apply a shear force across the uncompressed knee joint which damages knee connective tissues.

putting the weight at the end of the long lever of the uncompressed tibia. As the drawing shows, the lower leg hangs out in space. As you apply force to the ankle, especially in the extreme knee bend position built into some leg extension machines, the shear force at the knee end of the tibia pushes it diagonally away from the femur. The hamstrings, which would stabilize this motion if you were standing, are largely inactivated by the seated position.[4,5]

In many cases the athlete worsens the problem by using the back of the knee to push against the seat, further increasing the shear force, which is taken largely by the anterior cruciate ligament (ACL) and its associated cartilage.[4,5] The damage may not show while the knee is held by the machine. But subjected to heavy rotational or sideways force on the sports field, a small tear in the cartilage, which happened in the gym, rips into agony.

Don't Hack Or Leg Press

The hack squat machine is nearly as bad as the leg extension. By supporting the back, it isolates the quadriceps and inhibits the simultaneous contraction of the hamstrings necessary to stabilize the knee.[5] Seated and lying leg press machines are more of this mania. Again, the back is supported, so contraction of the hamstrings is reduced and shear to the knee increased. In addition, most seated leg press machines encourage the user to curl the back, thereby losing the natural lumbar curve and imposing large shear forces on the vertebrae.

These machines also fail to train the body for the integration of the muscle chains used in walking, running and jumping.[5,6] We cover this poor transfer of weight-trained strength to the sports field in Chapter 25, but I will mention it now to introduce you to the vital link required to join the weight room to your sport. **The neural output required to perform powerful movements is posture-specific.** That is, the neural output you learn from weight training supported by machines, differs radically from the neural output required to perform the free movements of sport. Machines train your nervous system to do all the wrong stuff.

Squat For Strong Knees

You often hear athletes dodging squats with complaints that it hurts their knees. Sure it does, if you do it with bad form, such as squatting too deep or using a heel block. Done right, however, the squat is one of the best knee exercises there is. As you come up to straighten the knee, the hamstrings contract strongly to straighten the hips, simultaneously pulling the tibia back to reduce shear. In addition, when standing under load, the soleus muscle of the lower leg, which runs from the back of the tibia to the Achilles tendon, contracts strongly to stabilize the knee front-to-back. Shear force is minimized.[4,7,8]

Calves Of Iron

The calf is not just one muscle as some books imply, but three layers of muscles as shown in the drawing ahead. The top layer is the two-headed **gastrocnemius** which crosses both knee and ankle joints. It attaches to the back of the femur and to the knee capsule, then runs down to join into the Achilles tendon which attaches to the calcaneus (heel bone).

The gastrocnemius is a major flexor of the foot and also helps stabilize the knee. Mostly, it acts as a braking force on the leg, especially so during downhill movement. To brake the leg it functions primarily in eccentric contraction (lengthening under load).

Top Layer   **Middle Layer**   **Inner Layer**

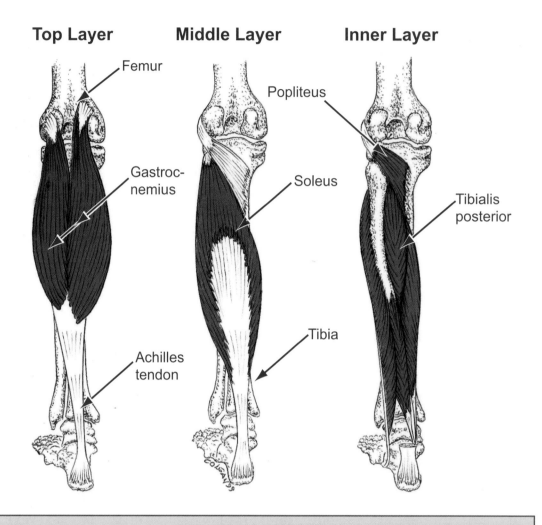

Femur

Gastroc-
nemius

Achilles
tendon

Popliteus

Soleus

Tibia

Tibialis
posterior

The calf is not just one muscle but three layers of muscles, all with different points of attachment and different functions. To train them all for power requires a lot more exercises than the usual calf machines.

That's why the calf is so hard to train. Running downhill puts a far greater eccentric force on the gastrocnemius than it can ever lift concentrically. Consequently, the usual calf exercises you see being done with donkey calf, seated calf and standing calf machines are next to useless, because they use weights that can be handled concentrically. These weights are not heavy enough to stress the gastrocnemius eccentrically. It gets greater eccentric stress every day. You can build stronger calves by just running down stairs.

The Power Program trains the leg stabilizers so well that you will be able to balance on the Swiss ball within minutes of first trying.

The secret is to lift concentrically with both calves, then take one away to provide a strong eccentric contraction for the other. When we first introduced two-leg concentric/one-leg eccentric exercises for calves and other leg muscles, they got a few snickers and jibes from big boys in the gym. Then they saw the results. Now many elite athletes use them. One-leg eccentric squats, for example, are a mainstay of Michael Johnson's weight routine. And he can out-sprint horses.

Soleus

Unlike the gastrocnemius, the **soleus** is a one-joint muscle crossing only the ankle. It runs from the fibula and tibia and joins into the Achilles tendon. It is a major flexor of the foot, a stabilizer of the ankle, and also helps stabilize the knee.

The soleus is also called the body's "second heart." It acts as a strong venous pump to return blood to your heart.[8] Standing immobile inactivates this pump, thereby pooling blood in the legs, which is why some soldiers standing at attention suddenly faint. The soleus is exercised strongly during the foot flexion accompanying gastrocnemius exercises, squats and lunges, and during plyometric and other jumping routines.

Tibialis Posterior

Underneath the soleus lies the **tibialis posterior**. It runs from the top of the tibia and fibula to attach to various bones in the arch of the foot. Not even mentioned in conventional weight training books, this muscle is vital to athletes, because it holds the foot to stop excessive pronation, and it prevents excessive loads on the foot arch by distributing the load at the ball of the foot among the metatarsal bones. Weakness in this baby is a major cause of foot and knee problems in athletes.

If you are one of those myriad of sufferers who spend endless hours in search of orthotics or arch supports that really work, or who rotate through thousands of dollars worth of anti-pronation sports shoes every year, a weak tibialis posterior may be the culprit. We try to take care of this problem in our calf exercises by simultaneously supinating the foot while flexing under load.

You will also do better wearing shoes with strong lateral stability at the heel, and a very snug heel counter. If you can get a finger in at the sides or back of the heel, it's too loose. Pad it firm with stick-on foam or dump the shoes fast.

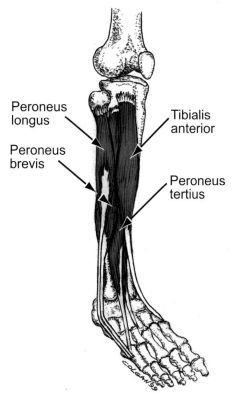

Peroneus longus

Peroneus brevis

Tibialis anterior

Peroneus tertius

Strong tibialis anterior and peroneus muscles are essential for good balance and energy-efficient foot fall during sports.

Popliteus

The little **popliteus** runs from the outside end of the femur to the back of the tibia. It laterally rotates the femur on the tibia as you stand up, walk or run. Together with the knee ligaments, it also holds the tibia and femur in line.

Running downhill or across sloping surfaces, stresses this muscle strongly. You will know you have overdone it from a distinctive pain at the inner side of the back of the knee.

Tibialis Anterior

The **tibialis anterior** runs down the front of the leg from the tibia to the medial cuniform bone of the foot that links to the bones of the big toe. It is essential to athletes for balance and to prevent foot-slap during running. It also lifts the foot clear of the ground for the next stride.

Folk with weak tibialis muscles have poor balance and also trip easily. Novice runners know all about tibialis weakness when they get shin splints. We tackle the tibialis by stretching and loading it during calf exercises. For runners with persistent shin problems we use Sorbothane heel cushions.

Peroneus

The **peroneus** is a group of three muscles on the front and outside of the lower leg. They run from the fibula to the metatarsal bones of the forefoot that lead to the little toe and the big toe. They work primarily in eccentric contraction to control foot movement rather than produce it, thereby contributing to balance and posture. We tackle these muscles by adduction and dorsiflexion of the foot during calf and adduction exercises.

Extensors Of Toes

It's worth mentioning the two **long extensors** of the toes. They run from the tibia and fibula to the phalanges bones of the toes. Like the tibialis, they help to prevent foot-slap following heel-strike when running. They also help to lift (dorsiflex) the foot for the next stride. They are vital to balance. Flexion of the ankles and toes during calf and other one-leg exercises strengthens these muscles well. We get problem cases to pedal the stationary bike against resistance for 30 minutes, twice a week for 10 weeks with conscious flexion and extension of the feet and ankles.

Power Principle 24: Use Single-leg Eccentrics and Lunges to Train Lower Legs.

Frank Shorter.
Kitchen utensil for trimming the puckered little ends off hotdogs.

10 Top Leg Exercises
Front Lunges

- Stand as shown with arms hanging loosely.
- Pull up on transversus and pelvic floor.
- Inhale.
- Step directly forward and touch back knee lightly to floor.
- Keep front knee tracking over second toe of foot.
- Keep arms loose.
- Return to start position while exhaling.
- Alternate legs.

The Front Lunge is an excellent leg strengthening and stabilization exercise for athletes.

This exercise is for Extension-Connection and Strength-Stabilization Cycles.

Back Lunges

- Stand as shown with arms hanging loosely.
- Pull up on transversus and pelvic floor.
- Inhale.
- Step directly back and touch back knee lightly to floor.
- Keep front knee tracking over second toe of foot.
- Keep arms loose.
- Return to start position while exhaling.
- Alternate legs.

The Back Lunge differs radically from the Front Lunge in that most of the resistance is on the stationary leg. It is the easiest lunge to start with.

This exercise is for Extension-Connection and Strength-Stabilization Cycles.

Plié Lunges

- Stand as shown with arms hanging loosely.
- Pull up on transversus and pelvic floor.
- Inhale.
- Step to side as shown in top photo.
- Sweep unweighted leg around behind weighted leg and lower knee to floor beside ankle of weighted leg.
- Keep front knee tracking over second toe of foot.
- Keep arms loose.
- Return slowly to start position while exhaling.
- Alternate legs.

Plié Lunges, which we took from ballet exercises are the best form to get the adductors and inner hamstrings. Be careful to keep the knee tracking directly over the front foot.

This exercise is for Extension-Connection and Strength-Stabilization Cycles.

Diagonal Lunges

- Stand as shown with arms hanging loosely.
- Pull up on transversus and pelvic floor.
- Inhale.
- Step diagonally to side but keep foot facing forward.
- Swivel feet and lower back knee to lightly touch floor.
- Keep front knee tracking over second toe of foot.
- Keep arms loose.
- Return to start position while exhaling.
- Alternate legs.

Diagonal Lunges are the most effective form of stabilizing the leg and knee under rotational force. Essential for athletes.

This exercise is for Extension-Connection and Strength-Stabilization Cycles.

Front To Back Lunges

- Stand as shown with arms hanging loosely.
- Pull up on transversus and pelvic floor.
- Inhale.
- Step directly forward as for a front lunge and touch back knee lightly to floor.
- Keep front knee tracking over second toe of foot.
- Step back toward start position but do not touch foot to floor at start position.
- Instead go directly into a back lunge.
- Return to start position while exhaling.
- Alternate legs.

This exercise is superb for stable balance on the playing field. When athletes have learned it well, we go them to do it with their eyes closed.

This exercise is for Strength-Stabilization Cycles.

CAUTION:
This is an advanced exercise. Not to be done until athlete is thoroughly practised in both front and back lunges.

Plié To Diagonal Lunges

- Stand as for previous lunges, arms hanging loosely.
- Pull up on transversus and pelvic floor.
- Inhale.
- Step forward diagonally as far a diagonal lunge, swivel feet and touch back knee lightly to floor.
- Keep front knee tracking over second toe of foot.
- Step back towards start position but do not touch foot to floor at start position.
- Instead go directly into a plié lunge.
- Return to start position while exhaling.
- Alternate legs.

The most difficult lunge combination, the Plié to Diagonal Lunge is the best for training balance, especially in side-to-sde movement. Once well learned, we get athletes to do it with their eyes closed.

This exercise is for Strength-Stabilization Cycles.

CAUTION:
This is an advanced exercise. Not to be done until athlete is thoroughly practised in both diagonal and plié lunges.

Cable Adduction/Rotation

- Stand as shown with foot attached to low cable by strap and rotated out as far as possible.
- Pull up on transversus and pelvic floor.
- Inhale.
- Swing leg rapidly diagonally across body and simultaneously rotate foot inward as far as possible.
- Return to start position while exhaling.
- Alternate legs.

The Cable Adduction/Rotation is the best exercise for training adductors and internal rotators of the thigh (muscles that pull the thigh in towards the groin and rotate the leg inwards).

This exercise is for Extension-Connection and Strength-Stabilization Cycles.

Cable Abduction/Rotation

- Stand as shown with foot attached to low cable by strap and rotated inward as far as possible.
- Pull up on transversus and pelvic floor.
- Inhale.
- Swing leg rapidly diagonally away from body and simultaneously rotate foot out as far as possible.
- Return to start position while exhaling.
- Alternate legs.

The Cable Abduction/Rotation is the best exercise for training the abductors and outer rotators of the thigh (muscles that move the thigh sideways and rotate the leg outwards).

This exercise is for Extension-Connection and Strength-Stabilization Cycles.

Seated Calf Eccentrics

- Sit as shown in seated calf machine.
- Lower heels and rotate them inward to touch each other at lowest position.
- Pull up on transversus and pelvic floor.
- Inhale.
- Raise heels and rotate them outward to fully contract calves.
- Take away one leg.
- Rotate leg down to low position while exhaling.
- Alternate legs.

The rotational one-leg eccentric calf exercise is so much more effective than conventional calf training, there's no comparison.

This exercise is for Strength-Stabilization Cycles.

Scott One-Leg Calf Eccentrics

- Stand with belt attached to low cable with heels together in low position as shown.
- Pull up on transversus and pelvic floor.
- Inhale.
- Raise heels and rotate them outward to fully contract calves.
- Take away one leg.
- Lower weight with other leg to low position while exhaling.
- Alternate legs.

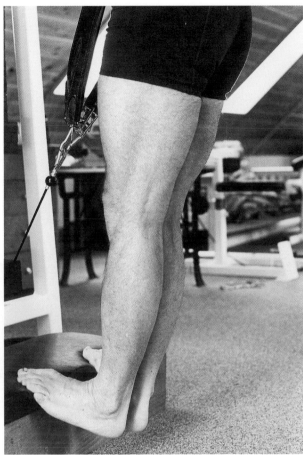

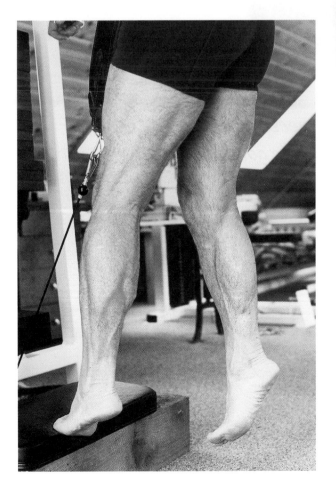

The best of the best calf exercises, this roational one-leg eccentric beauty will give you calves of iron.

This exercise is for Strength-Stabilization Cycles.

*Be kind to your knees: you'll
miss them when they're gone.*

25

The Vital Link

Throughout the Power Program, I have shown you how speed is the biggest component of athletic power, and how to train for the fast concentric contractions that modify your muscles and nervous system to react more rapidly. I have also shown you why conventional weight training fails miserably to give you this ability.

In his new book, worldwide expert on training for power, Tudor Bompa of York University in Toronto agrees:

> If an athlete is trained with bodybuilding methods, which is often the case, the neuromuscular system adapts to them. As a result the athlete should not be expected to display fast explosive power because the neuromuscular system was not trained for it.[1]

Remember, speed of reaction is the biggie for power. All three cycles of the 25-week Power Program, which emphasize acceleration of the concentric contractions, help you attain this speed. But you still need one more step to enable you to transfer the explosive power of the weight room into the specific movements of your sport. We call it **The Link Cycle**. Unlike the other three cycles, this one is incorporated into your competitive season. It can give you all the speed you need.

The Link Cycle

The Link Cycle is sport specific. That is, you use exercises which simulate particular skilled movements of your sport. Why? Because research shows clearly that, unless you train these sport-specific links, power gained during weight training transfers poorly to performance.

In a recent, representative study, researchers at the New South Wales Academy of Sport in Sydney, Australia measured changes in leg flexion and extension strength following heavy squat training. They then measured changes in the 40-meter sprint. There was so little relation between strength measured in the laboratory and improvements in sprinting speed, they concluded: "tests of muscular function cannot be used to monitor training-induced changes in performance."[2]

A lot of lab tests of strength are artificial movements, performed on isolation machines that bear little relation to the free movement of sport. But that's not the main reason why the weight room often fails to transfer to the sports field. Our pesky nervous system is the culprit. It's a wee bit complicated but stick with me. In a nutshell, **the neural output required to perform power movements is posture-specific**. That is, the changes you train into your nervous system to perform a movement in one posture, differ radically from the neural output required to perform a similar movement in another posture.

The bench press provides a great example, because it is a favorite power exercise in aggressive pushing sports such as football, wrestling, shotput and javelin. A recent study by Wilson and

The bench press is ineffective for training athletes to push powerfully on the playing field, because the neural output it trains only enables the athlete to push away from a back-supported horizontal posture. The bench is a power exercise for arm, shoulder and chest integration.

colleagues, at Southern Cross University, in New South Wales, Australia found that power gained in the bench press completely failed to transfer to pushing movements in an upright position.[3]

A squint at the biomechanics shows you why. In the lying-on-the-back-posture of the bench press, you train the nervous system to push away from a horizontal back supported by a bench. There is little back, core or leg involvement. On the playing field, however, you push from an unsupported standing position with major back, core and leg involvement. The nervous system of these bodyparts is not trained for such movement by the bench press. Consequently, the transfer of power from bench press to playing field is very poor.

Because of this problem, some European coaches scoff at the bench press calling it "the American exercise." They mistakenly think it is only useful for holding up the car while you change a wheel. By this point in the book you know otherwise. The bench is a great power exercise for integration of arms, chest and shoulders.

Neural Specificity

The whole Power Program, but especially the Link Cycle, is designed to optimize power transfer from the weight room to the sports field. You have gained a lot of that transfer already by using many

With a light weight, the cable woodchops are excellent link exercises for golfers, tennis players, baseball players, shot and discus throwers and martial artists.

movements with free weights and cables that simulate the postures and movements of sport. You have also made your muscles more flexible, and have seen how flexibility increases power transfer by increasing speed of reaction and range of motion.[3] And you have also learned the power posture. One big reason we advocate living the power posture during training and daily life, is that it facilitates the transfer of power to the same posture during sports.

To ice the cake, you now have to use exercises that closely simulate particular skilled movements of ***your*** sport. More than that. You and your coach have to devise a personal Link Cycle which focuses on movements of your sport in which you are weak. I can't give you the specifics for your particular sport here but I do include some good general link exercises ahead.

Speed Speed Speed

The first step in all link programs is to further increase your speed. You have gained a lot of speed already from our focus on fast concentric contractions throughout the 25-week Power Program. To get faster, you now have to use lighter weights. Why? Because no matter how many muscle fibers you recruit to move heavy weights, acceleration from rest is slow. Now you now have to train your nervous system for faster acceleration. So you have to perform the link exercises with faster acceleration. For the Link Cycle you use weights of only 20 – 60% of 1 RM, and in all exercises you focus on explosive concentric contractions.

The slow eccentric contractions which gave you most of your newfound strength are no longer your concern. The weights you use in the Link Cycle, are too light to cause much of the myofibrillar damage necessary for growth of muscle strength. Remember, the Link Cycle is primarily for training your nervous system.

You Have To Have Power To Link

Some coaches and athletes studying for **Colgan Power Program Certification** object that we don't tell them about the Link Cycle until near the end of the two-semester course. I have done the same in this book. It's deliberate. Some folk want to jump right into the Link Cycle in the same way that they want to jump into the Power Cycle. Don't even think about it. I see a ton of injured athletes who have been wrongly trained to do power exercises before their bodies are prepared with extension, connection, and stabilization. I see even more athletes doing link exercises, such as medicine ball throws, before they have sufficient power to link to anything.

Link exercises are for training the nervous system to transfer strength and speed gained in the weight room to explosive power on the playing field. They are next to useless, and downright dangerous, unless you have already gained the necessary muscle strength, general neural speed, and connective tissue toughness. In programs at the Colgan Institute, unless the athlete is already well trained with weights, we don't use the Link Cycle until the second year on the Power Program, and then only lightly. In the third year, you can go for broke!

When you do get into link training, you have to do it at the right time in your training routine. Don't make the common mistake of doing link exercises after skill training. After skill training, your nervous system is fatigued, from being focussed on one form of learning — sport-specific techniques. To switch immediately to learning neural speed is very difficult. Link training is best done in the early morning after a good sleep.

A final word about link exercises. In conventional training, they are often put under the heading **"plyometrics"**. Because strength is often confused with power in books and articles, plyometrics are often mistakenly used and adapted as strength exercises. They are ineffective for strength increase, but such is the confusion among athletes that I give the problem a separate chapter ahead.

Power Principle 25: Use the Link Cycle to gain speed.

10-Week Link Cycle

Workouts Per Week		**5**
Exercises Per Workout		**3 - 5**
Sets Per Exercise		**3**
Reps Per Set	Set 1	**8 - 12**
	Set 2	**6 - 8**
	Set 3	**3 - 6**
Weights	Set 1	**20% 1RM**
	Set 2	**40% 1RM**
	Set 3	**60% 1RM**
Rest Periods		**3 minutes**

9 Top Link Exercises
Spinal Rotation Lunge

- Stand holding medicine ball as shown.
- Pull up on transversus and pelvic floor.
- Generate tension in muscles antagonistic to the rotational movement.
- Inhale.
- Release antagonist muscles like a spring and swing ball diagonally up to side opposite as fast as possible.
- Return to start on alternate sides by striding forward while exhaling.

The Rotational Lunge is essential speed training for the core.

This exercise is for Link Cycles.

The Back Throw is an excellent link exercise for muscle chains on the back of the body for all jumping sports and martial arts.

This exercise is for Link Cycles.

Back Throw

- Crouch with medicine ball as shown.
- Pull up on transversus and pelvic floor.
- Generate tension in muscles antagonistic to the throwing movement.
- Inhale.
- Release antagonist muscles like a spring and throw the ball straight back overhead as fast as possible while exhaling.

Front Throw

- Hold medicine ball on chest as shown.
- Pull up on transversus and pelvic floor.
- Generate tension in muscles antagonistic to the throwing movement.
- Inhale.
- Release antagonist muscles like a spring and throw the ball forward as fast as possible while exhaling.

The Front Throw is a great speed exercise for all ball sports that use the hands.

This exercise is for Link Cycles.

Front Overhead Throw

- Hold medicine ball behind head as shown.
- Pull up on transversus and pelvic floor.
- Generate tension in muscles antagonistic to throwing movement.
- Inhale.
- Release antagonist muscles and throw ball forward overhead as fast as possible while exhaling.

The Overhead Throw is an excellent speed exercise for muscle chains on the back of the body, for all ball sports that use the hands, for all throwing sports, and for martial arts.

This exercise is for Link Cycles.

Seated Front Throw

- Sit holding medicine ball on chest as shown.
- Pull up on transversus and pelvic floor.
- Generate tension in the muscles antagonistic to throwing movement.
- Inhale.
- Release antagonist muscles like a spring and throw ball forward as fast as possible while exhaling.

The Seated Front Throw is an excellent speed exercise for core power in ball sports. Use a partner to forcibly throw the ball back at you.

This exercise is for Link Cycles.

Side Throw

- Sit holding medicine ball out to the side as shown.

- Pull up on transversus and pelvic floor.

- Generate tension in muscles antagonistic to throwing motion.

- Inhale.

- Release antagonist muscles like a spring and rotate spine to throw ball forward as fast as possible while exhaling.

- Alternate sides.

The Seated Side Throw is one of the best speed exercises for rotational core power and for sports utilizing extreme spinal rotation, including field throws, golf, tennis, cricket, baseball and martial arts.

This exercise is for Link Cycles.

Bounce Jump

- Stand on edge of bench as shown above left.

- Pull up on transversus and pelvic floor.

- Inhale.

- Jump forward off bench as shown above right.

- Resist folding the body and bounce high and forward off ground immediately on impact as shown above far right.

- Exhale after impact.

The Bounce Jump is an excellent speed exercise for all jumping and running motions.

Throughout impact and take-off in the Bounce, keep your body tight and do not permit impact to flex you.

This exercise is for Link Cycles.

Developed by the legendary Australian running coach Percy Cerutty, the Bound shown below, is a premier link exercise for runners.

The Bound is an essential speed exercise for all running and jumping movements and raquet sports. Using a 40 ft long elastic rope towed behind a car with 15 - 20 lbs pressure, increases bound rate and distance.

Caution. Do towing on soft surfaces only.

Bound

- Jog briskly.
- Pull up on transversus and pelvic floor.
- Inhale.
- Bound up and forward 10 - 20 times with bouncing motion, exhaling and inhaling rapidly just after each impact.

This exercise is for Link Cycles.

Band Twist

- Stand with elastic rope or band stretched as shown with about 15 lbs of pressure.
- Pull up on transversus and pelvic floor.
- Generate tension in muscles antagonistic to twisting movement.
- Inhale.
- Release antagonist muscles like a spring and rotate spine as fast as possible while exhaling.

The Band Twist is an excellent link exercise for core speed for all sports.

This exercise is for Link Cycles.

Side Bound

- Stand as shown with elastic rope or band pulled firm but without stretch.

- Pull up on transversus and pelvic floor.

- Inhale.

- Bound to the side as fast as possible with a bouncing motion while exhaling.

- Alternate sides by turning body 180º at start.

The Side Stride is a great link exercise for sports with erratic sideways motion, including basketball, tennis, football, hockey and other field games.

This exercise is for Link Cycles.

George got a lot stronger on that chimp testostreone.

Plyometrics

A whole lot of athletes suffer a whole lot of hokum under the name **plyometrics**. But this form of explosive exercise can be very effective, so I want to try and separate some of the gold from the dross. The good stuff is very similar to some of our link exercises

To define it simply, plyometric exercises load the muscle chain suddenly while it is lengthening (eccentric contraction). The idea is that the sudden load will permit the muscle chain to rebound into faster and more intense concentric contractions than you can achieve from rest. I wish it was that easy.

The sudden load causes two main effects which do not occur in concentric contraction from rest. First, it activates what is called the **stretch reflex**. This defensive mechanism in muscles, acts like a rubber shock cord to prevent the muscle chain from overstretching into injury. The stretch reflex momentarily stores some of the sudden load as "elastic strain energy," which then helps to rebound the muscle chain into explosive concentric contraction.

Second, sudden loading of the muscles facilitates learning of neural speed. Since the mid-80's, Hakkinen, Sale, and a whole raft of other researchers, have shown consistently that the more explosive you can make concentric contractions, the better the nervous system learns to increase the speed at which it can activate fast-twitch fibers.[1,2] Remember, speed and fast-twitch activation are the biggies for athletic power.

The Big Drop

All well and good, and theoretically accurate. Problem is, we humans are pesky overreaching creatures who just have to fix what ain't broke, gild the lily, and polish the rosebud. A good example of overreaching is one of the most popular plyometric exercises, the **drop jump**. In the drop jump you drop from a height and rebound into the air. The force you generate in a force plate on the ground, the height you jump up, and the speed from start to finish are the common measures of power.

Renowned golf coach David Leadbetter, seen here in his signature hat, is master of the athletic golf swing, now the leading (and most winning) swing in the world. He knows all about linking together muscle chains to take advantage of elastic strain energy.

Nothing could be simpler than the drop jump but here's how we screwed it up. As you increase the drop height, the force with which you hit the ground increases. That's basic physics. But it got some folk excited that greater and greater heights would be superior, because they generate more and more downward force to convert into upward motion. They must have been watching too many flying kung-fu movies.

Contrary to the virtual reality generated by hidden trampolines and computer simulation in these films, any basic anatomy text will show you that the human body is poorly constructed for storing elastic energy and converting it into upward motion. Nevertheless, dreams of Superman prevailed over science. Throughout the '70s and early '80s, athletes were dropped repeatedly from heights of 1.0 – 2.5 meters (3 feet 3 inches – 8 feet 2 inches).[3] The result — a mass of injuries — and virtually no increase in power.

Why? Four reasons. The gravitational force generated by dropping from such heights is enormous. It slams the feet flat, and bangs the heels hard into the ground, thereby dissipating much of the energy. It overwhelms the stretch reflex. It forces the athlete into extreme flexion at hips, knees and ankles. And it slows the motion. In 1980, Bosco and Komi showed that a drop height of even one meter (3 feet 3 inches) renders plyometric training ineffective.[4]

Shortly after, Bobbert and colleagues at the Free University of Amsterdam in the Netherlands, and others, showed that drop heights between 20 – 40 centimeters (8 – 16 inches) were the highest that achieve any results.[5] Even these heights may be too great. In a representative study at Liverpool John Moore's University in England, Lees and Fahmi compared six-drop heights from 12 – 68 centimeters (5 – 27 inches), in terms of height of subsequent jump, maximum force of jump and speed of jump. On all measures, the 12-centimeter (5-inch) drop proved superior.[6] Yet I still see modular plyometric benches advertised with tiers up to 1.5 meters. Go figure!

Another bit of lily gilding is the addition of barbells on the shoulders, or special weighted belts, to increase the drop force. Not only do these gismos pause the motion, thereby making the exercise ineffective, but they also introduce unbalanced point loading and extreme shear forces on the back and knees. Sow the seeds with these exercises and you will reap a fine crop of injuries on the playing field.

Bounce Baby, Bounce!

Despite all the evidence, excessive drop heights and added weights have spawned a whole cult of drop jump exercises, called **counter-movement jumps**. In these handy-dandies, the athlete allows his body to flex, pauses momentarily with feet flat, and swings his arms to assist the upward jump. It's a crock! The counter-movement jump loses most of the momentum and dissipates most of the drop force into the ground. It also misses the stretch reflex, which is long gone by the time the athlete takes off [7,8].

In contrast, the **bounce jump**, or **rebound jump** the original idea of plyometrics, minimizes the time the feet are in contact with the ground. By doing so it is

The Bound is an effective plyometric exercise, because it is quick enough to take advantage of the elastic strain energy of the stretch reflex.

Renowned author, trainer and masters athlete, Dr Bill Misner makes extensive use of elastic energy to achieve this rhythmic energy-conserving stride.

quick to utilize the elastic energy of the stretch reflex. It also converts the downward energy (supplied by gravity) reasonably efficiently into upward energy for the spring. Especially so, if it is done diagonally to gravity as detailed in Chapter 25. In biomechanical gobble, the efficiency of angular transfer of energy increases as the angle of transfer decreases. For you and me, that means more power is transferred when bouncing forward than straight up and down.

In a recent study representative of the evidence, Young and colleagues at Ballarat University in Victoria, Australia compared counter-movement jumps against bounce jumps. Both groups trained with 72 – 90 drop jumps per week for six weeks. The counter-movement group showed no significant increase in power. The bounce jump group improved their power by a massive 20%.[7]

A new analysis of the biomechanics of these jumps, by Kovacs et al, at Hungarian University, in Budapest, confirms why the bounce jump transfers more power into upward motion. For the same drop height, during counter-movement jumps, the feet strike the ground with about three times the force of the footstrike during bounce jumps. But the pause, essential to flex the hips, knees and ankles under load for the spring upwards, dissipates most of this extra energy into the ground. Results show that the power at the moment of take-off in the counter-movement jump is less than half the power of at the moment of stake-off in the bounce jump.[8] Remember, it is the intensity of concentric contraction and the speed of concentric contraction that determine power output. Counter-movement jumps are too slow and too weak. Bounce jumps are the way to go.

Plyometric Principles

I cannot cover the endless variety of plyometric exercises in this short account, but the drop jump example offers some general principles that hold for almost all of them.

1. Effective plyometrics focus on rapid bounce or rebound.

2. The transition between eccentric and concentric contraction should be as fast as possible.

3. The sudden load imposed during eccentric contraction should not be so great it overwhelms the stretch reflex.

4. The sudden load imposed should not be so great as to cause a pause or counter-movement.

Power Principle 26: Use Plyometric Training to Harness Elastic Strain Energy.

Top athlete of the US Armed Forces, Warrick Yeager took a Colgan program to help him fine tune his speed and economy of motion.

"Looks like it needs some of your vitamins, darling".

Power Nutrition

You body cannot grow optimally in response to training, unless you provide it with the right structural materials in sufficient amounts to repair and maintain existing tissues and grow new tissues. Obvious, yes, but many athletes still do not appreciate the power of nutrition to improve performance. I cover the subject in detail in my books **Optimum Sports Nutrition** and the new **Colgan: Sports Nutrition**.[1,2] Nevertheless, this book would be incomplete without basic power nutrition, because, unless you attend to it, you are throwing away a helluva'n edge.

The Right Stuff

To gain that edge, first you need to appreciate that you are simply a localized bit of the mass of solids, liquids, gases and vibrations that flow around you and through you every living day. The world, including you, is all one interacting system of chemistry. Changes in that chemistry completely determine your power and your performance, whether they occur "outside" in the environment or "inside" that hairy bag of salty water we call the "human body".

You are constructed from a mix of naturally occurring chemicals that have formed part of the chemistry of the Earth since life began. Every molecule of you has lived on Earth before. Every substance has been through the guts of millions of creatures before you. The calcium of your bones, for example, was digested by ancient sea creatures and grown into their shells. These shells decayed into the soils from which the plants and animals we use as food today obtain their calcium.

So it is with all the chemicals that make up your flesh. Over countless millennia, the human body evolved millions of precise mechanisms to utilize the chemicals in its ancient environment, and convert them into muscles, bones, glands, organs, and brain. Today, we call those chemicals **nutrients**.

The human body could develop mechanisms only for those chemicals that were present during its evolution. Today they are still the only chemicals it can use for growth, maintenance and repair[3]. These facts of evolutionary history give us the first principle of power nutrition.

> **First Principle of Power Nutrition: Design your diet so that you receive a complete mix of the ancient chemicals from which the human body evolved.**

To: Micheal
The Power Program
Has made the Difference!

Motocross champion Danny Smith lives on a Colgan Power Nutrition Program.

Avoid The Man-Made

During the last few hundred years, science has developed more than 100,000 chemicals that never existed on Earth before. But evolution takes millennia. So the human body has not had sufficient time to evolve mechanisms to deal with them. Consequently, almost all man-made chemicals are either useless or detrimental to health.

Vitamin E provides a good example. Naturally occurring Vitamin E is **d**-alpha tocopherol. The "d" stands for **dextrorotatory**, a right-hand twist of the molecule. This twist provides the precise chemical key that fits your body locks for Vitamin E, and enables you to use it to grow body tissues.

Man-made Vitamin E, however, is a mixture of two chemicals — trimethylhydroquinone and isophytol. It is called **dl**-alpha tocopherol, because nearly 90% of it is **levorotatory**, a left-hand twist of the molecule. This left-hand twist does not fit your body locks for Vitamin E, and most of the dl-alpha tocopherol is next to useless for human nutrition.[4,5]

A sunny morning in Los Angeles is typical of all major cities in industrialized nations that are mired in a toxic soup of man-made poisons.

Other man-made chemicals suffer similar faults. They do not fit your body's chemical locks. Consequently, it cannot use them properly. They are also often detrimental to growth, maintenance and repair, because they interfere with receptors for the good stuff. Prescription drugs provide telling evidence, because they are all examples of molecules that did not exist during our evolution. The antibiotic **vancomycin,** for example, is effective to kill some life-threatening infections. But because the body cannot deal with the drug, it has devestating effects on intestinal flora and on the immune system. Other examples are the anti-inflammatory drugs used to treat arthritis. As I document in my book, **Beat Arthritis,** though they relieve the pain, they also hasten the progress of the disease.[6]

Second Principle of Power Nutrition: Design your diet and lifestyle so that you avoid, expel or neutralize chemicals created by man.

Synergy and Completeness

Nutrients operate only in synergy, that is, by multiple interactions with each other. They cannot work alone. Benefits of vitamin C in reducing colds for example, depends as much on other nutrients as on the vitamin itself. If you take a large dose of vitamin C to stop a cold, it's multiple interactions require that you also increase your intake of vitamins B_6 and B_{12}, zinc, folic acid and choline.[7]

I document in my book **The New Nutrition** how complete nutrition is next to impoossible to obtain today from our degraded food supply.[8] Especially so for athletes, who need superior nutrition to that of couch potatoes. Consequently, we recommend all athletes to supplement their diets with a complete daily muli-vitamin/mineral. Formulas for these supplements for various purposes are given in my books **Optimum Sports Nutrition** and **Hormonal Health**.[1,9] A good general formula for athletes is given in the following table.

The synergy of your body is so precise that if even one essential nutrient is missing or deficient, the whole mix of your flesh becomes defective, and optimal function is impossible. You need only a tiny bit of Vitamin B_{12}, for example, a few millionths of a gram, an amount you could fit on the head of a pin. But if you don't get it, your energy declines within days, you cease to make healthy red blood cells, and you develop pernicious anemia. Left untreated this disease gradually destroys your brain, bringing insanity and certain death.[10]

A typical daily multi-vitamin/mineral usually includes enough vitamin B_{12}. But very few supplements on the market provide complete supplementation. For the latest scientific evidence and most complete scientific formulas visit our website at www.colganinstitute.com, or e-mail team@colganinstitute.com, or read any one of the books noted above.

**Third Principle of Power Nutrition:
Take a complete multiple vitamin/mineral supplement every day.**

Carbo Loading
Cunning commercial ploy to
sell mountains of pasta and
oceans of Chianti.

Vitamin/Mineral Formula for Athletes

Vitamin A (palmitate)	10,000 i.u.	Docosahexaenoic acid	120 mg
Beta-carotene	15,000 i.u.	Eicosapentaenoic acid	180 mg
Vitamin B1 (thiamin)	125 mg	Folic acid	1800 mcg
Vitamin B2 (riboflavin)	75 mg	Glucosamine sulfate	500 mg
Vitamin B3 (niacin)	40 mg	Hydroxy-methyl-butarate (HMB)	500 mg
Vitamin B3 (niacinamide)	200 mg	Inositol	100 mg
Vitamin B5 (pantothenic acid)	525 mg	Iodine	175 mcg
Vitamin B6 (pyridoxine)	75 mg	Iron (picolinate)	25 mg
Vitamin B12 (cyanocobalamin)	225 mcg	L-cysteine	350 mg
Vitamin C (ascorbic acid, calcium & magnesium		L-glutamine	334 mg
ascorbate, ascorbyl palmitate)	3750 mg	L-glutathione	60 mg
Vitamin D3 (cholecalciferous)	200 i.u.	L-methionine	112 mg
Vitamin E (d-alpha tocopherol)	800 i.u.	Magnesium	912 mg
Vitamin K	60 mcg	Manganese	22 mg
Arginine alpha-ketoglutarate	417 mg	Molybdenum	160 mcg
Bioflavonoids	100 mg	Para-amino-benzoic acid (PABA)	75 mg
Biotin	350 mcg	Phosphatidylcholine	632 mg
Boron	8 mg	Potassium	124 mg
Calcium (carbonate, citrate, ascorbate)	1033 mg	Selenium (selenomethionine)	350 mcg
Chromium (picolinate)	433 mcg	Silica	10 mg
Co-enzyme Q10	20 mg	Vanadyl sulfate	39 mcg
Copper (gluconate)	400 mcg	Zinc (picolinate)	47 mg

Physiological Dynamics

We live in an instant gratification society. Nutrients, however, works to Nature's rhythms. There's no quick fix. The business of improved nutrition is to build a better body. That takes a lot of time. You have to wait until Nature eliminates all the defective and worn out body cells. The enriched nutrient mix then steps in to build new, improved cells.

Your skin is replaced about every two weeks, and you get a whole new blood supply every three months. But it takes six months for most of the cells in your muscles to turn over. After a quarter century in sports nutrition, the shortest program we will give an athlete is six months.

Consider it this way. Neglect a houseplant and its stems and leaves will wither. When you care for it again with regular plant food, water and TLC, the old structure will perk up a bit. But you have to wait until Nature eliminates all the sick and dying cells before the plant can recover. Only after months, when the old neglected structure has fallen off, and new leaves and stems have had time to grow, will the plant return to glory. It is the same with your body.

Fourth Principle of Power Nutrition: Once you start a nutrient program stick to it. You will achieve telling results in about six months.

It takes a few turnovers of muscle cells to develop one-arm push up power. But then you can easily maintain it for life.

How Much Protein?

Half the dry weight of your body is protein. The structure of your muscles, organs, brain cells, even your genes is pure protein. The hemoglobin that transports your oxygen is a protein. The thousands of enzymes that control all bodily functions from the blink of an eye to the growth of a bone, are proteins every one.

None of these protein structures is fixed. But, unlike fats and carbohydrates, your body has no way to store spare protein. It grows new proteins from the protein that you eat. All are being replaced continuously. So, unless you eat the right amount of the right protein in the right way every day, your body cannot grow optimally.

First we have to know the right amount of protein. As I detail in **Optimum Sports Nutrition**, recommendations vary widely from the obsolete Recommended Dietary Allowance of 1.4 grams per kilogram bodyweight to excessive and toxic amounts of 5.0 grams per kilogram bodyweight.[1] These recommendations are usually inaccurate on two counts. First, they are generally derived from short-term nitrogen balance studies run over a few days or at most a few weeks. You are looking for long-term effects. Second, they use bodyweight. Athletes of the same bodyweight differ widely in bodyfat. Bodyfat does not need protein.

We base protein requirements on lean body mass, and take the 25-week Power Program as the period of lean mass gain each year. The amount of protein you need for drug-free training depends on the amount of muscle you carry now, and the amount of muscle you can expect to gain in that 25 weeks.

I cover the science in detail in my other books.[11,2] Here are the bare bones. The average protein content of your lean mass is about 21%. You need to eat one and one-third times this protein in 25 weeks in order to maintain your current lean mass. To gain new lean mass, however, you have to eat about eight times its protein content in order to grow it. When training for power, the maximum growth of new lean mass you can expect in 25 weeks is about 10% of your existing lean mass. So you have to eat an additional 8 X 10 = 80% of the protein in your existing lean mass in order to grow the new mass.

Following is a table with it all worked out. It is based on an ecto-mesomorph body type typical in athletes, and on numerous athletes measured by the Colgan Institute. All you need to know is your current lean mass.

Daily Protein Required For Power Training

| Current Lean Bodyweight | | Maximum Gain of Lean Mass in 6 months | | | | Daily Protein Requirements (grams) |
| | | Men | | Women | | |
(kg)	(lbs)	(kg)	(lbs)	(kg)	(lbs)	
25	55	1.70	3.74	1.25	2.75	58
30	66	2.00	4.40	1.50	3.30	67
35	77	2.30	5.06	1.75	3.85	76
40	88	2.70	5.94	2.00	4.40	85
45	99	3.00	6.60	2.25	4.95	94
50	110	3.30	7.26	2.50	5.50	103
55	121	3.60	7.92	2.75	6.05	113
60	132	3.90	8.58	3.00	6.60	123
65	143	4.30	9.46	3.25	7.15	133
70	154	4.60	10.12	3.50	7.70	143
75	165	4.90	10.78	3.75	8.25	153
80	176	5.30	11.66	4.00	8.80	162
85	187	5.70	12.54	4.25	9.35	172
90	198	6.00	13.20	4.50	9.90	182
95	209	6.30	13.86	4.75	10.45	192
100	220	6.70	14.74	5.00	11.00	201
105	231	7.00	15.40	5.25	11.55	211
110	242	7.30	16.06	5.50	12.10	220
115	253	7.70	16.94	5.75	12.65	230

The Quality of Protein Supplements

The next step is to get the right protein. Protein quality is often touted in terms of the Protein Equivalency Ratio (PER), or the Net Protein Utilization Index (NPU), or the Protein Digestibility Corrected Amino Acid Score (PDCASS). Forget them! The only index of protein quality worth a damn to athletes is Biological Value (BV), which measures the amount of protein retained in the human body per gram of protein absorbed.

When the BV scale was formed, whole egg was given a standard score of 100, as the best protein around at the time. Some of the new ion-exchange whey concentrates and isolates now rate up to 159.[11] Good whey protein mixes are well over the 100 mark in BV. Compare that with a BV of 80 for beef, 79 for chicken, 77 for casein, 74 for soy.

You should aim for the highest BV protein you can get. Select a brand by buying from a company with a reputation to lose. Taken in shakes of 30 grams, three times daily, this protein provides the right stuff to build all the muscle and its supporting neural and vascular structures for your new power.

> **Fifth Principle of Power Nutrition: Take sufficient first-class protein every day.**

Don't Sweat About Bodyfat

I can't cover nutrition and bodyfat in this short account. It's all done in my new book **Colgan: Sports Nutrition**. But here's the nub of it. Most people who have tried to lose bodyfat permanently and failed, have been fooled by commercial weight-loss schemes claiming that you have to submit to one or other of an increasingly bizarre parade of restrictive diets. By following such unbalanced eating plans they have taught their bodies to live directly on the energy produced from food in their stomachs.

With each bout of dieting, they make it increasingly more difficult for the body to access the energy stored in their structure as bodyfat and glycogen. Most of them become functionally hypoglycemic. They have to have food every three or four hours to avoid a precipitous drop in blood sugar. They will never lose fat permanently until they teach the body to live from its structure. To do so you have to avoid spiking your insulin for at least a year. The Power Nutrition principles are designed to enable you to do just that.

Especially pay attention to eating unprocessed foods grown without pesticides and uncontaminated with man-made chemicals. If the food comes in a cardboard carton or commercially sealed pack, then leave it for the chubs. There are now 120 million Americans who are waddling testimony to the power of food processing conglomerates to turn them into fat and sugar processing plants. It gets worse by the year.

Take a complete supplement of vitamins and minerals and sufficient protein, essential fats and pure water every day. Eat low glycemic carbohydrates, exercise correctly and exercise regularly with the Power Program. The fat should take care of itself.

Sounds miraculous in our age of diet fads and fancies. Below is Neville Yuen, one of the thousands who is a living testament to the efficacy of our programs. If it's not happening for you, email me at team@colganinstitute.com.

This is Neville Yuen, at 390 lbs in January 1997 before he began a Colgan Power Nutrition Program.

This is the new muscular Neville Yuen at 185 lbs in January 2000, demonstrating his old balloon pants.

Sixth Principle of Power Nutrition: Don't spike your insulin.

Antioxidants

Each of the stable atoms that compose your body has electrons spinning around its nucleus in pairs that balance each other's electromagnetic charge. Undisturbed, they all spin in harmony, and the miraculous mosaic of flesh they compose remains healthy indefinitely.

But if an atom gains or loses an electron, it becomes a **free radical** with an unbalanced electromagnetic charge. Like the draw of a magnet, this charge then pulls an electron from, or jumps the unbalanced electron to, an adjacent healthy atom of flesh, thereby creating another free radical and setting up a chain of free radical damage.

This scenario, called **uncontrolled oxidation**, is the most powerful process of decay on Earth. Rusting of steel, browning of a cut apple, rotting of meat, and decay of human flesh all occur by uncontrolled oxidation. In 1954, Denman Harman at the University of Nebraska was the first to show that free radicals are the major cause of human aging.[12]

We would all die of free radical damage tomorrow were it not for the body's production of endogenous antioxidants, primarily **superoxide dismutase**, **catalase** and **glutathione**. These antioxidants neutralize free radicals by receiving or donating an electron. This action turns the antioxidants themselves into free radicals. But they are of less damaging forms, which are neutralized in turn by other antioxidants, until eventually all that remains is harmless carbon dioxide and water.

Nutrient Antioxidants To The Rescue

The antioxidants produced in your body fight uncontrolled oxidation lifelong. But they are not enough, especially for athletes, because physical exercise dramatically increases free radical production. Use of oxygen and conversion of glycogen and fats to energy creates free radical damage even in couch potatoes.[13] Sports activity and training, in which a typical athlete uses 12 – 20 times the oxygen of sedentary folk, and 5 – 10 times the energy, increases the free radical burden manyfold. So much so, that there is good reason to believe many athletes are suffering **antioxidant deficiency**.

Numerous studies show that endogenous antioxidants cannot provide sufficient protection.[12] Nutrient antioxidants have to step in to fill the bill. But you can't get good results with any old antioxidant mix. Especially, do not rely on a single antioxidant. All those claims that this or that substance is the only antioxidant you'll ever need are just promotional flapdoodle.

Two reasons. First, in neutralizing free radicals, all antioxidants themselves become free radicals, and must be neutralized by others. So taking a single one such as vitamin E, or pine bark extract, or whatever else is flavor of the month in the fitness magazines, may *increase* your free radical burden not reduce it.

The second reason that any one or two antioxidants cannot suffice, is that free radicals come in many different forms.[12] Some are neutralized by one group of antioxidants, some by another. To get the bulk of them you need a mix of antioxidants. The mix we use with athletes is given in the following table. It specifically targets those forms of free radicals that are most increased by exercise. You will see that it includes numerous nutrients that also form part of the essential daily vitamin/mineral mix. So don't double up if you are making up your own mix of pills.

Because of space restrictions herein, the table is based on only two criteria, bodyweight and at least 15 hours training per week (including the Power Program). You can get closer to your personal antioxidant requirement by reading **Colgan: Sports Nutrition,** in which I use multiple criteria. Here, space permits only the basics.

There's no doubt antioxidants work. A comprehensive review of studies by Lester Packer of the University of Calfornia and a panel of experts, concluded that antioxidant supplements reduce tissue damage, increase tissue repair and enable athletes to train more effectively.[14] Don't leave home without them.

Seventh Principle of Power Nutrition: Take a personal antioxidant formula every day.

Weight Training:
Three meals a day of hamburger, fries and chocolate mousse.

Antioxidants Required For Power Training

Antioxidant Nutrient (Always take antioxidants with food)	Daily Amount	
	Up to 70 kg (154 lbs) bodyweight	Over 70 kg (154 lbs) bodyweight
Vitamin E (IU)* D-alpha-tocopheryl succinate**	800	1200
Vitamin C (gm) Ascorbic acid, mixed mineral ascorbates, ascorbyl palmitate	2.0	5.0
Beta-carotene (IU)*	15,000	30,000
Coenzyme Q10 (mg)	15	30
L-glutathione (mg)	100	150
N-acetyl cysteine (mg)***	100	175
Selenium (mcg) L-selenomethionne	200	300
Iron (mg) Iron picolinate	10	14
Zinc (mg) Zinc picolinate	15	25
Copper (mg) Copper gluconate	0.5	1.25
Manganese (mg) Manganese gluconate	2.0	4.0
Alpha-lipoic acid (mg)	100	200
Lycopene (mg)	50	100
Lutein (mg)	6	9
Rutin, hesperidin, naringin (mg) mixed citrus flavonoids	200	300
Procyanidins (mg) grape seed extract, standardized to 95%	150	200
Catechins (mg) green tea extracts standardized to 20%	20	40
Ginkgo Flavonoids (mg) ginkgo biloba extract standardized to 24%	8	12
Silymarin, taxifolin (mg) milk thistle extract standardized to 80%	50	100
Genestein, diadzein (mg) soybean extract standardized to 10%	10	20
Anthocyanins (mg) bilberry extract standardized to 25%	10	15
Melatonin (mg) **	1.0	1.75

*IU: Internatinoal Units are obsolete measures no longer used in nutrition science. But, because they continue to appear on most supplement labels, they are used here for your convenience.
**Preferred forms of nutrients used by the Colgan Institute are given, because different forms of the same nutrient have widely different absorption rates and degrees of efficacy. The figures cannot be applied to other forms.
***N-Acetyl cysteine should be used only in conjunction with at least three times its amount of vitamin C. Otherwise n-acetyl cysteine can precipitate as cysteine in the kidneys and possibly cause kidney stones in sensitive individuals.
** Melatonin should be taken at night immediately before bed.

Essential Fats

Athletes hate fat. But there are two essential fats your body cannot make, the omega-6 fat **linoleic acid** and the omega-3 fat **alpha-linolenic acid**. They must be obtained from your diet.

These fats are essential because they form parts of the structure of your brain, eyes, ears, testes, adrenals, the membranes that line your joints, and the membranes that surround and protect every cell in your body. Whenever the dietary supply is inadequate, body function declines.[15] In addition essential fats boost oxygen use,[16] reduce, yes *reduce* bodyfat[15] and improve insulin metabolism.[17]

Most folks are unaware that government recommendations for these two essential fats are higher than for any vitamin or mineral.[18] For athletes we use even more because of considerable research evidence of deficiency, especially of the omega-3 fat alpha-linolenic acid.[2] For detailed information read my book **Essential Fats**.[15] We recommend 20 – 40 grams per day of organic flax oil which provides a 4:1 ratio of alpha-linolenic acid to linoleic acid.

Eighth Principle of Power Nutrition: Take essential fats every day.

Masters bodybuilding champion, lecturer and outstanding supplement designer, Cory Holly, studied nutrition with Dr Colgan. Cory knows the value of daily essential fats.

Carbohydrates

As I document in **Colgan: Sports Nutrition**,[2] the best carbohydrate foods are those which do not spike insulin, do not cause gut acidity, and also provide undamaged vitamins, minerals, essential fats and accessory nutrients such as polyphenols. They should be **low-acid**, and **minimally processed**, or not processed at all, and **low-glycemic**.

Low-glycemic means that they are slowly absorbed from the gut and do not spike your insulin. For optimum growth, you should do all you can to keep your insulin steady all day long.[1] A brief table of low-glycemic foods follows, together with common high-glycemic foods that you should leave for the lulus.

Numerous foods widely touted as healthy fall into the "leave for the lulus" category. Orange juice, for example, is great for creating gut acidity. Rice cakes, so beloved of dumb dieters, have such a high glycemic index, they are equivalent to eating spoonfuls of sugar straight from the bowl. Carbo loading with the three P's, pizza, pasta and pudding, produces bodies that look and perform like Jabba the Hutt.

One time you *can* use high glycemic carbs beneficially is immediately after an intense workout which has depleted muscle glycogen. You have a window of about 60 minutes after the workout, during which carbs in the gut which quickly appear in the blood as glucose, are immediately snatched up and stored as glycogen by the depleted muscles, and do not spike insulin. We use 100 – 200 grams of high glycemic carbs (fruit juice) along with 30 – 60 grams of protein and 20 – 40 grams flax oil as a drink right after workout. It works both to reduce muscle catabolism and to restore muscle glycogen.[1]

> **Ninth Principle of Power Nutrition: Eat low-glycemic, low-acid carbohydrates every day.**

Glycemic Index

These are some of the foods that have been measure for their glycemic index. For power nutrition, we recommend foods with a glycemic index of 70 or less.

BREADS & PASTA *(cont.)*		**LEGUMES** *(cont.)*			
Bran	31	Oat, coarse	93	Lentils, green, dried	33
Oatmeal, long cooking	49	Rye, crisp bread	95	Lima beans	36
All bran	74	Crackers, plain	100	Navy beans	40
Brown rice	81	Wheat, whole meal bread	100	Kidney beans, dried	43
White rice, boiled 10-25 mins	81	Wheat, white bread	100	Butter beans	46
Oat bran	85	Wheat, French baguette	131	Chickpeas, dried	47
Instant oatmeal	85	Spaghetti, brown, boiled 15 min	61	Green peas, dried	50
Muesli	96	Spaghetti, white, boiled 15 min	67	Peas, frozen	51
Shredded wheat (Nabisco)	97	**DAIRY PRODUCTS**		White beans, Haricot, dried	54
Chinese glutenous rice	98	Yogurt, non fat	32	Pinto beans, dried	60
Weetabix	109	Skim milk	39	Garbanzo beans	61
Rice Krispies (Kellogg's)	121	Whole milk	41	Green peas, frozen	65
Corn Flakes (Kellogg's)	112	Yogurt	44	Baked beans, canned	70
Puffed wheat	122	Custard	59	**ROOT VEGETABLES**	
Puffed rice	132	**FRUIT**		Sweet potato	59
GRAINS		Cherry	23	Yam	62
Barley, pearled	36	Plum	25	Beet	64
Wheat kernels, steamed	41	Grapefruit	26	Potato, white (new), boiled	80
Rye kernels	47	Peach	29	Carrot	92
Wheat kernels	63	Pear	34	Potato, mashed	98
Bulgar	65	Grape	45	Potato, russet, baked	116
Couscous	66	Apple	49	Potato, peeled, sliced, microwaved	117
Wheat kernels, quick cooking	75	Orange	54	Potato, instant	120
Buckwheat	78	Banana, green	56	**DESSERTS**	
Sweet corn	80	Mango, ripe	81	Sponge cake	46
Millet	103	Papaya, ripe	81	Custard	59
BREADS & PASTA		Banana, ripe	90	Oatmeal cookies	78
Rye, whole grain	42	Raisin	93	Ice cream	80
Barley, coarse, scalded kernels	48	Apricot	94	Digestive biscuits	82
Barley, coarse	57	**LEGUMES**		Shortbread	88
Rye, pumpernickel	68	Peanuts	15	Tofu ice-cream substitute	155
Rye, whole meal	89	Soybeans, dried	20		
Barley, whole meal	93	Black-eyed peas	33		

Ergogenics and Protectors

There are many other beneficial foods and chemicals for athletic performance that I have no space to describe here. I cover them in **Colgan: Sports Nutrition**.[2] I will mention a few of the best however, that form a regular part of our nutritional advice to athletes.

PHOTO, ZACH TAYLOR

Super fit and gorgeous Cheri Lynn Ruddiman is a top trainer who learned the Power Program with Dr Colgan.

Creatine Monohydrate

Creatine phosphate is the chemical in your muscles which regenerates your primary energy molecule **adenosine triphosphate (ATP)**. In 1992 Paul Greenhaff of the University of Nottingham in England and Roger Harris of the Karolinska Institute in Stockholm, Sweden showed that a 5-gram oral dose of **creatine monohydrate** taken 4 – 6 times per day increases muscle levels of creatine phosphate,[19] which likely boosts ATP regeneration.

Increased regeneration of ATP allows an extension of anaerobic effort. In a series of studies in the mid '90s, supplements of creatine of 20 – 25 grams per day for only one week, were shown to increase maximum power output by a massive 5 – 6% in elite athletes.[20,21] Creatine quickly became one of the most popular and effective ergogenic aids in sports.

There are a few secrets to its correct use, however, all of which are detailed in my books, **Creatine for Muscle and Strength**[22] and **Colgan: Sports Nutrition**.[2] Here are the basics. The amounts of creatine required are related to lean bodyweight. After a few days of creatine loading, the muscles become saturated and you need only a maintenance dose. A male of 160 lbs lean bodyweight for example, requires 18 grams of creatine per day for 6 days to load, then 6 grams of creatine per day to maintain muscle levels for the rest of an eight-week cycle. A table follows from which you can work out your personal creatine program.

The only form of creatine shown to be effective in controlled studies is creatine monohydrate. Other forms of creatine, such as creatine citrate, might work but, despite all the marketing hype, there is ***no evidence*** that they do.

Creatine should be taken in divided doses of not more than five grams. Creatine should be taken with sugar to facilitate muscle uptake. We use a 50/50 mixture of grapefruit juice and grape juice or mix the creatine into a sweetened protein shake. You should cycle creatine eight weeks on, four weeks off.

For non-responders and to enhance creatine effects, boost insulin efficiency with daily supplements of 400 micrograms of chromium picolinate, 600 milligrams of eicosapentaenoic acid and 25 milligrams of dehydroepiandrosterone (DHEA).[22,2]

A note of caution. DHEA is an intermediate steroid in the steroid cascade from cholesterol to testosterone. As such it is banned by many sports authorities as a steroid drug that unfairly aids athletic performance. Our measurements, and those of other researchers, however, show that some athletes have very low levels of DHEA. It is clear to us (and should be to any sports official who takes off the blinders) that in order to truly level the playing field, these athletes should have their DHEA raised into the normal range. For athletes with normal DHEA levels, creatine usually works a treat.[22]

Creatine Loading and Maintenance

Lean Bodyweight		Males		Females	
		Loading gms	Maintenance gms	Loading gms	Maintenance gms
(lbs)	(kg)				
80	36	9	3	6	2
100	45	11	3.5	8	2.5
120	55	14	4.5	10	3
140	64	16	5	11.5	3.5
160	73	18	6	13	4
180	82	20	6.5	14.5	4.5
200	91	22.5	7	16	5
220	100	25	8	17.5	6

Acetyl-l-Carnitine

L-carnitine is well known as a fat transporter in the human body,[1] but its acetylated form **acetyl-l-carnitine (ALC)** has multiple other roles that can benefit athletes. We first became interested in this substance in the late '80s, when researchers showed that intense weight training causes the body to increase its conversion of l-carnitine into ALC, and that oral supplementation with l-carntine increased this conversion further.[23]

We have gradually discovered some of the reasons for this increase of ALC with intense effort. First, ALC stimulates testosterone production to support muscular growth.[24] It does so by increasing activity of the get-up-and-go neurotransmitter **dopamine** in the brain which has multiple other stimulatory effects on performance.[25] It also increases activity of the get-up-and-go neurotransmitter **acetylcholine.**[24]

Second, ALC reduces the exercise-induced rise in the catabolic hormone **cortisol.**[26] Third, ALC increases reaction speed and focus of attention under stress.[27] We figure that the increase in bodily ALC caused by neuromuscular stress, is part of the evolutionary fight/flight response that enabled humans to survive in the first place.

The discovery that oral supplements of ALC will boost the natural increase in ALC with stress is a boon to athletes of all stripes. We use 1000 – 2000 mg in the early morning and 1000 – 2000 mg at noon. Don't use ALC after 3 pm as it may disrupt sleep.

Phosphatidylserine

The stress of intense exercise raises body levels of **cortisol**, a catabolic hormone formed in the adrenal glands. The increased cortisol breaks down muscle to provide the amino acid **glutamine** to maintain immunity, and to provide the liver with amino acids to convert into glucose for energy. As cortisol continues to rise, however, it eventually suppresses both energy and immunity.[2]

Exercise also releases anabolic hormones, notably testosterone, which build muscle. The trick for an effective Power Program is to maximize the anabolic effects of exercise and minimize the catabolic.

That's one big reason I've advised you not to hit the weights for more than an hour at a time. About 60 minutes into a hard workout, testosterone levels start to drop in a lot of folk we measure, and cortisol starts to become dominant. Guys who spend a couple of hard hours in the weight room every day can **lose** strength.[1] Even a one-hour weight workout (plus stretching and warm-up) is pushing it for a lot of folk. Their cortisol levels go over the moon.

Without the hassle of blood tests, some fair indicators of time to quit that you can use on yourself are, headache, dizziness, weakness and goose bumps. And whenever you see athletes gulping high carb drinks or bars during workouts, it's a good bet they're heading for catabolism.

One supplement that may tip the scales a bit in your favour is a phospholipid which forms part of your cell membranes called **phosphatidylserine**. That's not the related phospholipids, lecithin, choline or phosphatidylcholine. They, and all the weird pseudo-scientific concoctions in muscle ads, don't work a damn, despite what the snake oil merchants may claim.

Recent studies with healthy men show that phosphatidylserine can substantially reduce the exercise-induced rise in cortisol, and hopefully reduce it's catabolic effects and enhance recovery.[28] It also seems to work with experienced athletes. In a recent study Thomas Fahey gave weight-trained athletes 800 mg of phosphatidylserine or a placebo, then seriously overtrained them. They did 65 sets per workout for four days a week, all at maximum intensity. Remember, the Power Program advocates 24 sets per workout as a maximum.

So as not to kill the subjects, the study ran for only two weeks at a time. Results showed they had less muscle soreness, recovered quicker and had better energy while on the phosphatidylserine. Even though the study was double-blind, all subjects correctly identified the two-week period they were on the supplement.[29] We use 400 – 800 mg of phosphatidylserine per day, with apparently good results.

Protection Against Hormones

Except during periods of extreme training, both male and female athletes tend to have higher testosterone and estrogen levels than their sedentory peers. They are also stronger, faster, more aggressive and more resistant to pain. These differences occur partly because sports tend to attract the genetically physically exceptional, and partly because the *right* diet, supplementation and training also increase testosterone levels and their effects on the body.

A large proportion of athletes also use anabolic steroids, and other drugs, plus over-the-counter, indirect testosterone boosters, such as tribulus and yohimbe. Many of them become walking hormone disasters.

The downside to testosterone is not only the damaging effects of high levels of the hormone itself, but also its conversion into dihydrotestosterone and estrogen. Dihydrotestosterone is best known for damaging the prostate, and excess estrogen is linked to female diseases of the breasts and male and female diseases of the reproductive system, including cancer. Consequently, after assessing their hormonal status, we frequently advise athletes to protect themselves from long-term effects of their natural, or induced, high testosterone and estrogen levels.

As documented in my book **Protect Your Prostate**, considerable protection is afforded by the antioxidant nutrients vitamins C and E and the minerals selenium and zinc[30] included in the antioxidant supplement earlier in this chapter. To directly inhibit the conversion of testosterone, we also advise supplementation with a daily herbal mixture of 300 mg saw palmetto, 200 mg pygeum and 500 mg urtica. Further protection is provided by 1000 mg *aged* garlic. Only aged garlic works.

Regular use of tofu, miso, natto and other traditional Japanese foods from soy also help to prevent hormone-based diseases. The isoflavones, **genestein** and **diadzien** that they contain, inhibit growth of aberrant cells in the male prostate and female reproductive system.[30,31] And regular use of green vegetables of the cabbage family provides **indole-3-carbinol** which helps to direct estrogen along benign pathways in the body.[9]

Junior skating champion Karen Clark. You are never too young to start on the Power Program.

Joint Protection

Athletes tend to wear out their joints, especially shoulders, hips, lower back and knees. It's no mystery why. Most joint problems, and the arthritic diseases they promote, occur from simple wear and tear. It starts when the rate at which exercise damages and wears away the structure of the joint, exceeds the rate at which the body can make the complex structural chemicals required to regrow it.

As documented in my book **Beat Arthritis**, one way to offset these problems is to provide your body with structural components of joints ready-made.[6] Two important chemicals are **glucosamine** and **chondroitin**. We have used them with athletes with good success for the last 12 years. A meta-analysis of all the controlled studies of their use in joint problems has just been published in the **Journal of American Medical Association**, concluding that they really do work.[32]

A third substance that is joint protective is **S-adenosylmethionine (SAMe)**. I have documented the evidence in its favor elsewhere.[6] We use these three substances in combination as essential daily joint protection: glucosamine sulfate 1.0 grams, chondroitin 1.0 grams, SAMe 200 mg. Joint problems are way easier to prevent than to cure.

Power Nutrition: Summary

There's a ton of other supplements: conjugated linoleic acid, zinc/magnesium aspartate. ECA stack for weight loss, OKG, KIC, HMB, ribose, glycerol and on and on. But you will have to read **Colgan: Sports Nutrition** to get the lowdown on them. Together they might be worth 1 – 2% if used correctly. But first you have to do the basics shown below.

First Principle of Power Nutrition: Design your diet so that you receive a complete mix of the ancient chemicals from which the human body evolved.

Second Principle of Power Nutrition: Design your diet and lifestyle so that you avoid, expel or neutralize chemicals made by man.

Third Principle of Power Nutrition: Take a complete multiple vitamin/mineral supplement every day.

Fourth Principle of Power Nutrition: Once you start a nutrient program stick to it. You will not achieve significant, lasting results for at least six months.

Fifth Principle of Power Nutrition: Take sufficient first-class protein every day.

Sixth Principle of Power Nutrition: Don't Spike Your Insulin.

Seventh Principle of Power Nutrition: Take a personal antioxidant formula every day.

Eighth Principle of Power Nutrition: Take essential fats every day.

Ninth Principle of Power Nutrition: Eat low glycemic, low acid carbohydrates every day.

Power Nutrition   *A Typical Daily Program*

6.00am	•	*Cardiovascular Training:*	On empty stomach. Water only.
8.00am	•	*Morning Shake:*	8 oz soy milk 1 tablespoon organic flax oil 3 grams creatine monohydrate Fresh Fruit to taste 30 grams ion-exchange whey concentrate

Take with shake:

Muliti-vitamin/mineral/antioxidant AM pak	500 mg aged garlic
200 mg SAMe	1000 mg acetyl-l-carnitine
Saw palmetto/pygeum/urtica	200 mg phosphatidylserine

10.00am	•	*Breakfast:*	Bowl uncut oatmeal Egg white omelet with cooked tomatoes Green tea
10.30 am	•	*Weight training*	
Noon	•	*Lunch:*	Mixed salad greens and root vegetable salad 4oz tofu, fish or skinless chicken or turkey breast Tea or coffee
1.00pm	•	*Nap 30 – 60 minutes*	
2.00pm	•	*Skill Training*	
3.00pm	•	*Afternoon Shake:*	8oz soy milk 30 grams ion exchange whey concentrate 1 tablespoon organic flax oil Fresh fruit to taste

Take with shake:

1000mg acetyl-l-carnitine	200mg phosphatidylserine
500mg aged garlic	

4.00pm	•	*Skill Training*	
6.00pm	•	*Dinner:*	Tofu miso sashimi or fish fillet Salad and cooked vegetables Fresh fruit Green tea

Take with dinner:

Multi-vitamin/mineral/antioxidant PM pak	Saw palmetto/pygeum urtica

8.00pm	•	*Snack or small protein shake or 1 glass white wine*	

Take with Snack:

	1mg melatonin

9.00pm	•	Bed	

Power Principle 27: Power Nutrition Every Day.

"You're taking those muscle pills again!"

Program Your Mind

Despite lifelong training, the physical power of the strongest man remains puny, compared with that of an ape. And any human is outrun with ease by a deer, overcome in seconds by a bear. Yet we have wrested control of the Earth from these and all other creatures. We have done so by learning to use the limitless power of the human mind.

Your final and most important goal in the Power Program is to program your mind to focus the physical power you have gained so that it is greatly magnified. Your body will always be constrained by the design of its structure. You will never leap tall buildings ina single bound. But the leap of your mind is unlimited. Given the right training, it can enable the body to accomplish feats you now believe impossible.

One of the greatest living martial artists, Mas Oyama, is legendary for his mental training. A documentary film shows him felling a charging bull with two successive blows to the head. There are men a-plenty as strong or stronger than Oyama. But very few who can command their minds to focus sufficient power into split-second movement that can stop a charging bull.

Gymnastics coach Bela Karoli is also a master of movement, one of the rare souls who can teach the balance, coordination and skills that allow his students to fly with the grace of angels. But technical mastery is only part of his curriculum. During the 1996 Olympics, I watched an injured Kerri Strug, the torn ligament in her left ankle heavily bound, explode down the runway and fly in a perfect Kurchenko vault to bring home the gold, then collapse on the mat to the roar of a standing ovation. The secrets of Karoli's genius lie in his training of the mind.

Kerri Strug, whose mental focus enabled her to perform perfectly at the 1996 Olympics with a torn ligament in her left ankle, leaves the medal ceremony triumphant wiht her gold medal, carried by her mentor Bela Karoli.

Sun Tzu wrote **The Art of War** about 500 BC. Yet this ancient book is one of the texts used in Japanese business today, and is a major aid to their commercial success. Sun Tsu stresses how the power of the mind is far superior to the power of weapons, or the numbers of soldiers, no matter how strong and well trained they are. He portrays a skilled general thus:

> His primary target is the mind of the o p p o s i n g commander: the victory a product of creative thought.[1,2]

If you would excel in sport, pin this advice on your bedroom wall, where you can learn from it every day. You may train your body to enormous power, but it is your mind which determines how well you can focus, direct and control it.

Seek A Mentor

This or any other book can give you only a few guidelines towards programming your mind. To help you follow the tortuous path you need a mentor to teach you personally.

You entered this world with your body naked, your mind a blank slate. Your most private beliefs, even belief in a Creator, were taught to you by someone else. And often it is only the belief which remains long after the source is forgotten.

Had you been born into a different culture, you would hold different beliefs, worship different gods. Yet, just as you feel certain about your own beliefs now, they would be as natural to you as breathing. And you would be hard put to define their sources.

So take great care to whom you give your mind. Don't sell it cheap for money or material possessions. And don't be seduced by university degrees, or professional memberships with gift certificates, or worse, those one-week whiz-bang courses with sets of shiny videos.

Ditch entirely the dross of newspapers, TV and the internet. These forms of virtual

Michael Colgan with his mentor New Zealand master coach Arthur Lydiard, at the Colgan Institute in San Diego in 1983.

reality are mostly unexamined speculation aimed at gaining market share. If, as millions do, you use them for your learning, then you train your mind to witlessness, all dust and bric-a-brac, with everything priced above its value.

I know plenty of talented but unsuccessful athletes. Every few months they get wildly enthusiastic about a different training program or new methodology or spiritual awakening. As Aikido master George Leonard says, "They love honeymoons but will never make a marriage." Don't be one of them. Seek out a flesh-and-blood mentor to teach you, one who is the embodiment of everything he or she espouses.

Avoid Conflicting Counsel

Once you have chosen a mentor who has agreed to teach you, reject any information that conflicts with the teaching. Avoid all other counsel, because clear and constant focus is the only basis from which you can learn to move in your sport without hesitation or doubt. Even the tiniest conflect inhibits your mind. To move with the certainty of a champion, you have to develop 100% confidence in what you have been taught.

A great example of the influence of conflicting counsel is the four-minute mile. In the early 1950s, numerous sports experts avowed publicly that a sub four-minute mile was impossible because of cardiovascular limits on human physiology. All the best milers heard many times and were influenced to think the barrier unbreakable.

Roger Bannister broke the four-minute mile in 1954. He used his medical training to reject the widely held but false belief that sub-four minutes was beyond the limits of human physiology.

Then, in 1954, Englishman Roger Bannister, a great miler but not world champion, applied his newly completed medical training to ridicule the limit. As Bannister explained, four minutes exactly is a completely arbitrary figure, part of what EE Cummings calls "man's hoax of clocks and calendars." Unlike gravity, it cannot possibly form a constant in the evolution of human physiology. Bannister programmed his mind to run specific times for each lap, and executed the plan perfectly in a demonstration race of 3:59.4.

Within months, a whole rash of runners began to break four minutes. The mental barrier created by conflicting counsel had been broken. Bannister wrote:

> Though physiology may indicate respiratory and cardiovascular limits to muscular effort, psychological factors set the razor's edge of victory and determine how closely the athlete approaches the absolute limit of performance.[3]

Subjugate Your Ego

One of my favorite poets and general curmudgeon, EE Cummings, said, "I never met a peripherally situated ego yet." We are all egocentric: it's part of the human condition. But if you want mastery of your sport, you will subjugate your ego to the master you have chosen, and accept his teaching completely.

It's an old saying: When you hire a master to paint you a masterpiece, don't allow amateurs to look over his shoulder and suggest improvements. You and your peers and all around you are the amateurs. Otherwise you would not need a master.

Even the masters know well that they remain amateurs in numerous ways that need a superior touch. Master classsical guitarist André Segovia took regular lessons and practiced four hours a day up till his death at age 84. Supreme sculptor, Henry Moore, took life drawing classes with a master every year to improve his "hand and eye and sense of scale."

It is the same in sport. Coach to more Olympic medalists than you have fingers and toes, and my mentor also, Arthur Lydiard in New Zealand is part running genius, mostly great spirit. American master Bill Bowerman, considered by many the greatest running coach ever acknowledged Lydiard's mastery, took his best athletes from the University of Oregon all the way to New Zealand to learn.

The advantage of learning from rare souls such as Lydiard, lies but lightly in the techniques they teach. Most of the growth is in what they give to your mind.

Master trainer Bill Bowerman (front) took his best athletes to New Zealand to run and learn with Arthur Lydiard and his runners.

Empty Your Mind

You cannot learn from a master until you reject past learning that conflicts with his teaching. Already, your mind may be clogged with fears and doubts and downright lies, sown by false instruction in your childhood. The interactions of these beliefs form emotion-bound habits that are hard to change. To re-program your mind you have to wipe the slate and start anew.

Samurai Miyamoto Musashi was never defeated in his lifetime. His mental mastery, portrayed in The Book of Five Rings shows you why.

Miyamoto Musashi's **The Book of Five Rings**, tells the old story of a self-important professor who came to learn about Zen from Zen master Nan-in. After listening patiently for some time, Nan-in served his guest tea. He continued to pour, though the cup overflowed. To the professor's protest he replied,

> Like this cup, your mind is full of opinions and speculations. How can I show you Zen unless you first empty your cup?[4]

Nothing that you see or hear when you look out of your eyes or listen with your ears exists out there. Everything you perceive is a construction of your mind made up of three components: your past learning, your physical mechanisms, and the stimulation of your senses.

Your past learning determines much of what you can perceive. Though my visual acuity is normal, my friend, naturalist Jonathan Grant sees a bear in the woods immediately, when I see nothing but trees. I'm looking for the regular boundaries and sharp contrasts, the crutches my brain has learned from the confines of our urban environment. I can see past them only with great difficulty. But Jonathan has learned a sharper, more advanced way of seeing. Until you free your mind of bad learning from the past, you will have similar difficulties. The jailkeeper is always ignorance. One potent aid to emptying the mind is meditation.

Meditate

You cannot speak of the immensity of the ocean to a frog that lives in a well. This wisdom is traced back at least to Chuang Tsu, Taoist master in 250 BC.[5] It refers to the difficulty of explaining the vast dimensions and power of the mind, except to those who have already experienced them. To attempt to introduce you in a page or two is so arrogant, I almost left it out of the book. Words cannot explain even as simple a thing as the taste of salt unless you have experienced it upon your tongue. But meditation is so important to athletic power I have to give it a shot.

We live in a world dedicated to distraction. We are trained from childhood to frantic external activity, to "busyness" which has become "business". We look outside ourselves so much, we rarely learn to look inside, that is, to meditate. Many folk fear it greatly. Some consider it the road to madness.

Remember, everything that keeps your mind distracted you learned from others, esspecially the triggers for negative emotional reactions of fear, anger, greed, jealousy, deception, hate and guilt. Achieving meditation, that is emptying your mind, is a very different form of learning. Western Society makes it especially difficult, because we overvalue what we call "intellect", which is usually defined in terms of crude measures of the ability to master the mechanics of school work or professional qualifications. Consequently, Western books and courses on meditation tend to separate it from life, as some mechanical habit you can learn that will benefit your welfare, like daily flossing your teeth.

You know the way it goes, "I've showered, pooped, flossed and meditated, now I'm ready for the day! We tend to focus on what Tibetan Buddhist master Sogyal Rimpoche calls, "the technology of meditation".[6] This effortful, mechanical approach is so far from the truth I don't know where to begin to refute it. So I will just state some simple principles that various Eastern masters advise as aids to meditation. [6-8]

First, you cannot "try" to meditate. Nor can you go to a course and learn meditation like you learn math or English. You can learn only to set up some conditions under which meditation may occur. Given the right conditions, and a good dollop of luck, meditation is something that happens to you. Nevertheless, those new to the practice can benefit from five "props", regular time, calm environment, posture, breathing and mantra.

Regular Time You need to reserve at least 20 minutes for meditation at the same time each day. Regularity helps the nervous system to learn change. You don't have to spend the whole time meditating. Allow your mind to return to everyday matters as it wants to. Meditative periods of three or four minutes are are sufficient. These alternating periods of meditation and daily thought help achieve your goal of integrating the practice into every living hour of your life.

Environment Medititate in a peaceful place, preferably outside in a natural setting, The stimuli of earth and water and plant life are the conditions under which the human body evolved and to which it responds best.

Practising meditation while floating in a parachute is a useful exercise we use to help empty the mind.

Posture The most used posture is sitting erect, cross-legged, "like a mountain", with hands on knees. Initially closed eyes may help. But gradually you should open them and look straight ahead, but at nothing in particular. Meditation is not a way of escaping the world or your senses into some type of trance. It is a way of sharpening your perception to the extent that your mind can begin to observe itself.

Breathing As recommended for daily stretching practice in Chapter 4, breathing should be soft and from the belly, with a light focus on exhalation and "letting go". Your goal is to "become one with the breath".

Mantra The mantra, said quietly, or simply thought, in rhythm with exhaling, can be as short as the sound "OM" or as long as a Christian prayer. The goal is to achieve a rhythm which resonate through the mind. It is a means of blocking distracting thoughts.

After a few months regular practice meditation, you will find less and less need for the props. In time you will be able to meditate in any situation without them. Achieving this calm state is an essential prelude to the advanced mental programming discussed ahead: power without effort and movement without thought.

Carry Your Sport With You

The next step towards programming your mind is to fill every day with what the master has given you to do. Your body and mind grow and function in accord with your habitual activities. You may not think so, but some 90% of your behaviour is habit and ritual. Only 10% is unprogrammed decision. You may dream otherwise, but you cannot grow beyond what you habitually do. You become your habits.

To grow in your sport, you have to make the new learning into automatic habit. To do so efficiently you must incorporate it into all your everyday activities. Carry what you are given to learn with you, to work and play, to boardroom, bathroom and bedroom. Build it into every working hour of your life.

Correcting a chronically tight muscle provides a simple example of the need for constant practice in order to effect change. As that wisest of physicians, Janet Travell, advises in her renowned books on muscle function,[9] if you stretch the muscle for only 10 minutes a day, then allow it to tighten again for the other 23 hours and 50 minutes it will always return to its habitual tightness.

Following this principle, I get gymnasts to practice one-leg balances while in the shower, while cleaning their teeth, while waiting for a bus. I get boxers to dodge and feint before the mirror while shaving, to practice tightening their core while driving. I get all athletes to practice the power posture all day long. That way they gradually become it.

Champion shooter T'ai Erasmus walks his talk. He knows the importance of carrying your sport with you.

Persist

We all experience the lingering fear that we don't have what it takes. Keep going anyhow, because persistence is worth far more than talent. I see hundreds of kids with athletic talent. Most of them flash briefly at school or college, then fade into obscurity. Their parents and teachers failed to realize that a vital ingredient of athletic success, is training the mind to persist.

Eminent sculptor, Auguste Rodin, failed three times before gaining entry to art school. Henry Ford went broke five times before succeeding with the Model T. And Winston Churchill was an unsuccessful politician all his life, until he became the greatest ever Prime Minister of England at age 62. If you would succeed as an athlete, then you must persist.

We all know the term "choke." It refers to the fear of failure that disrupts athletic performance which otherwise would be magnificent. Choking is an example of momentary failure to persist.Considered the greatest basketball player ever, Michael Jordan says:

Edson Sower, World Masters Triathlon Champion at age 82, and a long-time client of the Colgan Institute, is a fine example of persistence.

I can see how some people get frozen by that fear of failure … I think fear sometimes comes from a lack of focus or concentration. If I stood on the free-throw line and thought about 10 million people watching me on the other side of the camera lens I couldn't have made anything.[10]

Remember, fear does not exist in any object or situation. It is a construction of your mind, usually created from emotional remnants of past weakness or failure, or beliefs that you have learned from others. Whenever you become afraid, you have frightened yourself. Once you realize that you alone create every instance of your fear, you can begin to eliminate it.

Train For Toughness

It's the 1992 Winter Olympics at Albertville, France. World record holder in 1000 meter speedskating, Dan Jansen is the favorite for a gold. In the final he falls near the finish and fails to win anything. Then terrible personal tragedy hits his life with the death of his sister.

To overcome the stress he went to sports psychologist Jim Loehr in Orlando, Florida. Result: Dan won the 1000 meter Olympic speedskating title in Lillehammer in 1994, in world record time.

I applaud Loehr's approach because he understands the links between mental and physical power. He starts by getting clients to strengthen their core.

> If you want to develop a tremendous capacity for absorbing stress, strengthen your midsection. Your midsection determines your posture and breathing, and supports your lower back one of the core places where warriors store stress.[11]

A second Loehr strategy is to use every free moment to put yourself into the best emotional state possible. The better your emotional state, the more stress you can take. One way is to recreate past triumphs in your mind in every detail. Your body responds with real shifts in biochemistry towards that state.

Olympic speedskater Dan Jansen overcame terrible defeats in his sport and stresses in his personal life. He developed the mental toughness to win Olympic gold with a new world record at Lillehammer in 1994.

Next you should integrate training for mental toughness into everything you do. You don't have to sit under freezing waterfalls and meditate on zen koans. Simply facing the challenges of our devious corporate world today is far more taxing. Practice never turning your back on business or social stress, but responding with your own challenge, immediately and forcefully, but without anger. Loehr's latest book **Toughness Training For Life** tells you how to do it.[12]

Running champion Steve Prefontaine is a perfect example. He honed his toughness by challenging everything he didn't like. Like David facing Goliath, he took on the deceit of the governing bodies of sports at the time, and was instrumental in ending the farce of amateurism. Though "Pre" died in a car crash in the midst of his great career, his indomitable spirit lives on to fire the minds of thousands of athletes worldwide.

Eminent Oregon runner Steve Prefontaine, with coach Bill Bowerman, was killed in a car accident at the height of his career. "Pre's" indomitable spirit continues to fire the minds of athletes worldwide.

While teaching a sports nutrition course at the University of Oregon, I was out running one morning in bitter rain, reluctantly slopping along, whining to myself. Suddenly, I was passed by Pre and his mates laughing and chatting, all going like a train. They nodded indulgently to the old plodder. Sure gave me the kick in the ass I needed.

I learned later that Pre relished running in rain, snow, mud, whatever, because it toughened him to run ferociously when the weather was fine. He sums up his attitude to sports in words that form a touchstone for many an athlete seeking mastery:

I run to see who has the most guts.[13]

Move Without Thought

If you practice the principles of your master, the power program, the movements of your sport, meditation and training for toughness throughout the day, gradually they become automatic sequences in your brain. They become almost as automatic as breathing. Eventually they take over, and you become them.

When this mental programming occurs, you can perform without conscious effort or conscious thought. Your body acts by itself. This is the Zen state of **mushin** (no mind).[4]

When you achieve mushin, no thoughts or emotions intervene to disrupt or slow your actions. Movements flow and change as water, filling the space and time left empty by objects or opponents.

Masters, such as the samurai Musashi, who was never defeated in his lifetime, continued their learning of mushin until they became able to act directly in **kū** (emptiness).[4] To Western brains, kū is difficult to grasp. The nearest I can get to it in a sentence or two sounds like mush, but here goes.

Kū is being at one with the universe. When you know kū, you experience your body and mind not as separate from the world, but as science has shown them to be, an indivisible part of the mass of solids, liquids, gases and vibrations that swirl around us and through us every living day. If you become one of those who gain mastery of kū, you act effortlessly in concert

Hockey great Wayne Gretsky is a living example of a master who understands kū. Asked by reporters why he could beat everyone with such apparent ease he replied,

Most players chase the puck:

I go where the puck is going to be.

with all of these things. You are then undefeatable by anyone who has not reached this level of development.

Hockey great Wayne Gretsky is a fine example of a master who understands kū. Asked by reporters why he could beat everyone with such apparent ease, he replied, "Most players chase the puck, I go where the puck is going to be."

Watch the videos of Gretsky's games. Slow the motion at his shots. You will see numerous instances in which he skates to an empty point on the ice, and has already begun to swing his stick for the shot, while the puck is still distant in a meleé of other players.

If you think such mastery is forever beyond you, remember that Gretsky was born naked and witless, just like you and me. As Musashi says in every chapter of **The Book of Five Rings**,

It is a matter of learning the right principles.[4]

Power Principle 28: Program Your Mind.

29

The Whole Tamalé

It seems that we've climbed a mountain of evidence, but it covers only the basics of weight training for power. Nevertheless, with the 28 principles of the Power Program, the four periodization cycles and the right exercises, you can build a body that works well in any sports situation. With minimum maintenance it will continue to work well for the rest of your life. You have to invest a bit of puff to build a powerful body, but the lifetime return beats the hell out of anything you can make on the stock market.

This chapter gives you the whole program in summary from the Power Principles through to a sample workout for each of the training cycles.

Before I lay it all out, here are a few tips that will improve all your weight training.

1. For every rep, pull up and in on your tranversus and pelvic floor. For heavy reps, also lock your tongue by pressing it against your palate just behind your top teeth.

2. Center yourself before beginning a set. Assume power posture, inhale, exhale, inhale again and begin.

3. To improve balance and co-ordination and your sense of where your body is in space, close your eyes while lifting. Eventually you will be able to do weight training blindfold while standing on a Swiss Ball.

4. Don't use gloves. They inhibit kinesthetic feedback from the hands that triggers firing of arm stabilizers.

5. Don't use straps to increase your grip. Hand strength is diffcult to get. Take every chance you can to use bare hands.

6. Don't use weight belts or wraps. They are crutches that reduce bodily development.

7. Always sip water during training. Even 3% dehydration can reduce your strength by 10% [1].

8. Record your progress. Don't rely on memory. Note down your weights and reps for every exercise. It's the only way to really see the growth. You can obtain a Power Program Gym Record from the Colgan Institute, at www.colganinstitute.com.

Mike Stevenson, an Ironman Triathlon competitor at age 56, is on the Power Program and going like a bomb!

POWER PRINCIPLES

1: Periodize.	**14: Use precision zone negatives in every power workout.**
2: Train with weights for strength, balance, flexibility, coordination, reaction speed and mental focus.	**15: Use superset pairs of opposing exercises for a total of 20 – 24 sets, taking not more than one hour in the gym.**
3: Adopt Power Posture. Bum in, belly in, anus in, head in, and lock your tongue.	**16: Train each bodypart only once per week.**
4: Stretch every day.	**17: Do 6 – 8 of the best exercises per workout.**
5: First train joints and connective tissues with the Extension-Connection Cycle.	**18: Build abs and back for a core as firm as a fence post.**
6: After extension and connection training, train stabilizers and prime movers with the Strength-Stabilization Cycle.	**19: Stabilize the shoulder throughout its full range of movement.**
7: After extension, connection, strength and stabilization training, train with the Power Cycle for power.	**20: Train biceps and triceps together in opposing supersets.**
	21: Train back strength from inside to outside.
8: Train for maximum strength per pound of muscle, not for mass.	**22: Train the chest with wide-range precision.**
	23: Use the Big Four to power your legs.
9: Strengthen whole muscle groups in concert. Train the chain.	**24: Use single-leg Eccentrics and lunges to train lower legs.**
10: Use free-movement exercises with free weights and cables. Avoid isolation machines.	**25: Use the Link Cycle to gain speed.**
11: Go low reps and heavy to failure, or go home.	**26: Use plyometric training to harness elastic strain energy.**
12: Train for fast-twitch fiber growth.	**27: Power Nutrition every day.**
13: Use slow eccentrics all the time	**28: Program your mind.**

Periodization

To summarize the **Power Program** periodization system, the tables from previous chapters are set out below. The first 25 weeks of the year are divided into 8 weeks of Extension-Connection training, 10 weeks of Strength-Stabilization training and 7 weeks of Power training. One week of tapering, using only light Extension-Connection work should then see you at a power peak for the start of your competitive season.

During the competitive season, you do 10 weeks of Link training to increase your speed and to teach your nervous system to harness the new power to your sport. Then you do 15 weeks of a maintenance cycle of four short weight workouts per week using Extension-Connection training. Then you get a week off! That makes 52 weeks. Then you do the whole periodization cycle again. Stick with it. This system builds supermen.

Queen of Fitness, Victoria Johnson shows the stunning results of Power Program training.

Training heavy all year long inevitably leads to overtraining, injury and long-term fatigue of the nervous system. To avoid this, periodize your weight training by dividing the year into cycles of different forms of weight work.

52-Week Power Periodization

25-Week Power Training	Extension-Connection Cycle	8 weeks
	Strength-Stabilization Cycle	10 weeks
	Power Cycle	7 weeks
Taper		1 week
Link Cycle		10 weeks
Maintenance Cycle		15 weeks
Off		1 week

8-Week Extension-Connection Cycle

Workouts Per Week		5
Exercises Per Workout		6 - 8
Sets Per Exercise	*Exercises done in opposing pairs as supersets, to make supercycles of 6 sets.*	3
Reps Per Set	Set 1	10 - 12
	Set 2	8 - 10
	Set 3	6 - 8
Weights	Set 1	60%1RM
	Set 2	70% 1RM
	Set 3	80% 1RM
Rest Periods	*30 - 60 seconds between supersets* *2 - 3 minutes between supercycles*	

The Extension-Connection Cycle focuses on multi-joint, full-extension exercises that train the muscles and connective tissues in the complete movements they are designed to make. During this 8-week cycle, you are training your connective tissues to become stronger and your muscles to increase their range of motion, so as to be able to take the strain of the muscle strength gained in the next cycle.

10-Week Strength-Stabilization Cycle

Workouts Per Week		5
Exercises Per Workout		6 heavy plus 2 light
Sets Per Exercise	*Exercises done in opposing pairs as supersets, to make supercycles of 6 sets.*	3
Reps Per Set	Set 1	8 - 10
	Set 2	3 - 5
	Set 3	4 - 7
Weights	Set 1	70%1RM
	Set 2	90 - 110% 1RM
	Set 3	85 - 95% 1RM
Rest Periods	*60 seconds between supersets* *3 minutes between supercycles*	

The Strength-Stabilization Cycle focuses on free weights and cable exercises that demand full participation of the muscles that stabilize the joints while you are working the prime movers. During this 10-week cycle, you are increasing the strength of the prime movers and stabilizing the joints to withstand the added stress when the increased strength is applied during the next cycle.

The Power Cycle focuses on whole-body movements which involve multiple muscle chains simultaneously. This 7-week cycle links strengthened joints and connective tissues to strengthened prime movers and stabilizers, in a network of complementary muscle chains that permit smooth, efficient transfer of power from the ground, or any fixed point of limb connection. This cycle is designed to bring you to a power peak right before your competitive season begins.

7-Week Power Cycle

Workouts Per Week		3
Exercises Per Workout		4
Sets Per Exercise		4 - 5
Reps Per Set	Set 1	5 - 6
	Set 2	2 - 4
	Set 3	1 - 3
	Set 4	1 - 2
	Set 5	1 - 3
Weights	Set 1	80 - 85% 1RM
	Set 2	95% 1RM
	Set 3	95 - 105 % 1RM
	Set 4	100 - 125% 1RM
	Set 5	100% 1RM
Rest Periods		3 minutes

The Link Cycle is designed to optimize power transfer from the weight room to the sports field. During this 10-week cycle you use exercises that closely simulate particular skilled movements of your sport. You do these exercises fast and with lighter weights, to train your nervous system to perform the movements at the accelerated pace necessary for explosive power.

10-Week Link Cycle

Workouts Per Week		5
Exercises Per Workout		3 - 5
Sets Per Exercise		3
Reps Per Set	Set 1	8 - 12
	Set 2	6 - 8
	Set 3	3 - 6
Weights	Set 1	20% 1RM
	Set 2	40% 1RM
	Set 3	60% 1RM
Rest Periods		3 minutes

Workouts

In this book, I have the space to give you only one set of workouts. Many different workouts are given at my training camps on Saltspring Island, British Columbia, San Diego, USA, and Queenstown, New Zealand. At these training camps, we can tailor workouts for individual athletes and for different sports. These workouts are detailed in a forthcoming Power Program Workout Book. Here, I give one good program which fits many sports, and which provides a life-long power maintenance program. Ahead are the four workouts for an Extension-Connection Cycle, the five workouts for a Strength-Stabilization Cycle, the three workouts for a Power Cycle and the three workouts for a Link Cycle. Go for it!

Extreme sports demand extreme power. Here, top climber Craig Calonica prepares to fly a wing at 25,000 feet off Mt Everest. He made it!

Extension-Connection Cycle
Do each of the following 4 workouts once per week for 8 weeks.
Then move on to the Strength-Stabilization Cycle.

Workout 1: Shoulders   MONDAY

Repeat each superset 3 times: 12 reps, 10 reps, 8 reps, to make a Supercycle.
Between each supercycle, rest 2 min and stretch.

SUPERSET 1

External Rotation Bottom to Top   **Internal Rotation Top to Bottom**

SUPERSET 2

External Rotation Top to Bottom   **Internal Rotation Bottom to Top**

SUPERSET 3

Cable Lateral Raise   **Cable Lateral Pull-down**

SUPERSET 4

Labrada Rear Deltoid   **Lying Dumbbell Internal Rotation**

TOTAL 4 SUPERCYCLES (4 x 3 supersets) = 24 SETS

Extension-Connection Cycle (cont.)
Do each of the following 4 workouts once per week for 8 weeks.
Then move on to the Strength-Stabilization Cycle.

Workout 2:   Arms and Abs   TUESDAY

Repeat each superset 3 times: 12 reps, 10 reps, 8 reps, to make a Supercycle.
Between each supercycle, rest 2 min and stretch.

SUPERSET 1

Twisting Dumbbell Curl   **Twisting Dumbbell Kickback**

SUPERSET 2

Preacher Dumbbell Curl   **Cable Concentration Triceps**

SUPERSET 3

Overhead Rope Curl   **Overhead Rope Tricep**

SUPERSET 4

Swiss Ball Crunch   **Hanging Knee Kick**

TOTAL 4 SUPERCYCLES (4 x 3 supersets) = 24 SETS

Extension-Connection Cycle (cont.)
Do each of the following 4 workouts once per week for 8 weeks.
Then move on to the Strength-Stabilization Cycle.

Workout 3: Chest and Back   THURSDAY

Repeat each superset 3 times: 12 reps, 10 reps, 8 reps, to make a Supercycle.
Between each supercycle, rest 2 min and stretch.

SUPERSET 1

Colgan Diagonal Pull-down   **Scott Incline Dumbbell Press**

SUPERSET 2

Jockey Row   **High Cable Crossover**

SUPERSET 3

Bent Arm Pullover   **Kneeling Dumbbell Row**

SUPERSET 4

Flat Dumbbell Press   **Seated Row to Neck**

TOTAL 4 SUPERCYCLES (4 x 3 supersets) = 24 SETS

Extension-Connection Cycle (cont.)
Do each of the following 4 workouts once per week for 8 weeks.
Then move on to the Strength-Stabilization Cycle.

Workout 4: Legs — FRIDAY

Repeat each superset 3 times: 12 reps, 10 reps, 8 reps, to make a Supercycle.
Between each supercycle, rest 2 min and stretch.

SUPERSET 1

Cable Adduction/Rotation   Cable Abduction/Rotation

SUPERSET 2

Forward Lunges   Backward Lunges

SUPERSET 3

Plié Lunges   Diagonal Lunges

SUPERSET 4

Back Extension Curl-up   Reverse Back Extension

TOTAL 4 SUPERCYCLES (4 x 3 supersets) = 24 SETS

Strength Stabilization Cycle

Do each of the following 5 workouts once per week for 10 weeks.
Then move on to the Power Cycle.

Workout 1: Shoulders   MONDAY

Repeat each superset 3 times: 8 reps, 5 reps, 7 reps, to make a Supercycle.
Between each supercycle, rest 3 min and stretch.

SUPERSET 1

Scott Dumbbell Press   **Dumbbell Shrug**

SUPERSET 2

Scott Scapular Pull-up   **Front Dumbbell Raise**

SUPERSET 3

Lying Rear Deltoid Dumbbell Raise   **Lateral Dumbbell Raise**

SUPERSET 4

External Rotation Bottom to Top   **Internal Rotation Top to Bottom**

TOTAL 4 SUPERCYCLES (4 x 3 supersets) = 24 SETS

Strength Stabilization Cycle (cont.)
Do each of the following 5 workouts once per week for 10 weeks.
Then move on to the Power Cycle.

Workout 2: Arms and Abs   TUESDAY

Repeat each superset 3 times: 8 reps, 5 reps, 7 reps, to make a Supercycle.
Between each supercycle, rest 3 min and stretch.

SUPERSET 1

Drag Dumbbell Curl

Overhead Rope Tricep

SUPERSET 2

Arnold Concentration Curl

Cable Concentration Tricep

SUPERSET 3

Kneeling Rope Curl

Scott Kneeling Rope Tricep

SUPERSET 4

Vertical Scissors

Reverse Back Extension

TOTAL 4 SUPERCYCLES (4 x 3 supersets) = 24 SETS

Strength Stabilization Cycle (cont.)
Do each of the following 5 workouts once per week for 10 weeks.
Then move on to the Power Cycle.

Workout 3: Back   WEDSDAY

Repeat each superset 3 times: 8 reps, 5 reps, 7 reps, to make a Supercycle.
Between each supercycle, rest 3 min and stretch.

SUPERSET 1

Cable Woodchop   **Cable Reverse Woodchop**

SUPERSET 2

Weighted Pronated Pull-up   **Scott Cable Row**

SUPERSET 3

Scott Isolation Pull-down   **Jockey Row**

SUPERSET 4

Back Extension Curl-up   **Swiss Ball Curl-up**

TOTAL 4 SUPERCYCLES (4 x 3 supersets) = 24 SETS

Strength Stabilization Cycle (cont.)
Do each of the following 5 workouts once per week for 10 weeks.
Then move on to the Power Cycle.

Workout 4: Chest   FRIDAY

Repeat each superset 3 times: 8 reps, 5 reps, 7 reps, to make a Supercycle.
Between each supercycle, rest 3 min and stretch.

SUPERSET 1

Incline Barbell Press   **Lying Cable Pullover**

SUPERSET 2

Weighted Push-up   **High Cable Crossover**

SUPERSET 3

 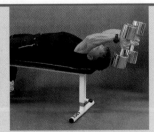  

Bent-arm Dumbbell Pull-over   **Straight-arm Pull-down**

SUPERSET 4

Practice High Pull (up to 30kg only)   Practice Power Clean (up to 30kg only)

TOTAL 4 SUPERCYCLES (4 x 3 supersets) = 24 SETS

Strength Stabilization Cycle (cont.)
Do each of the following 5 workouts once per week for 10 weeks.
Then move on to the Power Cycle.

Workout 5: Legs	SATURDAY

**Repeat each superset 3 times: 8 reps, 5 reps, 7 reps, to make a Supercycle.
Between each supercycle, rest 3 min and stretch.**

SUPERSET 1

Front to Back Lunge   **Plié to Diagonal Lunge**

SUPERSET 2

Light Squat (up to bodyweight only)   **Practice Barbell Deadlift (up to bodyweight only)**

SUPERSET 3

Cable Abduction/Rotation   **Practice Clean (up to 50 kg only)**

SUPERSET 4

Seated Calf Eccentrics   **Scott One-leg Calf Eccentrics**

TOTAL 4 SUPERCYCLES (4 x 3 supersets) = 24 SETS

Power Cycle
Do each of the following 3 workouts once per week for 7 weeks.
Then move on to the Link Cycle.

Workout 1:   MONDAY

Repeat each exercise 5 times: 6 reps, 4 reps, 3 reps, 2 reps, 3 reps to make a Superset.
Between each superset, rest 3 min and stretch.

EXERCISE 1	EXERCISE 2

Barbell Squat   **Barbell High Pull**

EXERCISE 3	EXERCISE 4

Weighted Horizontal Scissors   **Weighted Reverse Back Extension**

TOTAL 4 EXERCISES (4 x 5 sets) = 20 SETS

Power Cycle (cont.)

Do each of the following 3 workouts once per week for 7 weeks.
Then move on to the Link Cycle.

Workout 2:	WEDNESDAY

Repeat each exercise 5 times: 6 reps, 4 reps, 3 reps, 2 reps, 3 reps to make a Superset.
Between each superset, rest 3 min and stretch.

EXERCISE 1	EXERCISE 2

Barbell Deadlift

Weighted Pronated Pull-up

EXERCISE 3	EXERCISE 4

Woodchop

Reverse Woodchop

TOTAL 4 EXERCISES (4 x 5 sets) = 20 SETS

Power Cycle [cont.]
Do each of the following 3 workouts once per week for 7 weeks.
Then move on to the Link Cycle.

Workout 3:   FRIDAY

**Repeat each exercise 5 times: 6 reps, 4 reps, 3 reps, 2 reps, 3 reps to make a Superset.
Between each superset, rest 3 min and stretch.**

EXERCISE 1	EXERCISE 2

Barbell Bench Press   **Jockey Row**

EXERCISE 3	EXERCISE 4

Barbell Clean   **Weighted Back Extension Curl-up**

TOTAL 4 EXERCISES (4 x 5 sets) = 20 SETS

Link Cycle

Do each of the following 3 workouts once per week for 10 weeks.
Then move on to the Maintenance Cycle.

Workout 1:   MONDAY

Repeat each superset 3 times: 8 reps, 6 reps, 3 reps to make a Supercycle.
Between each supercycle, rest 5 min and stretch.

SUPERSET 1

Bounce Jump   **Bound**

SUPERSET 2

Back Throw   **Front Overhead Throw**

TOTAL 2 SUPERSETS (2 x 6 sets) = 12 SETS

Link Cycle (cont.)

**Do each of the following 3 workouts once per week for 10 weeks.
Then move on to the Maintenance Cycle.**

Workout 2: WEDNESDAY

**Repeat each superset 3 times: 8 reps, 6 reps, 3 reps to make a Supercycle.
Between each supercycle, rest 5 min and stretch.**

SUPERSET 1

Band Twist **Side Bound**

SUPERSET 2

Front Throw **Spinal Rotational Lunge**

TOTAL 2 SUPERSETS (2 x 6 sets) = 12 SETS

Link Cycle (cont.)
Do each of the following 3 workouts once per week for 10 weeks.
Then move on to the Maintenance Cycle.

Workout 3:   FRIDAY

Repeat each superset 3 times: 8 reps, 6 reps, 3 reps to make a Supercycle.
Between each supercycle, rest 5 min and stretch.

SUPERSET 1

Light Woodchops   Light Reverse Woodchops

SUPERSET 2

Seated Front Throw   Side Throw

TOTAL 2 SUPERSETS (2 x 6 sets) = 12 SETS

You now have all the components necessary to build a powerful and functional body. Using this program, we have not had a single failure in the last decade in anyone who has stuck with it. You may have had only mediocre results from conventional weight training or have given up because of injury and disillusionment. This is a different program altogether, building your body the right way from the inside out. If you have the guts and persistence, then the Power will surely be with you.

30

Postscript

This book gives you the basics of weight training for athletic power. But it only scratches the surface of what we cover in my Sports Training Intensives. Send us e-mails at team@colganinstitute.com and we will try and answer your questions with the latest and the best.

A final word. As training fads rise and fall in ever increasing parade, steer your course steadily by the compass of science. Remain always a seeker after truth, and glory in the gift of your body that can play the games of gods.

ALIVE

Flee fast the ordinary
Of everyday.
Reject the counsel
Of the saviours and the sane.

Feel for the pulse of your heart
Seek out those souls
Who animate its passion.
Cultivate those labors
That quicken its beat.
And count only little the cost.

For days without risk,
Without trembling emotion,
Crescendos of triumph,
Despairs of defeat,
Let the bondage of commonplace
Bind you spectator,
Condemned but to watching
The living of others,
Who dance with the fire of a passionate heart.

Michael Colgan

Appendix

Predict Your MAX

Use these tables to find your one-repetition-maximum for any exercise. Perform as many reps as possible (up to 10), with a weight you can handle between 90 and 400 lbs (or 40 and 195 kg). Then find that weight under the number of reps completed, and read across to the 1 REP MAX column to know your maximum.

Predict Your Max In Pounds									
Number of Reps Completed									**1 REP MAX**
10	**9**	**8**	**7**	**6**	**5**	**4**	**3**	**2**	
90	94	98	102	105	108	111	114	117	125
100	14	18	112	115	118	121	124	127	135
110	114	118	122	126	130	134	138	142	150
120	124	128	132	136	140	144	148	152	160
130	135	140	145	150	154	158	162	166	175
140	146	151	156	161	166	171	176	181	190
150	156	161	166	171	176	181	186	191	200
160	166	172	178	184	190	195	200	205	215
170	176	182	188	194	199	204	209	214	225
180	187	193	199	205	211	217	223	229	240
190	197	204	211	218	225	231	237	243	255
200	207	214	221	228	235	241	247	253	265
210	218	225	232	239	246	253	260	267	280
220	228	236	244	252	260	268	275	282	295
230	238	246	254	262	270	277	284	291	305
240	249	258	266	274	282	290	298	306	320

Continued…

Predict Your MAX

Use these tables to find your one-repetition-maximum for any exercise. Perform as many reps as possible (up to 10), with a weight you can handle between 90 and 400 lbs (or 40 and 195 kg). Then find that weight under the number of reps completed, and read across to the 1 REP MAX column to know your maximum.

Predict Your Max In Pounds (cont'd)

| Number of Reps Completed | | | | | | | | | 1 REP MAX |
10	9	8	7	6	5	4	3	2	
250	260	269	278	287	296	304	312	320	335
260	269	278	287	296	305	314	322	330	345
270	280	290	300	309	318	327	336	345	360
280	290	300	310	319	328	337	346	355	375
290	300	310	320	329	338	347	356	365	385
300	310	320	330	340	350	360	370	380	400
310	321	332	343	354	365	375	385	395	415
320	331	342	353	364	375	385	395	405	425
330	342	354	365	376	387	398	409	420	440
340	352	364	376	388	400	412	424	435	455
350	362	374	386	398	410	422	434	445	465
360	373	386	399	412	424	436	448	460	480
370	383	396	409	422	434	446	458	470	495
380	394	407	420	433	446	459	472	485	510
390	404	417	430	443	456	469	482	495	520
400	414	427	440	453	466	479	492	505	540

© The Colgan Institute, 1993.

Predict Your Max In Kilograms

Number of Reps Completed									1 REP MAX
10	**9**	**8**	**7**	**6**	**5**	**4**	**3**	**2**	
40	42	44	46	48	49	50	52	53	55
45	47	49	51	52	54	55	56	57	60
50	52	54	55	58	61	63	65	67	70
55	56	58	60	62	64	65	67	71	75
60	61	64	66	67	69	70	72	76	80
65	66	68	71	73	75	76	82	87	90
70	72	74	76	78	80	82	85	87	95
75	77	79	81	83	85	86	87	95	100
80	82	84	86	88	89	90	95	101	105
85	87	88	89	90	92	95	101	105	110
90	92	94	96	98	100	105	110	115	120
95	97	99	101	103	110	115	119	123	130
100	102	104	106	108	115	119	123	130	135
105	107	109	111	114	119	123	130	133	140
110	112	114	118	123	129	133	139	145	150
115	117	119	121	124	129	135	141	147	155

Continued…

Predict Your Max In Kilograms (cont'd)

| Number of Reps Completed | | | | | | | | | 1 REP MAX |
10	9	8	7	6	5	4	3	2	
120	122	124	126	130	136	142	148	154	160
125	127	129	131	135	142	148	154	160	165
130	132	134	136	142	148	154	160	165	170
135	137	139	141	146	152	157	162	167	175
140	142	144	146	151	158	164	170	176	185
145	147	149	151	154	155	169	176	186	195
150	152	154	160	168	174	180	186	191	200
155	157	159	166	174	180	186	194	200	205
160	162	164	166	174	180	186	194	202	210
165	167	169	171	175	184	193	202	211	220
170	172	174	176	184	193	202	211	220	230
175	177	179	181	187	199	208	217	226	235
180	182	184	186	193	202	212	221	230	240
185	187	189	191	197	208	217	226	235	245
190	192	194	196	200	210	220	230	240	250
195	197	199	204	213	222	231	240	249	260

Percentages of 1 REP MAX

Use these tables to calculate the weights to use for the Extension-Connection, Strength-Stabilization and Power Cycles.

Percentages of 1RM In Pounds

1RM (lbs)	50%	60%	70%	80%	90%	100%	110%	120%	130%
50	25	30	35	40	45	50	55	60	65
60	30	36	42	48	54	60	66	72	78
70	35	42	49	56	63	70	77	84	91
80	40	48	56	64	72	80	88	96	104
90	45	54	63	72	81	90	99	108	117
100	50	60	70	80	90	100	110	120	130
110	55	66	77	88	99	110	121	132	143
120	60	72	84	96	108	120	132	144	156
130	65	78	91	104	117	130	143	156	169
140	70	84	98	112	126	140	154	168	182
150	75	90	105	120	135	150	165	180	195
160	80	96	112	128	144	160	176	192	208
170	85	102	119	136	153	170	187	204	221
180	90	108	126	144	162	180	198	216	234
190	95	114	133	152	171	190	209	228	247
200	100	120	140	160	180	200	220	240	260
210	105	126	147	168	189	210	231	252	273
220	110	132	154	176	198	220	242	264	286
230	115	138	161	184	207	230	253	276	299
240	120	144	168	192	216	240	264	288	312
250	125	150	175	200	225	250	275	300	325
260	130	156	182	208	234	260	286	312	338
270	135	162	189	216	243	270	297	324	351
280	140	168	196	224	252	280	308	336	364
290	145	174	203	232	261	290	319	348	377
300	150	180	210	240	270	300	330	360	390

© The Colgan Institute, 1999.

Continued…

Percentages of 1RM In Pounds (cont'd)

1RM (lbs)	50%	60%	70%	80%	90%	100%	110%	120%	130%
310	155	186	217	248	279	310	341	372	403
320	160	192	224	256	288	320	352	384	416
330	165	198	231	264	297	330	363	396	429
340	170	204	238	272	306	340	374	408	442
350	175	210	245	280	315	350	385	420	455
360	180	216	252	288	324	360	396	432	468
370	185	222	259	296	333	370	407	444	481
380	190	228	266	304	342	380	418	456	494
390	195	234	273	312	351	390	429	468	507
400	200	240	280	320	360	400	440	480	520
410	205	246	287	328	369	410	451	492	533
420	210	252	294	336	378	420	462	504	546
430	215	258	301	344	387	430	473	516	559
440	220	264	308	352	396	440	484	528	572
450	225	270	315	360	405	450	495	540	585
460	230	276	322	368	414	460	506	552	598
470	235	282	329	376	423	470	517	564	611
480	240	288	336	384	432	480	528	576	624
490	245	294	343	392	441	490	539	588	637
500	250	300	350	400	450	500	550	600	650
510	255	306	357	408	459	510	561	612	663
520	260	312	364	416	468	520	572	624	676
530	265	318	371	424	477	530	583	636	689
540	270	324	378	432	486	540	594	648	702

© The Colgan Institute, 1999.

Percentages of 1RM In Kilograms

1RM (kg)	50%	60%	70%	80%	90%	100%	110%	120%	130%
40	20	24	28	32	36	40	44	48	52
45	23	27	32	36	41	45	50	54	59
50	25	30	35	40	45	50	55	60	65
55	28	33	39	44	50	55	61	66	72
60	30	36	42	48	54	60	66	72	78
65	33	39	46	52	59	65	72	78	85
70	35	42	49	56	63	70	77	84	91
75	38	45	53	60	68	75	83	90	98
80	40	48	56	64	72	80	88	96	104
85	43	51	60	68	77	85	94	102	111
90	45	54	63	72	81	90	99	108	117
95	48	57	67	76	86	95	105	114	124
100	50	60	70	80	90	100	110	120	130
105	53	63	74	84	95	105	116	126	137
110	55	66	77	88	99	110	121	132	143
115	58	69	81	92	104	115	127	138	150
120	60	72	84	96	108	120	132	144	156
125	63	75	88	100	113	125	138	150	163
130	65	78	91	104	117	130	143	156	169
135	68	81	95	108	122	135	149	162	176
140	70	84	98	112	126	140	154	168	182
145	73	87	102	116	131	145	160	174	189
150	75	90	105	120	135	150	165	180	195
155	78	93	109	124	140	155	171	186	202
160	80	96	112	128	144	160	176	192	208
165	83	99	116	132	149	165	182	198	215

Continued…

Percentages of 1RM In Kilograms (cont'd)

1RM (kg)	50%	60%	70%	80%	90%	100%	110%	120%	130%
165	83	99	116	132	149	165	182	198	215
170	85	102	119	136	153	170	187	204	221
175	88	105	123	140	158	175	193	210	228
180	90	108	126	144	162	180	198	216	234
185	93	111	130	148	167	185	204	222	241
190	95	114	133	152	171	190	209	228	247
195	98	117	137	156	176	195	215	234	254
200	100	120	140	160	180	200	220	240	260
205	103	123	144	164	185	205	226	246	267
210	105	126	147	168	189	210	231	252	273
215	108	129	151	172	194	215	237	258	280
220	110	132	154	176	198	220	242	264	286
225	113	135	158	180	203	225	248	270	293
230	115	138	161	184	207	230	253	276	299
235	118	141	165	188	212	235	259	282	306
240	120	144	168	192	216	240	264	288	312
245	123	147	172	196	221	245	270	294	319
250	125	150	175	200	225	250	275	300	325
255	128	153	179	204	230	255	281	306	332
260	130	156	182	208	234	260	286	312	338

References

Due to space limitations, the references quoted throughout this book are only a few representative examples of the research. They are selected to lead the scientifically minded reader to the main body of evidence behind our conclusions. More detailed evidence for each concept is given at our training camps and Anti-Aging Intensives held at Saltspring Island, British Columbia, Queenstown, New Zealand and San Diego, California.

For details contact:

E-mail: team@colganinstitute.com   Internet: www.colganinstitute.com

Introduction

1. Brink WD. **The Advisor**, 1994;Winter:2.

Chapter 1: Got Power

1. Bompa TO. Periodization of strength; The most effective methodology of strength training. **Nat Strength Condit Assoc J,** 1990;12:49-52.

2. Freeman W. Coaching, periodization and the battle of artist versus scientist. **Track Technique,** 1994;127:4054-4057.

3. Cissik J. **The Basics of Strength Training**. New York: McGraw Hill, 1998.

4. Fleck SJ, Kraemer WJ. **Periodization Breakthrough.** New York: Advanced Research Press, 1996.

5. Colgan M. **Sports Nutrition Guide.** Vancouver: Apple Publishing, 2001.

6. Lieber RL. **Skeletal Muscle: Structure and Function.** Baltimore: Williams and Wilkins, 1992.

7. Scott L. **The Bio-Phase Training System.** Salt Lake, Utah: Larry Scott and Associates, 1998.

8. Ho K et al. Skeletal muscle fiber-splitting with weight-lifting exercise in man. **Am J Physiol,** 1980;157:433-440.

Chapter 2: Power Parts

1. Delorme TL, Watkins AL. Technics of progressive resistance exercise, **Arch. Phys. Med,** 1948;29:263.

2. Poliquin C. **The Poliquin Principles.** Napa, CA., Dayton Writer's Group,1997.

3. Scott L. **The Bio-Phase Training System.** Salt Lake Utah: Larry Scott and Associates, 1998.

Chapter 3: Power Posture

1. Travell JG et al, **Myofascial Dysfunction and Pain, The Trigger Point Manual, Upper Half of The Body. Vol 1, Second Edition,** Baltimore: Williams and Wilkins, 1999.

2. Travell JG et al, **Myofascial Dysfunction and Pain, The Trigger Point Manual, The Lower Extremities. Vol 2, Second Edition,** Baltimore: Williams and Wilkins, 1999.

3. Rolf I. Rolfing: **Reestablishing the Natural Alignment and Structural Integration of the Human Body, Revised Edition.** Inner Traditions, 1990.

4. Feldenkrais M. **Awareness Through Movement.** New York, New York: Harper & Row Publishers, Inc., 1977.

Chapter 4: Elastic Muscle

1. Pope RP et al. A randomized trial of pre-exercise stretching for prevention of lower limb injury. **Med Sci Sports Exerc,** 2000;32:271-277.

2. Shrier I. Stretching before exercise does not reduce the risk of local muscle injury: a critical review of the clinical and basic science literature. **Clin J Sports Med,** 1999;9:221-227.

3. Smith CA. The warm-up procedure: to stretch or not to stretch. A brief review. **J Orthop Sports Phys Ther,** 1994:19:12-17.

4. Fyfe I, Stanish WD. The use of eccentric stretching in the treatment and prevention of tendon injuries. **Clin Sports Med,** 1992;11:601-624.

5. Safran MR. Warm-up and muscular injury prevention. An update. Sports Med, 1989;8:239-249.

6. Pink MM, Tibone JE. The painful shoulder in the swimming athlete. **Orthop Clin North Am,** 2000;31:247-261.

7. Terara M et al. Influence of passive torque offered by soft tissue on oxygen consumption during movement in men and women. **J Strength and Condit Res,** 1997;11:214-218.

8. Wilson GJ et al. Stretch-shorten cycle enhancement through flexibility training. **Med Sci Sports Exerc,** 1992:24:116-123.

9. Hortobagyi T et al. Effects of intense stretching – flexibility training on the mechanical profile and on the range of movement of the hip joints. **Int J Sports Med,** 1985;6:317-321.

10. Travell JG et al, **Myofascial Dysfunction and Pain, The Trigger Point Manual, Vol 1, Upper Half of The Body, Second Edition,** Baltimore: Williams and Wilkins, 1999.

11. Cox VM et al. Growth induced by incremental static stretch in adult rabbit latissimus dorsi muscle. **Exp Physiol,** 2000;85:193-202.

12. Sapega AA et al. Biophysical factors in range of motion exercises. **The Physician and Sportsmed,** 1981;9:57-65.

13. Light KE et al. A low-loading prolonged stretch versus high-loading brief stretch in treating knee contractures. **Phys Ther,** 1984;64:330-333.

14. Cornelius WI. **International Gymnast Tech.** 1981,2; Supplement.

Chapter 5: Extend And Connect

1. Travell JG et al. **Myofascial Dysfunction and Pain, The Trigger Point Manual, Upper Half of The Body. Vol 1, Second Edition,** Baltimore: Williams and Wilkins, 1999.

2. McFarlane S, Tan MH. **Complete Book of Tai Chi.** DK Publishing, 1997.

Chapter 6: Stable Strength

1. Kendall FP et al. **Muscles: Testing and Function, Fourth Edition.** Baltimore: Williams and Wilkins, 1993.

2. Colgan M. **Sports Nutrition**. Vancouver: Apple Publishing, 2001

Chapter 7: Power Cycle

1. Bompa TO. **Serious Strength Training.** Champaign Il: Human Kinetics, 1998.

2. Poliquin C. **The Poliquin Principles.** Napa, CA., Dayton Writer's Group,1997.

Chapter 8: The Power Equation

1. Einstein A, Infeld L. **The Evolution of Physics.** New York: Simon and Shuster, 1938.

Chapter 9: Train The Chain

1. Bompa T. **Periodization Training For Sport.** Champaign Il: Human Kinetics, 1999.

Chapter 10: Free Movement

1. Bompa T. **Periodization Training For Sport.** Champaign Il: Human Kinetics, 1999.

2. Magill L. **Paul Chek's Strong and Stable.** Vols 1-3, San Diego, CA: Paul Chek, 1997.

3. Colgan M. **Optimum Sports Nutrition.** New York: Advanced Research Press, 1993.

Chapter 11: Power Reps

1. Lieber RL, Friden J. Mechanisms of muscle injury after eccentric contraction. **J Sci Med Sport**, 1999:253-265.

2. Bompa T. **Periodization Training For Sport.** Champaign Il: Human Kinetics, 1999.

3. Westcott W. **Strength Fitness: Physiological Principles and Training, Fourth Edition.** Dubuque: William C Brown, 1991.

4. Atha J. Strengthening muscle. **Exerc Sports Sci Rev,** 1981;9:1-73.

5. Colgan M. **Creatine for Muscle and Strength.** Vancouver: Apple Publishing, 1999.

6.   Kraemer WJ, Fleck SJ. **Strength and Health Report,** 1998;2:1-2.

7.   Poliquin C. **The Poliquin Principles.** Napa, CA: Dayton Writer's Group, 1997.

8.   Friden J et al.   Myofibrillar damage following intense eccentric exercise in man.   **Int J Sports Med,** 1983;4:170-176.

9.   Newham DJ et al. Ultrastructural changes after concentric and eccentric contractions in human muscle. **J Neurol Sci,** 1983;61:109-112.

10.   Galloway J. **Marathon.** Atlanta: Phidippides Publications, 1996.

Chapter 12: Fast-Twitch

1.   Lieber RL. **Skeletal Muscle: Structure and Function.** Baltimore: Williams & Wilkins, 1992.

2.   Hautier CA et al. Optimal velocity for maximal production in non-isokinetic cycling is related to related to muscle fiber type composition. **Eur J Appl Physiol,** 1996;74:114-118.

3.   Linossier MT et al. Performance and fiber characteristics of human skeletal muscle during short sprint training and detraining on a cycle ergometer. **Eur J Appl Physiol,** 1997;75:491-498.

4.   Delecluse C. Influence of strength training on sprint running performance. Current findings and implications for training. **Sports Med,** 1997:24:147-156.

5.   Staron RS et al. Muscle hypertrophy and fast fiber type conversions in heavy resistance trained women. **Eur J Appl Physiol, 1990;60:71-79.**

6.   Dawson B et al. Change in performance, muscle metabolites, enzymes and fibre types after short sprint training. **Eur J Appl Physiol,** 1998;78:163-169.

Chapter 13: Essential Eccentrics

1.   Armstrong RB et al. Eccentric exercise induced injury in rat skeletal muscle. **J Appl Physiol,** 1983;54:80-93.

2.   Friden J et al.   Myofibrillar damage following intense eccentric exercise in man.   **Int J Sports Med,** 1983;4:170-176.

3.   Staron RS et al. Strength and skeletal muscle adaptations in heavy- resistance-trained women after detraining and retraining. **J Appl Physiol,** 1991;70:631-640.

4.   Collander EB, Tesch. PA. Effects of eccentric and concentric muscle actions in resistance training. **Acta Physiol Scand,** 1990;140:31-39.

5.   Collander EB, Tesch PA. Responses to eccentric and concentric resistance training in females and males. **Acta Physiol Scand,** 1990;141:149-156.

6.   Dudley GA et al. Importance of eccentric actions in performance adaptations to resistance training. **Aviat Space Environ Med,** 1991;62:543-550.

7.   Hather BM et al. Influence of eccentric actions on skeletal muscle adaptations to resistance training. **Acta Physiol Scand,** 1991;143:177-185.

8.   Tesch PA et al. Effects of eccentric and concentric resistance training on skeletal muscle substrates, enzymes activities and capillary supply. **Acta Physiol Scand,** 1990;140:575-580.

9. Dudley GA et al. Importance of eccentric actions in performance adaptations to resistance training. **Aviat Space Environ Med,** 1991;62:543-550.

10. Ho K et al. Skeletal muscle fiber splitting with weight-lifting exercise in rats. **Am J Physiol,** 1980;157:433-440.

11. Yarasheski K et al. Effect of heavy resistance exercise training on muscle fiber composition in young rats. **J Appl Physiol,** 1990;69:434-437.

12. Mauro A. Satellite cells of skeletal muscle fibers. **J Biophys Biochem Cytol,** 1960;9:493-494.

13. Vracko R et al. Basal lamina: the scaffold for orderly cell replacement. **J Cell Biol,** 1972;55:406-419.

14. Darr K, Schultz E. Exercise induced satellite cell activation in growing and mature skeletal muscle. **J Appl Physiol,** 1987;63:1816-1821.

15. Giddings CJ, Gonyea WJ. Morphological observations supporting muscle fiber hyperplasia following weight-lifting exercise in cats. **Anat. Rec,** 1992;233:178-195.

16. Sjöström M et al. Evidence of fiber hyperplasia in human skeletal muscles from healthy young men. **Eur J Appl Physiol,** 1992;62:301-304.

17. Mikesky AE et al. Changes in muscle fiber size and composition in response to heavy-resistance exercise. **Med. Sci. Sports Exerc,** 1991;23:1042-1049.

18. Gonyea WJ et al. Exercise induced increases in muscle fiber number. **Eur J Appl Physiol,** 1986;55:137-141.

19. Wong TS, Booth FW. Protein metabolism in rat gastrocnemius muscle after stimulated chronic concentric exercise. **J Appl Physiol,** 1990;69:1709-1717.

20. Fleck SJ, Kraemer WJ. **Periodization Breakthrough!** New York: Advanced Research Press, 1996.

Chapter 14: Negatives Are King

1. Friden J et al. Adaptive response in human muscle subjected to prolonged eccentric training. **Int J Sports Med, 1983;4:177-183.**

2. Johnston BL et al. A comparison of concentric and eccentric muscle training. **Med Sci Sports,** 1976;8:35-38.

3. Pearson DR, Costill DL. The effects of constant external resistance exercise and isokinetic exercise training on work-induced hypertrophy. **J Appl Sport Sci Res,** 1988;2:39-41.

4. Hortobaggi JP et al. Adaptive responses to muscle lengthening and shortening. **J Appl Physiol,** 1996;80:765-772.

5. Hakkinen K, Komi PV. Effect of different combined concentric and eccentric muscle work regimes on maximal strength development. **J Human Mov Studies,** 1981;7:33-44.

6. Godard MP et al. Effects of accentuated eccentric resistance training on concentric knee extension strength. **J Strength Cond Res,** 1998;12:26-29.

7. Bishop R et al. Changes in myoelectric activity of the biceps brachi and bracialis muscles under different eccentric loads. **Med Sci Sport Exerc,** 1998;30:S65.

Chapter 15: How Many Sets?

1.   Poliquin C. **The Poliquin Principles.** Napa, CA.: Dayton Writer's Group, 1997.

2.   Colgan M. **Sports Nutrition Guide.** Vancouver, B.C., Apple Publishing, 2001.

Chapter 16: Bodyparts

1.   Colgan M. **Optimum Sports Nutrition.** New York: Advanced Research Press, 1993.

2.   Stryer L. **Biochemistry, Fourth Edition.** New York: W.H. Freeman, 1995.

Chapter 17: How Many Exercises?

1.   Pearl W. **Keys to the Inner Universe, Vol 1.** Phoenix OR: Bill Pearl Enterprises, 1982.

2.   Barnett C et al. Effects of variations of the bench press exercises on the EMG activity of five shoulder muscles. **J Strength Condit Res,** 1995;9:222-227.

Chapter 18: Abdominals: Power Core

1.   Basmajian JV, Deluca CJ. **Muscles Alive, Fifth Edition,** Baltimore: Williams and Wilkins, 1985.

2.   Carter BL et al. **Cross-Sectional Anatomy.** New York: Appleton-Century-Crofts, 1977.

Chapter 19: Shoulder Power

1.   Poliquin C. **The Poliquin Principles.** Napa, CA: Dayton Writer's Group, 1997.

2.   Fleck SJ, Kraemer WJ. **Periodization Breakthrough!** New York: Advanced Research Press, 1996.

3.   Travell JG. **Myofascial Dysfunction and Pain. The Trigger Point Manual. Vols 1 and 2, Second Edition.** Baltimore: Williams and Wilkins, 1999.

Chapter 20: Arm Power

1.   Clemente CD. **Anatomy: A Regional Atlas of the Human Body, Third Edition.** Baltimore: Urban & Schwarzenberg, 1987.

2.   Travell JG. **Myofascial Dysfunction and Pain. The Trigger Point Manual. Vols 1 and 2, Second Edition.** Baltimore: Williams and Wilkins, 1999.

Chapter 21: Back: Power Lift

1.   Bollet AS. The relationship of the gluteus maximus to intelligence. **Medical Times,** 1984;112:109-112.

2.   Mundt DJ et al. An epidemiological study on non occupational lifting as a risk factor for herniated lumbar

intervertebral disc. **Spine,** 1993;18:595-602.

3.   Broer MR et al. **Patterns of Motor Activity In Selected Sports Skills.** Springfield, Ill: Charles C Thomas, 1967.

4.   Johnson G et al. Anatomy and actions of the trapezius muscle. **Clin Biomech,** 1994;9:44-50.

5.   Travell JG et al, **Myofascial Dysfunction and Pain, The Trigger Point Manual, Upper Half of The Body. Vol 1, Second Edition,** Baltimore: Williams and Wilkins, 1999.

6.   Basmajian JV, Deluca CJ. **Muscles Alive, Fifth Edition**. Baltimore: Williams & Wilkins, 1985.

7.   Kendall FP et al. **Muscles Testing and Function, Fourth Edition with Posture and Pain**. Baltimore: Williams and Wilkins, 1993.

8.   Agur AM. **Grants Atlas of Anatomy, Ninth Edition,** Baltimore: Williams and Wilkins, 1991.

9.   Bogduk N, Twomey IT. **Clinical Anatomy of the Lumbar Spine.** New York: Churchill, 1987.

10. Knapp ME. Function of the quadratus lumborum. **Arch Phys Med Rehab,** 1951;32:505-507.

Chapter 22: Chest: Power Push

1.   Toltt C. **An Atlas of Human Anatomy, Second Edition.** New York: MacMillan, 1919.

2.   Agur AM**. Grant's Atlas of Anatomy, Ninth Edition.** Baltimore: Williams & Wilkins, 1991.

3.   Madson N, McLaughlinT. Kinematic factors influencing performance and injury risk in the bench press exercise. **Med Sci Sports Exerc,** 1984;16:376-381.

4.   Algra B. An in-depth analysis of the bench press. **NSCA Journal,** 1982;October/November;6-11:70-72.

Chapter 23: Legs: Power Base

1.   Inman VT. Human Locomotion. **Can Med Assoc J,** 1996;94:1047-1054.

2.   Bollet AS. The relationship of the gluteus maximus to intelligence. **Medical Times,** 1984;112:109-112.

3.   Travell JG. **Myofascial Dysfunction and Pain. The Trigger Point Manual. Vol 2, Second Edition**. Baltimore: Williams and Wilkins, 1999.

4.   Basmajian IV, Deluca CJ. **Muscles Alive, Fifth Edition,** Baltimore: Williams & Wilkins, 1985.

5.   Ekberg O et al. Longstanding groin pain in athletes: A multidisciplinary approach. **Sports Med,** 1988;6:56-61.

6.   Perry S. The mechanics of walking. **Phys Ther,** 1967;47:778-801.

7.   Lander JE, et al. The effectiveness of weight belts during multiple repetitions of the squat exercise. **Med Sci Sports Exerc,** 1992,24:603-609.

8.   Poliquin C. **The Poliquin Principles.** Napa, CA: Dayton Writer's Group, 1997.

9.   McLaughlin T et al. The squat and its application to athletic performance. **NSCA Journal,** 1984;June/July:10-22,68.

Chapter 24: Steel Knees & Iron Calves

1. Broos MG et al. Knee injuries. In Shahady EJ, Petrizzi MJ (eds). **Sports Medicine for Coaches and Trainers, Second Edition.** Chapel Hill: ONC Press, 1991.

2. Hamill J, Knudson KM. **Biomechanical Basis for Human Movement.** Baltimore: Williams and Wilkins, 1995.

3. Palmitier RJ et al. Kinetic chair exercise in knee rehabilitation. **Sports Med,** 1991;11:402-413.

4. Yack HJ et al. Comparison of closed and open kinetic chair exercise in the anterior cruciate ligament-deficient knee. **Sports Med,** 1993;21:49-54.

5. Yack HJ et al. Comparison of closed and open kinetic chair exercise in the anterior cruciate ligament-deficient knee. **Sports Med,** 1993;21:49-54.

6. Yack HJ et al. Comparison of closed and open kinetic chair exercise in the anterior cruciate ligament-deficient knee. **Sports Med,** 1993;21:49-54.

7. Stone MH, Borden RA. Modes and methods of resistance training. **Strength and Condit,** 1997;19:18-24.

8. Steinkamp LA et al. Biomechanical considerations in patelofemoral joint rehabilitation. **Am J Sports Med,** 1993;21:438-444.

9. Ludbrook J. The musculovenous pumps of the human lower limb. **Am Heart J,** 1966;71:635-641.

Chapter 25: The Vital Link

1. Bompa T. **Periodization Training For Sport.** Champaign Il: Human Kinetics, 1999:162.

2. Murphy AJ, Wilson GJ. The ability of tests of muscular function to reflect training induced changes in performance. **J Sports Sci,** 1997;15:191-200.

3. Wilson GJ et al. Stretch shorten cycle performance enhancement during flexibility training. **Med Sci Sports Exerc,** 1992;24:116-123.

Chapter 26: Plyometrics

1. Hakkinen K. Neuromuscular and hormonal adaptations during strength and power training. **J Sports Med Phys Fitness,** 1989;29:9-26.

2. Sale D. Neural adaptation in strength and power training. In Jones et al,(eds). **Human Muscle Power,** Champaign, IL: Human Kinetics, 1986;289-304.

3. Zannon S. Consideration for determining some parametric values of the relative strength and elastic relative strength for planning and controlling the long jumper's conditioning training. **Athletic Coach,** 1977;11:14-20.

4. Bosco C, Komi PV. Influence of countermovement amplitude in potentiation of muscular performance. **Biomechanics VII.** Baltimore: University Park Press, 1980:129-135.

5. Bobbert MF et al. Drop jumping. I. The influence of jumping technique on the biomechanics of jumping. **Med Sci Sports Exerc,** 1987;19:332-338.

6. Lees A, Fahmi E. Optimal drop heights for plyometric training. **Ergonomics.** 1994;37:141-148.

7. Young WB et al. A comparison of drop jump training methods: effects on leg extensor strength qualitis and jumping performance. **Int J Sports Med,** 1999;20:295-303.

8. Kovacs I et al. Foot placement modifies kinematics and kinetics during drop jumping. **Med Sci Sport Exerc,** 1999;31:708-716.

Chapter 27: Power Nutrition

1. Colgan M. **Optimum Sports Nutrition.** New York: Advanced Research Press, 1993.

2. Colgan M. **Sports Nutrition Guide.** Vancouver, B.C: Apple Publishing, 2001.

3. Lovelock J. **The Ages of Gaia: A Biography of the Living Earth.** New York: WW Norton, 1988.

4. Oqihara T et al. Comparative changes in plasma and RBC alpha tocopherol after administration of dl-alpha tocopherol and d-alpha tocopherol. **J Nutr Sci Vitanimol,** 1985;31:169-177.

5. Burton GW et al. Vitamin E: Application of the principles of physical organic chemistry to the exploration of its structure and function. **Acc Chem Res,** 1986;19:194-201.

6. Colgan M. **Beat Arthritis.** Vancouver: Apple Publishing, 1999.

7. Philips M, Baetz A, (eds). Diet and resistance to disease. **Advances in Experimental Medicine and Biology, Vol 35,** New York: Plenum, 1981.

8. Colgan M. **The New Nutrition.** Vancouver: Apple Publishing, 1995.

9. Colgan M. **Hormonal Health.** Vancouver: Apple Publishing, 1996.

10. Lendenbaum JE et al. Neuropsychiatric disorders caused by cobalamin deficiency in the absence of anemia or macrocytosis. **New Engl J Med,** 1988;318:1720-1728.

11. Colgan M. **The Right Protein.** Vancouver: Apple Publishing, 1998.

12. Harmon D. Free radical theory of aging: Increasing the average life expectancy at birth and the maximum life span. **J Anti Aging Med,** 1999;2:199-208.

13. Colgan M. **Antioxidants The Real Story.** Vancouver: Apple Publishing, 1998.

14. Report on American College of Sports Medicine Annual Meeting, Dallas, Texas 27 May 1992. Abstracts.

15. Colgan M. **Essential Fats.** Vancouver: Apple Publishing, 1998.

16. Kabara J. **Pharmacological Effects of Lipids.** Champaign, IL: AOCS, 1989.

17. Storlien LH et al. Science. 1987;237:885.

18. Food and Nutrition Board US National Academy of Sciences. **Recommended Daily Allowances.** Washington, DC: National Academy Press, 1989.

19. Harris RC et al. Elevation of creatine in resting and exercise muscles of normal subjects by creatine supplementation. **Clin Sci,** 1992;83:367-374.

20. Greenhaff P. Creatine and its application as an ergogenic aid. **Int J Sports Nutr,** 1995;5:S100-S110.

21 Balsom PD et al. Creatine in humans with special reference to creatine supplementation. **Sports Med,** 1994;18:269-280.

22. Colgan M. **Creatine for Muscle and Strength.** Vancouver: Apple Publishing, 1997.

23. Harris RC et al. Acetyl-l-carnitine formation during intense muscular contraction in humans. **J. Appl Physiol,** 1987;63:440-442.

24. Bidzinska B et al. Effect of different chronic intermittent stressors and acetyl-l-carnitine on hypothalamic beta endorphon and GnRH and on plasma testosterone in male rats. **Neuroendocrinology,** 1993;57:985-990.

25. Sershow H et al. Effect of acetyl-lcarnitine on the dopiminergic ystems in aging animals. **J Neurol,** 1991;30:555-559.

26. Taglialagel G et al. Acetyl-lcarnitine enhances the response of Pc12 cells to nerve growth factor. **Brain Res Dev Brain Res,** 1991;39:221-230.

27. Lino A et al. Psycho-functional changes in attention and learning under the action of acetyl-l-carnitine in 17 young subjects. **Clin Ther,** 1992;140:569.573.

28. Monteleone P et al. Blunting by chronic phosphatidylserine administration of the stress-induced activation of the hypotrolamo-pituitary-adrenal axis in healthy men. **Exerc J Clin Pharmacal,** 1992;41:385-388.

29. Fahey TD Pearl MS. Hormonal and perceptive effects of phosphatidylserine administration during two weeks of weight training-induced over-training. Reported in Burke ER, Fahey TD. **Phosphatidylserine.** New Canoon CF: Keats, 1998.

30. Colgan M. **Protect your Prostate.** Vancouver: Apple Publishing, 2000.

31. Colgan L, Colgan M. **You Can Prevent Cancer.** (in press).

32. McAlindon TE et al. Glucosamine and Chondroiton for Treatment of Osteoarthritis. **JAMA,** 2000; 283:1469-1484.

Chapter 28: Program Your Mind

1. Su Pu Pei Yao (ed). **The Sun Tzu With Commentaries.** Shanghai: Chung Hua Shu Chu, 1931.

2. Griffith S (trans). **Sun Tzu: The Art of War.** London: Oxford University Press, 1963.

3. Smith T. It's all in your head. **Today's Chemist,** 1996; September:49-52.

4. Miyamoto Musashi. **Gorin No Sho: The Book of Five Rings.** Trans, Brown BS et al. New York: Bantam Books, 1982.

5. Merton T. **The Way of Chuang Tzu.** New York: New Directions, 1969.

6. Rinpoche S. **The Tibetan Book of Living and Dying.** San Francisco: Harper Collins, 1994.

7. Thich Nhat Hanh. **Old Path, White Clouds.** Berkeley, CA: Parollox Press, 1991.

8. Matics ML. **Entering the Path of Enlightenment.** London: George Allen and Unwin, 1971.

9. Travell JG et al, **Myofascial Dysfunction and Pain, The Trigger Point Manual, Upper Half of The Body. Vol 1, Second Edition,** Baltimore, Williams and Wilkins, 1999.

10. Jordan M. **I Can't Accept Not Trying.** San Francisco: Harper, 1994.

11. Callan K. Your warrior spirit. **Success,** 1996; September:22.

12. Loehr J. **Toughness Training For Life.** New York: Penguin Books, 1993.

13. Walsh C. **The Bowerman System.** Los Altos CA: Tafnews Press, 1983.

Dr Michael Colgan
Ph D, CCN

Michael Colgan, PhD, CCN, is one of the world's most popular scientific experts in nutrition. He is a best-selling author, and travels the world lecturing on anti-aging, sports nutrition and hormonal health.

From 1971 to 1982, Dr Colgan was a senior member of the Science Faculty of the University of Auckland, where he taught in Human Sciences and conducted research on aging and physical performance. Startling results of his early research convinced him to write his first book for the public, **YOUR PERSONAL VITAMIN PROFILE** (*William Morrow, New York*), during his tenure as a visiting scholar at the Rockefeller University in New York. This revolutionary book rapidly became a definitive guide for accurate, scientifically researched nutritional information.

From 1979 to 1997, Dr Colgan was President of the Colgan Institute of Nutritional Science. He is now Chairman of the Board. The Colgan Institute is a consulting, educational and research facility formed in 1974, primarily concerned with effects of nutrition and exercise on athletic performance, aging and degenerative disease.

With a distinguished reputation for expertise in sports nutrition, Dr Colgan advises hundreds of elite athletes including: track and field Olympians Donovan Bailey, Quincy Watts, Leroy Burrell, Steve Scott, Michelle Burrell, Meredith Rainey Valmon and Regina Jacobs; three-time world boxing champion Bobby Czyz; rowers Francis Reininger and Adrian Cassidy; powerlifter Rick Roberts; two-time world triathalon champion Julie Moss; shooting champion T'ai Erasmus; Australian heavy-weight boxing champion Chris Sharpe; motor-cross champion Danny Smith; and bodybuilding champions Lee Labrada, Lee Haney, Laura Creavalle and Lenda Murray.

TESTIMONIALS FROM PEERS

"Listen to this man. He's the best in sports nutrition."
Arthur Lydiard, New Zealand Olympic Coach

"His theoretical development of concepts of preventive nutrition...could make an important and unique contribution to the development of preventive medicine in the United States."
Dr Jonas Salk, The Salk Institute

"Crammed with wicked wit and wisdom, irreverent and impertinent, his clear, concise and easily understandable writing is a treat. Ramrod straight, he goes for the jugular of science every time, each conclusion strapped tight to impeccable medical references. And the man himself is a living example of everthing he advocates."
Ben Weider, PhD
President, International Federation of Bodybuilders

"The work of the Colgan Institute is an especially valuable contribution to human knowledge."
Dr Andrew Strigner, London

PROFESSIONAL MEMBERSHIPS

American College of Sports Medicine
New York Academy of Sciences
British Society for Nutritional Medicine
American Academy of Anti-Aging Medicine

CLIENTS Digital Equipment, Dupont, Twinlabs, Weider Health & Fitness, US National Institute on Aging, Price Waterhouse

email team@colganinstitute.com   www.colganinstitute.com

Index

C

G

H

Q

R

T